D0830996

Social Structure in Italy

CRISIS OF A SYSTEM

This book demonstrates that twentieth century social stratification and the distribution of political and economic power in Italy cannot be properly understood without carefully analyzing the historical dynamics of the development of Italian society. This analysis is also needed to explain the woeful economic, and governmental and administrative performance of the strata that finally reached the levers of power. The Italian society and social and political system are in a crisis: development is uneven and the bureaucratic structures are in shambles. The roots of this crisis lie in the endemic underdevelopment typical of the second half of the nineteenth century. Clearly, they cannot be attributed to the historic failures of Fascism, Democracy, Catholicism or Marxism in Italy, but they are the outcome of a long history of underdevelopment followed by extremely uneven regional evolution leading to tremendous cleavages between ultra-modern and utterly antiquated phenomena, the juxtaposition of flexibility and rigidity, of optimistic enthusiasm and hidebound traditionalism, of extreme wealth and abysmal poverty, of high and low levels of earnings, and of a maladjusted, ill-functioning, uneasy combination of agricultural, industrial, and post-industrial society. All this is aggravated by the crisis in the church and by the North-South situation in which many millions of people have migrated from the South to the North, and by the ensuing struggle between a mass of lumpen proletarians and proletarian immigrants from the South, who are exploited as a work force for the industrial development of the North.

Mario Santuccio holds a law degree from the University of Ferrara and is Professor of Sociology at the Dept. of Psychology at the University of Padua. He is Director of Research on the *Organization and Social Dimension of Scientific Research in Italy*, a project of the Italian National Council of Research. Sabino S. Acquaviva is one of Italy's most distinguished social scientists. He holds a law degree from the University of Padua and taught at the Universities of Trento and Nice. He is now Professor of Sociology at the University of Padua. He is the author of thirteen books.

Social Structure
in Italy
CRISIS OF A SYSTEM

S. S. Acquaviva
M. Santuccio

Translated from the Italian by Colin Hamer

WESTVIEW PRESS · BOULDER · COLORADO

Published 1976 in London, England by Martin Robertson & Co. Ltd.

Published 1976 in the United States of America by Westview Press, Inc.
1898 Flatiron Court Boulder, Colorado 80301
Frederick A. Praeger, Publisher & Editorial Director

Printed and bound in Great Britain

Library of Congress Cataloging in Publication Data

Acquaviva, Sabino S
   Social structure in Italy.

   Bibliography: p.
   Includes index.
   1. Italy – Social conditions.   2. Social classes – Italy
History.   3. Italy – Economic conditions.   4. Social
institutions – Italy.   5. Italy – Politics and government.
I. Santuccio, Mario, joint author.   II. Title.

HN475.A6   309.1'45   76–13602
ISBN 0–89158–615–6

Contents

Contents

Foreword

In addition to a table of contents we have provided an analytical summary of the argument. While the main body of the work reproduces all the headings and sub-headings contained in the table of contents, references to the more detailed analytical summary consist simply of bold numerals. These serve to break down our line of argument into all its main individual steps, however small, so that the reader can more easily appreciate their logical place in the lay-out of the book as a whole. This should make it easier to understand what we are trying to say, and may prove particularly helpful to students using it as a text.

In writing this book each author has made himself responsible for the sections more closely relating to his own particular interests. Mario Santuccio has dealt with emigration (pp. 31–35), the lower middle and lower social strata (pp. 66–80), education (pp. 149–57), the Christian Democrat and Italian Communist parties and the trade unions (pp. 180–200). Sabino Acquaviva has written the remainder of the work. However, the general line of the argument results from prolonged mutual discussions that have resulted in a broad measure of agreement on most questions at issue; the differences of opinion that remain will be clear enough to the attentive reader.

Full references to other sources will be found in the general bibliography at the end of the book. In the notes, references will usually be of the form 'Salierno, 1973', corresponding to the entry 'Salierno G. (1973) *Il sottoproletariato in Italia*, Roma, Samonà e Savelli'.

We are especially grateful to Dr Leslie Sklair of the London School of Economics, and to Professors I. De Sandre, G. Guizzardi, and G. Sarpellon, who lecture in the University of Padua on sociology, the sociology of knowledge and economic sociology respectively; they have all read our work in manuscript and put forward useful suggestions and observations.

Analytical Summary

Introduction

1. Purpose behind this study. 2. Both the crisis within and the structure of Italian society have historical origins. 3. The three phases leading up to the present crisis: underdevelopment (1860–1900), slow development (1900–1948), rapid development (1948–1972). 4. Underdevelopment, male-dominated family groupings and a closed value-system in the first phase. 5. A liberal-minded ruling-class and the beginnings of change: a socio-economic two-way split with the South 'colonized' by the North. The new power-system. 6. The beginnings of development. The primitive accumulation of capital, and its social and cultural implications. The new value-system from liberalism to fascism: the broadening of the gulf between North and South. 7. First signs of rapid development: concluding remarks about the historical background to the present-day structure of Italian society and the crisis facing the system.

Part one: Vertical and horizontal structures in Italian society

1. Theoretical models to explain the structure of Italian society and the crisis within it: (a) a model of the structure, (b) two models in conflict – development and underdevelopment, (c) a model of the power-system. 2. The vertical structure: how GNP is distributed between the different sectors – a dynamic structure. 3. The two-way split in the vertical structure: the difference between North and South. How this dualism is partly superseded by imbalances of

another sort. 4. Distribution of the active population: its overall decrease and the reserve labour force. The evolution of the vertical structure. 5. The place of emigration. Proportions of this phenomenon and its social and cultural implications. The rate of emigration as it affects the various sectors. 6. Conclusions and a theoretical model for the evolution of the vertical structure. 7. The horizontal structure: the thinking behind a stratification based on relationships to the means of production. 8. Other factors that help to differentiate between strata: the way in which the relationship to the means of production is developed; the way in which incomes are obtained; level of earnings; bargaining power (political, the strength of skilled labour); position within the organization; employment in the public or private sector; extent to which there is a division of labour and the form this takes; further factors. 9. The strata derived from the foregoing considerations: some definitions. Upper stratum, upper middle stratum, lower middle stratum, lower stratum. 10. The strata in reality. 11. Quantitative considerations. 12. Typical features of the different strata: (a) the upper stratum – the old and new capitalist ruling-class, the average entrepreneurs among the bourgeoisie, the state bureaucrats, the cultural élite, other adherents; (b) the upper middle statum – it partly coincides with the corporate structures of the *ceti* and the bureaucracies, other categories in this stratum, its increase in size and power; (c) the lower middle stratum – consisting mainly of workers, with characteristics closely dependent on the speed with which and the way in which Italian industry has developed – changes within this stratum; (d) the lower stratum – the traditional lumpenproletariat in an underdeveloped country and its modern counterpart, the marginal labour force, women, pensioners, and others belonging to the reserve labour force. 13. Concluding remarks: the more recent socio-cultural changes and their repercussions within the class-system and the *ceti*. Different customs and a new style of collective behaviour. The evolution of the average *ceti* and the levelling-down process within them. The socio-cultural melting-pot as a catalyst of further change.

Part two: The pyramid of power – power-systems and value-systems

1. *The pyramid of power.* How power is legitimated (prevailing values) within the overall social system. 2. Interdependence of the

economic break-through, social change, and a revised value-system within Italian society. 3. The theoretical frame of reference for the change-over: a model in which underdevelopment and development are in conflict with three cardinal features: the value system invoked to legitimate authority, the socialization system and the institutional system. 4. Theoretical characteristics of underdevelopment. The challenging of the position of male-dominated family groupings. 5. A makeshift model for a changing society, and the first signs of development. 6. How this makeshift model challenged traditional social structures and values. The reshaping of the value-system in the light of an up-dated Catholicism. 7. The challenge facing the Catholic system: the falling off in religious observance, the decrease in those choosing priesthood, the credibility crisis. 8. The changes in religious outlook and in social behaviour. 9. The value-system, socialization system and institutional system in Italy. 10. Final observations regarding the industrial model of society in transition: the Catholic and Marxist cultural systems, their transformation and its implications; counter-culture; the challenge facing the two rival value-systems as legitimators of the social structure.

11. *The distribution of power:* how power is connected with income-making. 12 Power associated with agricultural investment. The challenge confronting capitalism in this sector. The resulting crisis among small-holders. The notable decline in power deriving from land ownership. 13. Power in the industrial and commercial sectors. The decline in private ownership and investment, and the increase in the public sector. 14. Land-investment in connection with urban development. 15. The emergence and rise to power of the new class of public managers and entrepreneurs.

16. *The structures of social administration.* The development of the administrative bureaucracy, manipulation and social conditioning. Historical and recent factors in its inefficiency and parasitic character. 17. The 'client' system and the private exploitation of the public sector. 18. Administrative and economic consequences: bankruptcy threatening the government and the national economy. 19. Other bureaucracies in the service sector. 20. The education system as an agent of selection and social stratification. The rapid expansion of provisions for instruction, their failure to meet the needs they are

supposed to cater for, and the extent to which they are out of touch with the overall needs of the technostructure. 21. Some conclusions regarding education. 22. An overall model of structures in the service sector. 23. Some further bodies and organizations within it. 24. Scientific research organizations. 25. Groups with special interests. 26. The general inefficiency of the public administration and the tertiary sector as a whole, its diagnosis and derivation.

27. *Political power in the strict sense.* The social and cultural background of the Italian politician class and Italian politics. The influence of the traditional culture. 28. The Catholic and Marxist sub-cultures as structural and cultural features of the Italian political scene. Mass-membership of the corresponding political parties. 29. The Christian Democrat Party: place within the electorate, membership, power-system. 30. The Italian Communist Party: place within the electorate, membership, power-system. 31. The other political parties, the party system as an almost two-party system with no changes taking place in the composition of the ruling-class. 32. The trade unions, some mainly Catholic and others mainly Marxist – their emergence as a new concentration of power alongside the political parties and parliament itself (including the government). 33. Final remarks: power-sharing is restricted to an élite. 34. A general model of the Italian power-system.

35. *Conclusions:* out of underdevelopment and into crisis.

Introduction

1   The object of this study is to build up a general picture of the overall structure of Italian society, and at the same time to show how the crisis confronting it can be understood as a crisis within the social system. The crisis itself is linked with at least five ranges of phenomena:

(1) the dualism of a society split into two parts roughly corresponding to the geographical division of the country into North and South – this is true from several points of view;
(2) certain features of the power-system and social stratification that derive from the very early days of a united Italy, which took for granted the social structures of underdevelopment;
(3) the nature and pace of development in the twenty-year period that ended in the early 1960s – this was fairly slow at first, but soon became a stampede;
(4) the prevailing value-systems and their evolution;
(5) the actual structure of the Italian capitalist system and the way in which capital accumulates.

2   Such factors in the present crisis as uneven development and a disproportionate growth of the administrative bureaucratic structures already characterized the state of society and the way in which it was developing in the second half of the nineteenth century. They cannot simply be attributed to the historical failures of Fascism, Democracy, Catholicism or Marxism in the country, but are the outcome of a long history of underdevelopment. It might be hard to find a civilization of equal antiquity that exhibits such characteristics so clearly as Italy.

1

Her history has made of her a society that in some ways is developed, in others underdeveloped; here modern, there antiquated; flexible after a fashion but possessed of a certain rigidity; clinging to tradition while adopting the most up-to-date forms of development. Side by side we find development and underdevelopment, high and low levels of earnings, an agricultural, an industrial and a post-industrial society – and the reasons for this situation stand out in Italy's political, economic and social history.

The power-system, the class-system and social stratification are based not simply on economic foundations, but on such ill-assorted value-systems as Catholicism and Marxism, on a primitive religious attitude among the people as well as a widespread religious (and political) scepticism, on such mutually exclusive codes of conduct as the Mediterranean-type, male-dominated, family spirit of the South and the total lack of interest in moral considerations in the North (as in other advanced, industrial societies), on the startling inefficiency of the state bureaucracy in Central and Southern Italy and the comparative efficiency of the industrial bureaucracy in the North, and on considerable imbalances in matters of economics, science and technology.

Italy's power-system, the balance between its political forces, the value-system invoked to legitimate the power structure, and the economic set-up until recently and still to some extent today, are a function of her character as a relatively underdeveloped country.

In other words, development has been conditioned by the overall, historically determined structure of society, especially in the nineteenth century. This was a complex manifold, varying from region to region, the culture and the economy being in some places fairly developed and in others scarcely developed at all. Thus, the pace of change varies in the different regions along with the form it takes. The economic and social structures of today still owe their basic orientation and unmistakable characteristics to the sometimes quite considerable remnants of these several antiquated social models, which ride on the crest of the tide of change, and without which many present-day social phenomena cannot be understood. The crisis in contemporary Italian society is largely due to its history; a shrewd observer of past events might possibly have been able to foresee much of what is now taking place.

The five points from which we began will provide the basis for our subsequent analysis of the country's social structure. As well as grouping the different problems together in this way in the light of the general historical background, we shall take into account the more salient distinguishing features of the successive phases of Italy's more recent history.

3   At least three phases are of particular importance for an understanding of the contemporary social structure and the crisis afflicting it: a period of general lack of development with an economy at subsistence level; a period (roughly 1900–1948) in which the pre-existing social structures and economic conditions along with the underlying value-systems are absorbed into a process of industrialization and modernization, while development is slow; a further period (1948–73) of rapid development producing a certain amount of upheaval in some parts of the country, affecting both the social structure and the value-systems.

4   Throughout the greater part of the country the first period lasted until about the end of the last century. On the whole the picture is one of an economy at subsistence level, where the majority of the population barely manage to survive and the accumulation of even the minimum of capital needed for development to get under way is either very difficult or impossible. During this period the industrial zone occupies no more than a very small area, and it was not until the end of the century that Turin, Milan and Genoa came to be regarded as the apexes of an industrial triangle – a triangle that became an established reality during the interval between the two World Wars, while it was only after the Second World War that industrialization came to the whole of the peninsula.

Economic conditions in this first period are accompanied by backward socio-cultural institutions and structures. Economic power is concentrated in a small number of hands, political power is similarly centralized, and the value-system is that of the Mediterranean-type, male-dominated family group. The family itself occupies a privileged position within society and in the value-system, and represents a stable reference-point for each individual and a space within which he can defend his own interests and those of the rest of the family.

Widespread hostility to society outside one's own family characterizes this period, reflecting personal psychological insecurity and the economic and social insecurity of Italian society in general.[1] In Southern society especially, individualism is marked with a deep-seated hostility to the state and to authority in general. Such hostility diminishes step by step as one moves up through the country from the South with its large estates, to the Centre where share-cropping is common in several regions, and on to the North where ownership is already on a smaller scale, more differentiated conditions of both ownership and employment being a quite well-established situation.

The level of earnings also rises as one works one's way up from South to North, and this is reflected in the economic and social standard of living.

However, throughout the whole of the nineteenth century, these differences notwithstanding, the overall situation is one of wide-spread underdevelopment against the background of a family-centred organization of life and a closed value-system inspired by a Christianized paganism and a male-dominated family spirit. So closely does the family respond to the individual's moral and psychological needs that other forms of association hold less appeal than elsewhere, and there is little urge to participate in local, regional or national community affairs.[2] This sort of attitude prevails throughout the whole country in one degree or another, but flourishes particularly in the South under the form of the 'client' system, with influential families bringing into their orbits steadily increasing numbers of individuals tied to them for reasons of economic interest in one way or another. Such networks of clients hinder the creation of other associations or of the economic, cultural and political infrastructures that make development possible. Together with the inadequacies of such structures as do exist, this serves to reinforce the position of the families and their dependent clients, resulting in a vicious circle. The passage of time has modified and to some extent meant a development out of the original situation, but in some regions similar conditions persist even today, as we shall see, and explain many of the political and economic conditions surrounding life in Italy (and in some other southern European societies in the Mediterranean basin).

Thus, in this first period, against a background of distrust, suspicion and hostility vis-à-vis authority in society at large, the system of legitimation based on a closed value-system and a family-centred socialization system is employed to maintain the status quo, while the institutional system, linked to the continuing concentration of economic power, is centralized and authoritarian.

As a result, until this vicious circle of depression is broken, society remains closed and static as regards (a) the power-system; (b) any taking of the economic initiative; (c) the cultural milieu and the value-system; and (d) the structure of the family. In other words, the cult of the family flourishes alongside hostility to civil authority which, in a closed society, rests on a backward economy, with capital in the hands of a few – this central fact supporting each of the others in turn. An economy at subsistence level, a rigid institutional system, the cult of the family and the attitude towards authority combine together to obstruct change and hinder its progress.

We leave to historians and anthropologists the task of analysing such phenomena in detail, but they or their caricatures survive, so our insight into contemporary society is greater if we understand them.

5   It was against this background that between the beginning and the middle of the nineteenth century there emerged a liberal-minded entrepreneur class, who consolidated their position in the second half of the century. This was partly because of the repercussions within Italy of the French Revolution, and partly on account of the slow beginnings of a progressive accumulation of agricultural and even industrial capital (though the latter was largely induced by factors outside Italy and consisted of foreign investments in the country). It was at this time that this fringe-group of liberal-minded, anti-clerical and 'enlightened' bourgeoisie, favouring a free-trade economy, proposed their alternative plans for society, which gradually became the foundations of their control of Italy and its changing fortunes.

This, then, was the class that broke out of the vicious circle of underdevelopment, when, principally for motives of economic self-interest, they severed a few links in the chain that brought together the subsistence-level economy, familism, and the traditionally accepted values. Their main interventions were directed against the traditional structures of the Catholic Church and the economic interests of the old Italian states, particularly the features surviving from the feudal system. Simultaneously the new class strengthened the social structures of capitalist enterprise, and in this way changed the face of society.[3]

However the development this new class instigated was far from integrated: it was the beginnings of what was to become the uneven development of contemporary Italy – the South, which was in some respects more agricultural and had a fragile industrial set-up, ill-equipped to defend itself against the concentration of (at least political) power in the North, collapsed and became an agricultur-ally backward area from which manual workers could be taken to help in the slow industrialization of the North. This meant a thoroughly dualistic society – the shotgun marriage of development and underdevelopment, fossilized traditional values and new values, enterprise and sloth, frenzied activity and unemployment, inefficiency and the quest for hyper-efficiency.

Spreading from Piedmont and Lombardy the new system of values invoked in support of the power structure tended to impose itself on the whole country, though never with entire success; the difficulties increased the further South one went, partly because of the different conditions of community life and the different position of capitalism.

The traditional system weakens its hold as time goes on, but retains a certain weight, becoming indeed, as we shall see, almost the deciding factor during periods of serious social crisis, when its weight is enough to tip the scales in a particular direction when added to the sum of the other factors involved. Nevertheless, emigration and two World Wars have made serious inroads into it, since they have necessitated a profound rethinking of values and provoked severe economic crises.

Even in the nineteenth century the ruling-class were not simply seeking to reshape institutions in the interests of national unity and by means of education to provide a single culture, at least for all the upper strata: they wished to establish a solid economic basis for the new order by bringing into being one national economic market.

One of the main moves in this shift in the economy was the confiscation of ecclesiastical property, an act which also struck a blow against the main institutional structure supporting the tradi-tional value-system. This expropriation of the Church's wealth strengthened, and sometimes sufficed to make possible the establish-ment of a capitalist land-owning class, and in North Italy it was this class that then encouraged industrial investment.

Thus the confiscation of ecclesiastical lands, the seizure of the common land belonging to the various communes, and the subsequent juridical regulation of all questions of ownership in a way that favoured the bourgeoisie, combined to bring about the emergence of a new group of rich people, so making possible an initial accumulation of capital. This was the foundation for the subsequent economic development.

Such economic, political and social measures are the roots of many of the ills in society today, and by adopting them the liberal, capitalist class did not really solve the old problems. By taking over the Church's property they merely altered the way in which ownership was concentrated in the hands of the few. The dualism already afflicting the country was worsened by the new ruling-class's development programme, which meant in practice an uneven and unbalanced development with marked differences between North and South, the latter being for a long time exploited by the North as if it were some sort of colony. Development always supposes a division of labour, and here it meant specialization in the various industries, and specialization between regions.

Any mercantile economy rests on the division of labour, and, whatever their ideas in the abstract, this was what in practice the ruling-class of the newly united Italy brought into being. It was compatible with the pre-existing situation, which they could not or did not wish to change, and in some ways it made matters worse. Capital and industrial production came to the North; the South, with its agriculture hardly, if at all, modernized, provided a consumer market and a reserve of manpower. An industrial bourgeoisie and a working-class were emerging in the North, too, within the context of the liberal, democratic value-system of private enterprise; while the South maintained the closed, traditional value-system, with capitalist landlords and farm-hands. Italy is still experiencing the consequences of this dualism.

Moreover, the standard of education improved much more rapidly in the North than in the South, so that here, too, one could soon say there were two Italies rather than one. Basic education came to the country as a whole between 1861 and 1911. (In 1861 74.7 per cent of the population could neither read nor write; this figure was to drop to 69 per cent in 1871, 63 per cent in 1881, 48 per cent in 1901 and 38 per cent in 1911.)[4] However, in 1871, although there was a single corpus of laws for the whole country, only Piedmont, Liguria and Lombardy had reached the minimum educational standard then needed for development, though Tuscany and Veneto had almost reached it. Along with the other factors this served to concentrate the development in those areas where there was a sufficiency of cultural openness, technical knowledge and basic education for the process to get under way.[5] The other parts of the country only reached the required standard at the beginning of the present century, and so were practically excluded from the first phase of Italy's industrial development[6] – when they came on the scene, they had to take things as they found them.

It is, therefore, clear that the continuing existence and in some ways the deterioration of the country's dualistic structures together with her uneven development stemmed from both economic and political causes – the result of the old situation of uneven and inadequate economic development, and the emergence of an exclusive class of liberal politicians with restricted economic resources. The upshot was likewise economic and political: the dualism is still an economic reality today, and the present-day ruling-class are still conditioned, which is in many ways a bad thing, by these past political attitudes, values, and ways of justifying the social system.

The political unification of Italy in this first period, when the economy was still at subsistence level, was the achievement of a minority: 'Italy became a nation almost without realizing it had done so.' It was held together more by the resolve of the élite than by the will of the people, and was subject to a centralized power exercising control and overlordship through Prefects in the provinces, with little recourse to political parties or groups and with little attempt to win popular support. The ruling-class themselves were provincial in outlook for quite a time, with a very limited vision, not much national culture, and many ties to the old regional cultures.

Having brought about the national unification, these classes remained in power for some considerable time without any real popular support, and never succeeded in communicating to the rest of the country their ideal of renewal – all that the average citizen received was a fragmented and distorted image, a mere shadow of what their rulers dreamed of as a reality. The mass of the people were still Catholics for the most part, and acknowledged the value-system their rulers had rejected; they saw the new régime as something alien. The rise of new popular groups, such as the Mazzinians and the Republicans, and later the Socialists and the

Communists, also increased the isolation of the ruling-class and, indeed, opposed them.

Semi-feudalism and a sort of caste structure in society may have been superseded, but only by another power-system based on privilege; a class-system with more up-to-date features and values to its credit, but still one that confined power to a very small group. It was to be several decades before the basis for democracy became much broader, and almost a hundred years before one could say there was some sort of real democracy.

Throughout this period, then, Italy was characterized by: a mainly stagnant economic structure in which one could detect the beginnings of development; marked economic dualism at all levels dividing the North from the South and splitting up the individual regions into conflicting sectors; contrasting value-systems, one of them closed, conservative and attuned to underdevelopment, the other theoretically progressive, but harnessed in practice to the self-interest of a restricted élite; an élite controlling the country's political life, the means of production, the police and the army, ostensibly in the interests of a liberalized system of social institutions, but actually, as is quite obvious, to satisfy their own needs and aspirations; a markedly centralized bureaucratic structure controlled by the same élite; a social stratification in which the rights of the subordinate strata (and classes) were severely restricted by a ban on strikes, by other laws and social controls, and by economic and social unrest, low pay, unemployment, and widespread poverty.

This situation changed very slowly, and it was only at about the end of the nineteenth century that it began to assume quite different features.

6   One result of this situation was that by the end of the century Italy was lagging behind other industrial nations both economically and socially, even more than had been the case at the time of her unification. In 1895, for instance, the gross national product of the United Kingdom was, taking the relative numbers of each country's population into account, three times that of Italy, which was only half that of France or Germany. Yet, despite the ruling-class's isolation and lack of efficiency, and despite the persisting dualism, Italian enterprise showed an upward trend at the turn of the century. 'During the fifteen years of Europe's *belle époque*, the Edwardian

period known in Italy as the *età giolittiana*, this late arrival at the
feast of development managed, thanks to her own looms, her own
lathes and her own water-turbines, to move so rapidly as to recover
some of the ground she had lost to the established industrial giants
of the North',[7] Great Britain being the first among them – though,
in fact, Britain still influenced the peninsula's development,[8] especially in the industrial sector.[9]

This brings us to phase two. By the beginning of the present
century Italian society already possessed all the basic features of its
subsequent structure and stratification, some of them only in germ,
others in embryo, and some in a more organized form. Capitalism
in Italy might not have grown to the dimensions it had achieved in
northern Europe, but it had already obliged the old rival participants
in the power game to form new alliances, reorganize their forces,
and decide whether to oppose or rally to the support of the new
forces coming into play as the economy was gradually transformed.
Most of the factors that were later to bring about a change in Italian
social stratification were already present: agricultural capitalism
having by then been joined by the capitalist interests of industry,
commerce and banking; investment in agricultural land by investment in urban development sites and the building industry[10] (especially in the main centres such as Rome and Milan[11]); and
agricultural labourers by factory and office workers.

These new social and economic conditions seemed to have a
rather dampening effect on the traditional ruling-class, and signs of
an impending divorce between politics and economic development
became increasingly obvious. Development, in other words, was no
longer the result of the efforts of the political class who had united
the country and thought of her economic growth as some sort of
continuation of the same political programme; by this time it was
taking place to some extent independently of the whims of politicians, had assumed more definite contours of its own, and involved
actively competing social, economic and political groups, classes
and *ceti*. (We use the Italian term *ceto* to refer to any association of
individuals, mainly drawn from the intermediate strata of society,
who share some common interest and have in part a common
culture, and are linked to one another by organizational, corporate
or bureaucratic structures only partly connected with their relationship to the means of production.) If development had previously
been a single and on the whole a single-minded process, by this

time it had been transformed into the dialectical interplay of rival interests.

The characteristics exhibited just after the First World War by the ruling-class and by the dominant social strata, whose members had thrived on the earlier economic expansion, were not without their ambiguities and contradictions: upholders of the traditional values, old-fashioned Catholics, anti-clericals, free-thinkers, the new bourgeoisie, and non-dogmatic pragmatists competed with each other while multiplying the bonds that gradually committed them all equally to the pluralist society. That complex labyrinth out of which Fascism would for a time emerge to produce the illusion of a united front, consisted of such disparate elements as the old and new economic strata ranging from the bourgeois land-owners to the modern bourgeois industrialists, with their clearly conflicting ideologies – some of the demands of fidelity to the old value-system were impossible to reconcile with the need for efficiency in the interests of industrial development.

The period extending from the start of the economic development proper at the beginning of the century to the downfall of Fascism marked the evolution of Italy out of her first industrial apprenticeship as a nation into an established industrial state.[12] Meanwhile, her former closed, clear-cut value-system opened up and became more differentiated, partly due to the rise of the working-class, and partly because of the growing importance (which continues today) of the only moderately affluent or relatively poor bourgeois elements. Even under Fascism attitudes towards work and business initiative and enterprise were no longer influenced by the traditional value-system to the same extent as in the past. There was, on the other hand, a widespread desire for a better social standing, better pay, a higher standard of living, and increased scope for initiative. Henceforth, people were valued in proportion to their economic prestige and success. This change in attitudes fostered the economic development under Fascism and after it.[13]

Fascism itself, unconsciously perhaps, called a halt for the time being to the critical reappraisal of the traditional Catholic institutions and prolonged the life of many male-dominated familistic traditions. However, it also set in motion processes which after the Second World War were to give rise to many innovations. For instance, the war-time economy centred on the industrial North paved the way for accelerated industrialization and industrial development in the post-war period. Fascism had inherited dualistic structures from the liberal ruling-class previously in power, but heightened the tensions within society even more, preserving the traditional values within the 'protective' environment of a structurally different society, while increasing the economic dualism between North and South.

7   With the end of the war many things changed.

Undoubtedly the second phase was concluded with several traditional features of the Italian landscape intact, despite the various changes, but probably partly because of the way in which these had been introduced; there was still an unbalanced dualistic structure, uneven growth, the value-system of underdeveloped Italy competing with the newly accepted values, a concentration of wealth (and especially of the ownership of land) in the hands of the few, and the polarization of the nation around the twin banners of Catholicism and Marxism – all things that ante-dated Fascism.

Yet the novelty cannot be denied. For a variety of reasons, as we shall see, there was a profound change in the ruling-class and, to some extent, in all the upper strata. The economic reconstruction of Italy brought with it a new stratum of industrial investors and a new cultural élite; Catholicism disentangled itself from Fascism and projected a new image; the traditional liberals ceased to be a popular political force and, at least until very recently, the Italian political scene was dominated at first by the competition and later by the increasing collaboration between Catholicism and Marxism – the latter gradually growing in strength at the expense of the former, or so it seems. This was the backcloth against which Italy's economy made its great leap forward.[14]

The history of the development of Italian society is also that of those economic, social and cultural factors which explain the imbalance within it; they determined its structure until very recently, and to some extent still determine its structure today. In our analysis the theoretical models we shall use to explain the structure of Italian society and the crisis within it have been constructed in the light of these historical considerations regarding Italy's economy, her social and political reality, and her value-systems.

Notes to the Introduction

1. See Crespi, 1966; Acquaviva and Eisermann, 1971, p. 160; Banfield, 1958, p. 147.
2. See Acquaviva and Eisermann, 1971, for ample documentation and a supporting bibliography; see also Corrain, 1962, pp. 1 and 15, as well as the 1966 reports issued by the Sociology Department of Padua University.
3. See Sereni, 1947.
4. The regional figures for illiteracy show the split between North and South:

Illiterate percentage of the population over 6 years old in different parts of Italy

Region	1871	1911	1951	1961	1971
North Italy (West)	45.3	13.0	2.8	1.8	1.3
North Italy (East)	67.8	28.4	6.3	3.9	2.0
Central Italy	71.8	38.4	11.5	7.3	4.3
South Italy	83.5	58.1	24.6	16.3	10.9
Italian Islands	85.4	56.9	24.0	15.5	10.3
Italy as a whole	68.7	37.0	12.9	8.3	5.2

Based on ISTAT 'Sviluppo della popolazione', with the tables re-expressed; ISTAT, *IX censimento, 1951*, vol. 5, various tables and references; *X censimento, 1961*, vol. 7, pp. 68ff. Illiteracy in North Italy in the recent past is mainly confined to immigrants from the South.

5. United Italy began as a nation of illiterates, at least in the Centre, the South and the islands. The available regional figures for 1861 provide a sufficient indication of the state of affairs: in Piedmont and Liguria, for instance, illiterates accounted for 54.2 per cent of the population, in Lombardy for 53.7 per cent, but for Southern Italy the figure was 86.3 per cent, Sicily having 88.6 per cent and Sardinia as many as 89.7 per cent illiterates. See ISTAT, *Sommario di statistiche.*

6. See Zamagni, 1973, pp. 187–240.
7. Toniolo, 1973, p. 6. The most important and certainly the most obvious factors that made development possible are well known and generally admitted: emigration, money sent to Italy by those who had emigrated, low wages permitting employers to increase their capital and compete with foreign industrial concerns, unemployment which ensured that cheap labour was available, tariff barriers, improved standards of culture and education, and other factors – some of them permanent, others incidental in character. Thus, because wages remained steady, capital accumulation was more easily achieved, and was particularly notable in the light industrial sector, the textile industry being especially favoured by such factors as low wages, tariff barriers, and government support. A clear indication of the economic break-through in certain sectors was the rise in steel production between 1881 and 1889 from 3600 to 158,000 metric tons, while iron production rose from 94,000 to 181,000 tons. However, Italian heavy industry remained insignificant in comparison with that of the more advanced industrial nations, such as the United Kingdom which in 1890 was producing 8,960,000 tons of cast iron and, in 1895, 3,260,000 tons of steel.
8. Representing the 1938 figures as 100, production stood at 27 in 1874, dropped to 25 in 1880, rose to 30 in 1885, only to drop again to 26 in 1886, before rising to 31 in 1887. The first sharp rise was at the turn of the century from 31 in 1898 to 55 in 1908. After that, however, there was no general

improvement until the First World War. If the 1912 figure was 60, it dropped back to 56 in 1914. Italian industry at the turn of the century was no great thing despite the money invested in it, the tariff barriers, the changes in the social structures, in education and in the value-system, or the government's centralizing influence in favour of a free-trade economy and increased administrative control. See ISTAT, *Sommario di statistiche.*

9. The so-called heavy industries were largely controlled by foreigners and dependent on foreign capital. The management and technicians in the engineering factories were very often English, Swiss, German or French. Italian personnel were only introduced very slowly – indeed, in the chemical industry only after the Second World War. Northern European bankers and industrial magnates presided over the key development sectors. To mention just one example, it was an Englishman, Philip Taylor, who founded the still existing firm of Ansaldo in Genoa; in 1891 this was the largest and best-equipped firm of its kind, and it is still one of the largest. English influence was dominant towards the close of the nineteenth century, but the Germans were in the ascendant in the decade immediately prior to the First World War. Italy's economic subservience also extended into the sectors of half-finished and finished products. See Morandi, 1959.

10. There was quite a rapid development in the electrical industry and others connected with urban expansion, such as the cement industry where the output rose from 104,000 metric tons in 1890 to 846,000 in 1910 and 31,792,000 in 1971. The rise in electricity production was just as sharp. See ISTAT, *Sommario di statistiche;* ISTAT, *Compendio statistico 1971.*

11. This expansion was accompanied by a parallel urban development that, in addition to its economic effects, created the necessary social space for new forms of culture to take root and flourish in an atmosphere of overall development. The population of Rome, for instance, rose from 244,484 in 1871 to 423,943 in 1901 and that of Milan from 192,182 in 1861 to 490,084 in 1901.

12. After the First World War the expansion continued steadily, the gross national product between 1920 and 1925 showing an annual increase of almost 4 per cent. Meanwhile, Italy established herself as the exporter of industrial manufactured goods, the annual increase in turn-over being of the order of 15.5 per cent. There was a proportionate increase in the national income, and between 1921 and 1925 the unemployment figure dropped from 541,775 to 122,000.

If we take the 1938 figures for the production of manufactured goods as 100, the pre-war level was regained and improved upon: 59 in 1921, 61 in 1922, 66 in 1923, 73 in 1924, 83 in 1925, 80 in 1927, 88 in 1928, 90 in 1929. The world crisis in 1929 brought the figures down again, but the wars in Ethiopia and Spain helped them to rise once more – 86 in 1935, 109 in 1939, 110 in 1940. There had been a rise of 25 points in a mere five years, but Italy's economy was already on a war-time footing. Different authorities, including the Central Institute of Statistics itself, have challenged these figures, proposed alternative ones, and suggested different ways of assessing the country's economic expansion. However, broadly speaking they present a fair picture of the situation.

The most recent expansion did, of course, take place in exceptional circumstances, since the country was in an almost continuous state of war. There was the Fascist revolution (1919–22), the re-taking of Libya (which had been almost completely lost to Italy in the First World War), which dragged on until 1930, the war in Ethiopia (1935–36), the

Spanish war (1937–39), the conquest of Albania (1939) and the Second World War (1940–45).

Notwithstanding her economic expansion, Italy's industrial resources at the start of the Second World War were extremely slight when compared with those of other European nations. The electricity output was 15,544 million kilowatts as against the United Kingdom figure of 24,372 million. Italy had 2214 locomotives while the United Kingdom had about 22,000. The national income was 5320 million dollars in comparison with the United Kingdom's 21,854 million. In 1938 Italy produced little more than 52,000 cars, while Germany made 348,000 vehicles, France and Great Britain about 300,000 each, and the United States 4,446,000.

At the end of the war Italy's economy showed signs of collapse. Agricultural production was only 63.3 per cent of the 1938 figure, and industrial production also dropped. See the ISTAT figures (*Compendio statistico 1971*) and De Rosa, 1973, p. 41, where there is a useful overall synthesis of the available data.

13. It is usually reckoned that the post-war reconstruction had been completed by 1949, and in the twenty years between then and 1969 there was a fourfold increase in industrial production. Taking the industrial output in 1938 as 100 it was up to 123 by 1950 and rising rapidly: 140 in 1951, 145 in 1952, 159 in 1953, 358 by 1962 and 546 in 1969.

The manufacturing industries were extremely active and it was here that the development was most obvious. During the period of the economic miracle (1953 to 1969) production rose by 191 per cent, the rise in light engineering being one of 96 per cent, while that in car production was one of 700 per cent. The production of machine tools rose by 57 per cent and that of precision tools by 399 per cent. This uneven development introduced an imbalance between the various sectors, and the consequent problems were aggravated by Italy's membership of the Common Market, which meant even more specialization: those sectors that were thriving prospered even more, while those in difficulty found the situation increasingly hard to face. See Lettieri, 1967b.

14. Despite the imbalances we have noted, the rapidity of the country's economic growth is clear from an examination of the figures for what are regarded in Italy as key sectors of the economy, such as electricity and the metal industries. The following table shows the rise in the production of cast iron and steel:

Average annual production of cast iron and steel (metric tons)

Year	Cast iron	Steel
1861–70	21,699	—
1891–1900	12,321	75,053
1911–20	345,208	960,689
1931–40	714,551	1,961,122
1951–60	1,694,426	5,365,682
1961–65	3,868,143	10,302,591
1966–70	7,298,218	16,039,480
1971	8,536,336	17,451,926
1972	9,415,098	19,814,605
1973	10,032,493	20,994,980

See Romeo, 1961, p. 171; ISTAT *Sommario di statistiche*, p. 79; ISTAT *Compendio statistico 1972*, p. 188.

The rise in per capita incomes has been equally rapid, though not as fast as that of industrial production considered separately, the latter having expanded more rapidly than it has in other countries. The national income in 1948 equalled the 1938 figures, and had doubled by 1955, when it represented 464 dollars per head of the population. This may seem little when compared with 1152 dollars per head in the United Kingdom, 975 dollars per head in Germany, or 969 dollars per head in France, but it was clear evidence that Italy was catching up. In these twenty years of rapid economic expansion both earnings and savings increased as never before, whether taken absolutely or in relation to the numbers of the population, so that by 1972 the average income for each inhabitant was 1,158,500 lire, or 2000 dollars at the 1972 rate of exchange. If prices are considered as having been stable at 1963 levels, the net national income from 1958 to 1972 rose by as much as 85 per cent. The gross national product was rising more rapidly than in most other industrial countries, with the exceptions of Germany and Japan. See ISTAT, *Compendio statistico 1972.*

PART ONE

Vertical and Horizontal Structures in Italian Society

CHAPTER 1

Theoretical Models of the Structure of Italian Society and the Crisis within it

1   One point at least stands out from the various considerations brought forward by way of introduction: the study of Italian society today must take into account the sort of development that brought it into existence. Any theoretical model or schema used to explain its structures and their transformations presupposes this background of facts. To the extent that Italy has passed from underdevelopment to development, she can be understood in terms of some sort of model of a closed society dialectically related to the model of an advanced industrial society. In practice, however, each region of the country from North to South, from the most industrialized to the most agricultural, has its own place on a continuum between these two extremes, and needs to be seen in terms of its own particular model of transition.

If this is the general picture, our present task is to construct first of all a theoretical model of Italy's social structure to help us in our efforts to understand it, and then a variety of models designed to account more specifically for such phenomena as the power-system, the value-system, the way in which authority is legitimated, etc. It is not something to be undertaken lightly, since it is all too easy to focus too exclusively on sociological considerations or else to lose one's way in the labyrinths of ethnology and cultural anthropology. The uneven quality of the developments experienced by Italian society does, in fact, lend itself in some ways to a sociological model

19

and in others to more ethnological models of interpretation. We have opted for a compromise solution to some at least of these problems, viz. two general models and one more specific model set in relationship to each other.

The model we have chosen to represent and explain the structures themselves is mainly socio-economic in character, and we shall deal with this presently, while we have used a dynamically bipolar model of development and underdevelopment to shed light on the cultural shifts in the value-system, the socialization system and the institutional system, and it is against this background that we consider more specific problems and proceed to analyse the dynamics of Italy's social evolution. At a subsequent point in our investigation we shall also propose another model, dependent on the cultural one, and use it to describe and explain the power-system. First, then, the structural model.

It is clear that we cannot discuss structure unless we attempt to show how the various members of the society we are considering are related both to one another and to the various groups and sub-groups of which that society is composed. Hence, our treatment needs to be logical and organic.

For our purposes we see no need to define social structure directly, but we shall indicate some aspects of this notion as it applies to Italian society, and point at the same time to four specific fields of inquiry:

(a) into Italy's vertical structure;
(b) into her horizontal structure;
(c) into the structures at the top; and
(d) into her lateral structures.

Without pretending to define structure itself exhaustively, we shall take it here to mean the sum of overall relationships binding together the various parts and members of Italian society on the basis of some definite factors which alone render intelligible these relationships between individuals, infrastructures and sub-systems.

By *vertical structure* we mean the way in which the population belong or fail to belong to the different productive sectors of Italian society: agricultural, industrial, services, inactive or only marginally active. When we speak of *horizontal structure* we are referring to the general division of society into different strata, identified principally in terms of their relationship to the means of production and certain other factors to be mentioned later. The *structure at the top* comprises both those with direct power, such as the political parties and the upper grades in the administration, and those who use their authority to endorse the prevailing value-system: the cultural élite, the Church, etc. *Lateral structures* are agencies which do not run society directly, or control the means of production wholly or in part, or identify themselves with any value-system or source of authority as such, but which either support the main structure (as the education system does, for instance) or provide for those on its fringe in a way consistent with its overall requirements (e.g., old people's homes, mental hospitals, prisons, etc.).

We shall deal separately with the vertical structure, the horizontal structure and the structure of power at the top, in such detail as our topic seems to require, but any remarks we have to make about

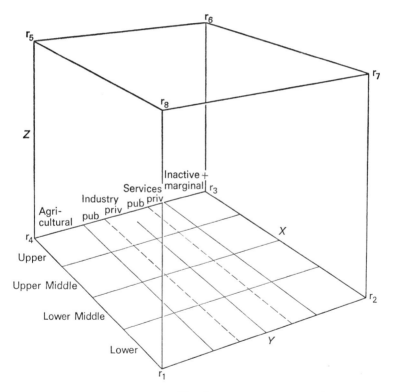

FIG. 1

lateral structures will occur most naturally alongside the discussion of the other three structures, with which they are so closely interwoven.

How, then, are these three structures themselves interrelated? We can refer to any individual within society by three indices to fix his position within society in terms of vertical membership of a particular productive or non-productive sector, horizontal stratification, and proximity or otherwise to the structure at the top. A diagram will make this clear (see Fig. 1). XY is a plane area in which the line X and those parallel to it represent the sectors within the vertical membership of society (agriculture, industry, services, inactive members) while the line Y and its parallels represent the horizontal stratification of society into the lower, the lower middle, the upper middle and the upper strata. The whole plane XY can then be imagined to rise upwards along the Z axis, which is used to indicate the structure of power at the top. If we consider the public and private sectors of industry and services as separate, there are 24 small squares in the plane XY, which yields 360 small cubes in the cube XYZ, supposing fifteen centres of real or direct power (why this number, we shall explain in chapters 5 and 6) – all of these 360 are real and not just theoretically possible combinations. Of course, such a cuboid classification cannot give any indication of the relative significance of any particular position within it.

CHAPTER 2

The Vertical Structure

A. Imbalances in the distribution of incomes and the division of labour

2   There is wide agreement as to how gross products and incomes are to be analysed and classified in terms of their distribution among various sectors of society, so that it will not take us long to provide the reader with an overall picture of the vertical structure of Italian society. We shall be summarizing existing conclusions, not arriving at new ones. The important thing is to appreciate the dynamics of this structure in relation to our preceding inquiry into the economic development.

Take, for instance, the gross national product and its distribution

Table 2.1   **Gross National Product Distributed Between the Various Sectors of Economic Activity**

Year	Woodlands, Agriculture and Fisheries %	Industry %	Services and Public Administration %	Total GNP
1861–70	54.40	18.69	26.90	52,425*
1881–90	48.33	19.66	31.99	60,194
1901–10	43.77	21.97	34.25	80,854
1921–30	36.03	29.42	34.61	119,311
1941–50	37.06	20.09	33.83	130,742
1951–60	17.54	32.95	49.50	18,292†
1961–65	14.25	38.27	47.46	27,360
1966–70	12.65	40.50	46.84	35,336
1971	11.56	40.80	47.63	39,953
1972	10.65	41.06	48.28	41,240

* millions of lire at 1938 rate
† billions of lire at 1963 rate

between the economic sectors at different points in time, as shown in table 2.1. The part played by services or tertiary production (excluding the public sector) has been relatively stable, but there has evidently been a steady growth in the industrial sector at the expense of agriculture and forestry,[1] so that by 1972 agriculture accounted for only about 10 per cent of the gross national product.[2] Moreover, recent developments favour expansion in the tertiary sector at the expense of both industry and agriculture. Since the 1950s the tertiary sector has been about as large as the agricultural and industrial sectors combined, accounting for nearly 50 per cent of GNP.[3] Increasing growth continues to occur in both industry and the services at the expense of agriculture, which is only what our study of Italian economic development would have led us to expect.

3   Granted, then, that increasing growth was predictable, we still have to ascertain whether or not the imbalance already noted in the geographical distribution of industrial production at its inception has remained a permanent feature of the overall development.

In fact, development has changed the proportions of the economic relationships between the different sectors, but there has been no change in the basic split between North and South. Consequently, when development first really got under way incomes in some areas were already comparable with those in other advanced European nations, while in others they were below the average for under-developed countries. In some places growth was very slow, in others astonishingly rapid. One example from the South: while incomes in immediately adjacent regions remained stagnant, in the province of Foggia they rose from the equivalent of 159 dollars per inhabitant in 1951 to 342 in 1961 and about 1000 in 1971, with some variation in the calculations of different authorities.

This, too, was only to be expected. When economic growth first got off the ground the imbalance between average individual incomes in the North and in the South was already evident. In terms of population, involvement in agriculture and average earnings for 1950, the dualism between these two Italies just before the economic breakthrough was quite remarkable.[4]

The split and imbalance between North and South becomes clearer still if we consider the distribution of the labour force between the various sectors in the different regions on the basis of the 1951, 1961 and 1971 census returns.[5] The initial situation was hard enough for the South with only 23–24 per cent of the national income, scant possibilities of capital accumulation, and only moderate economic drive. The way in which the sources of wealth were distributed obliged the South to supply 60 per cent of the normal additions to the national labour force during the period of the country's main economic expansion. Again, in 1951 the gross regional income in the South amounted to little more than one-fifth of the gross national product, although the South accounted for rather more than one-third of the population.

The imbalance between North and South, which had not varied much from unification days up to 1950, remained throughout the course of the subsequent rapid economic expansion.[6] The way in which economic development has polarized does not favour the South, but holds incomes there at a low level, with an adverse effect on cultural opportunity and choice of employment. Backwardness, unemployment, illiteracy, a high infant mortality rate, etc., are still problems in the South. While their causes partly lie in the past, the displacement of money and workers from the South to areas of greater economic opportunity undoubtedly helps to maintain them in being.

There have been some recent improvements in earnings in the South in the last few years, but there has been no great change in the general North-South situation of imbalance and economic dualism.

Many authors would say that since the early 1960s this is no longer so. There were always a few spots where there was a greater economic development and a measure of political and administrative organization, but on the whole the South was for a long time almost a colonial dependency of the North, which supplied her with industrial products to consume in exchange for her readily available labour force. Now, however, it has been integrated into the economic and social life of the country as a whole, and participates directly and intrinsically in the overall growth of the country, just as the North does; once more industrial expansion is the explanation.[7]

Yet one cannot say the imbalance in the development has been done away with, or that it no longer concerns society as a whole. In discussing this imbalance and bipolar split several authors refer to the consequences of 'uneven development':

The historically evident split between North and South, which once largely coincided with that between town and country, industry and agriculture, craftsmen and peasants, is being gradually replaced by one between central and fringe areas of urban and industrial development on the one hand and squalor, stagnation and redundancy on the other.

The disproportion between industrial and urban expansion means that more people now live in towns than can reasonably hope to work in them.

In other words, only a limited proportion of the lower classes have any meaningful place in the process of production, which alone could give them a sense of belonging to and being involved in modern life as members of the 'working-class', in which factory workers take a central position.

A lack of social unity is expressed by this uneven distribution of job-opportunity, which in its turn obstructs the rise of a properly integrated working-class, and correspondingly leads to a certain lack of political, social and economic cohesion in the rival middle-classes due to differences in development, overemployment in the service sector, contrasting standards of living, and imprudent speculation.

In the South real power resides with the coalition of forward-looking investors, politicians, bureaucrats and members of the new urban middle-class – all of whom are regarded as the enemies of the lower classes, whom they no longer control, but keep in disarray by stifling their aspirations to autonomy, regulating their standard of living, and setting limits to their economic opportunities of advance.[8]

A century has gone by since political unification, and economic unity is now also a fact, but imbalances persist, though economic integration is certainly increasing. These imbalances once revolved around agriculture, and now also relate to the abnormal escalation of the civil service, especially in the South, as is clear from the 1971 census returns, where it accounts for 30.4 per cent of total wages (20 per cent is the figure for Italy as a whole). Industrial earnings in the South come to 33 per cent of the total earnings, in comparison with 47 per cent throughout the whole country. In 1961 only 15.4 per cent of the Southern labour force was employed in industry, and in 1971 the figure was 14.9 per cent.

The actively employed fraction of the population has declined in the country as a whole, but particularly in the main Southern regions. Thus the 1971 figure for Naples was 25.3 per cent with Palermo and Bari at 30.3 per cent, in comparison with the national average of 34.7 per cent actively employed.

Differences between the South and the rest of Italy generally are also reflected in differences in average salaries among the professional classes,[9] (as we shall see more in detail later).

Enough has been said for the present about the differences in wages between individuals, geographical regions, and sectors of employment, and we shall now relate this to the distribution of the labour force itself.

The bipolarity within the situation is clear and hardly surprising. Salaries and pay rises have been higher in industry than in agriculture and more recently have risen even more in the tertiary or service sector. The geographical distribution of the economic cake has remained uneven, and this has contributed to the overall imbalance.

However, the situation is changing quickly, and all these changes have had important repercussions on the development of the vertical structure in relationship to the available labour force.

Italian society today is the consequence of a cultural, social and economic upheaval. There have been massive displacements of the population from agricultural labour to industry and the tertiary sector, from the countryside to the towns, with millions moving from the South to the North to seek employment in the rapidly expanding post-war industrial centres.

4 It is also particularly important to keep in mind the distinction between the active and inactive members of the population, since from unification times till the present day the proportion on the active list has steadily gone down.

Recently there has been a tremendous expansion of the tertiary sector in Italian society. This is partly due to the enormous development of the tourist industry which, in the space of a few years, has completely changed the appearance and life-style of entire regions. In addition, however, there is a pathological element, particularly serious in Italy, which involves the great extent to which state bureaucracy has spread throughout society.

Let us try and see how this situation affects the way in which the population fits into the vertical structure already mentioned. As regards the actively employed members of the population the economic development has obviously entailed a certain redistribution between the three sectors of the economy, similar to that which has taken place in other European countries, but in many ways more simple and straightforward.

Between 1951 and 1971 the percentage of the actively employed population engaged in agriculture dropped from 42.2 to 17.3 (51.7 in 1931), while the rise in industrial employment was from 32.1 to 44.5 per cent (26.3 per cent in 1931), with the tertiary sector expanding from 25.7 to 38.2 per cent (22 per cent in 1931).[10] Within each sector this development has been accompanied by a steady decrease in the percentage of those who are self-employed, and this trend is still apparent over the last three years.[11]

Moreover, taken as a percentage of the overall population, the proportion of those actively employed has dropped steadily from 59.5 per cent in 1861 to 49.3 per cent in 1931, 43.5 per cent in 1951, and 34.7 per cent in 1971.[12] This low percentage of actual workers is connected with the persisting imbalance in the Italian economy, and, as we have seen, there are sharp differences between North and South. The less industrialized regions account for a higher proportion of the inactive members of the population. Thus, in the highly industrialized North we find a labour force of 40.8 per cent in Piedmont and 40.7 per cent in Lombardy, while in the less developed South we find a labour force of only 29.8 per cent in Basilicata and 30.0 per cent in Calabria at the tip of the peninsula. The figures for the Italian islands are also low.[13]

The low percentage of the actively employed population stems from the well-known social and economic conditions of imbalance; but one cannot ignore the closed culture that still retains its hold on certain regions in the South. The temporarily unemployed are, by the way, treated as actively employed, and the inactive non-workers are such for cultural, psychological, conventional, economic, social, political and other reasons, so that the extent to which they are present in particular areas does mirror, at least to some degree, the cultural differences between North and South.

Of course, there is also a positive side to the drop in the active labour force. To some extent it reflects the rise in the school-leaving age and the drop in truancy, not to mention the recent boom in university education which now keeps perhaps as much as 2 per cent of the potential labour force otherwise occupied. The retirement age has also dropped, as it usually does in any advanced industrial society, even if in Italy retirement often coincides with re-employment in some forbidden occupation. The frequent need for retraining also often has the effect of squeezing certain workers out of their jobs in the competitive field of technology.

In any case, we have to remember that the drop in the labour force is not entirely real. It was due in part to the relative abandonment of agriculture and to the introduction of new ways of classifying jobs. The farmer's wife was regarded as actively employed because she helped with the work on the farm and in the fields, while in the city the housewife is not regarded as employed unless she also takes on some outside job. Women have been unable by and large to secure such work without first acquiring some specific training for it, and the result has been that the number of women workers in a rapidly changing economy remains small.

The actual figures available regarding the percentage of women actively employed are unreliable. For instance, it is clear that when the general census took place in 1971 the nature of the work women were engaged in their own homes was not always taken properly into account. Yet there are reliable indications that between one and two million women work at home.

Research in one town near Bologna revealed that while the 1971 census reckoned 3.0 per cent of women as working at home, the real figure was 13.4 per cent, and that the real figure for women employed in agriculture was 24.4 per cent instead of 17.4 per cent. In other towns with up-to-date agricultural and industrial economies the percentage of inactive housewives was 12.8 per cent although the census figure was 40.2 per cent; women working at home were 12.3 per cent in contrast with the census estimate of 3.6 per cent; and women manual-workers were 9.1 per cent and not the 7.5 per cent of the census returns, etc![14]

Even if, then, the active population has decreased, it has not done so as steadily as the figures suggest, especially in the North, and there is certainly not as close a relationship between the decrease in the active labour force and the unemployment figures as a superficial view might suggest.

In Italy today the unemployment problem is similar to that in other industrial countries. It fluctuates round about 3.5 per cent of the labour force, and it will be remembered that Keynes' theory favours unemployment of 2 or 3 per cent to maintain a fluid situation on the labour market. In 1970, 250,000 were unemployed and this had increased to 312,000 in 1971. The numbers of partially employed persons for these years stood at 272,000 and 281,000. Seasonal workers abroad and others temporarily employed outside Italy amounted to 233,000 and 210,000. It must be admitted that the percentage unemployed is higher if we examine the situation more closely, and take into account the potential labour force, the partially employed, those in compulsory retirement, etc. – but even then the figures are probably proportionally the same as those for other industrialized countries.

Some reckon that 15–18 per cent of the total labour force are in casual jobs.[15] If this figure is taken in conjunction with the number of those not officially trying to come off the inactive list, then the fraction of the potential labour force not being really used is somewhere between 29 and 33 per cent. Casual labour is not confined to the lower classes but comprises all those who for some reason or other work part-time or spasmodically. Perhaps Meldolesi exaggerates when he says that 'nationwide estimates show that more than 5 million are employed in casual labour, which is 25.7 per cent of the actual labour force, taking this to include those unemployed at present who are actually seeking work and have worked some time in the past'. Certainly the dualistic nature of the Italian economic structure prevents this phenomenon from being present to the same degree in the various regions or the different categories of employment. On the whole, casual work is more common in agriculture and rarer in the tertiary sector, where it is masked to some extent by the presence of a large number of workers in purely nominal or unnecessary occupations – the social parasites. The percentage of casual labour varies from region to region, and is generally in inverse proportion to the degree of development reached in the up-to-date sectors of the regional economy.[16]

The imbalance afflicting the nation, and more specifically that deriving from the disproportionate relationship between the active and inactive portions of the population, is clear if we examine this latter phenomenon more closely in the individual geographical regions.[17]

The census returns reveal that since 1951 employment in the agricultural sector has dropped more in the North than in the South, the ratio between the numbers actively engaged in agriculture in the South and those in the North being three to one in 1971 as against two to one in 1961. A similar imbalance in the basic situation and the sort of changes taking place in it can be noted in the overall employment figures, and the South is still the victim.[18]

However, the distinction between active and inactive population that is presupposed by these figures is now being increasingly questioned. If there is this distinction, it is certainly less clear-cut than the census returns suggest, especially with regard to the way in which employment in the tertiary sector is distributed.[19]

These findings put a question mark over other available figures, and the difficulty of reaching any certain conclusions is increased by the obvious fact that it is wrong to classify housewives as unemployed, though they are all too often so classified and figure in available and especially in official statistics as quite a high proportion of the so-called inactive population. Census returns and the analyses of economists are drawn up as if housewives were not productive workers in the tertiary or service sector, which is to ignore the child-care and other benefits they bring to society. However, the majority of housewives taken as a labour force belong in fact to the lumpenproletariat, the lower stratum, or the lower middle stratum, and some of them to the upper middle stratum. Unfortunately available statistics are insufficient for us to arrive at any realistic assessment of their true position, and we cannot as yet assign them accurately to the lower or lower middle stratum on the basis of their modes of occupation.

Despite these unresolved problems, we can nevertheless reach some sort of reliable conclusions, and we can agree that the developments within the vertical structure of society all point in much the same direction: a series of changes is taking place which amounts to a sort of minor revolution in the constitution of the population.

B. Emigration and movements between sectors

5   There is still a steady migration from country to town and from South to North. As a result, the population of North Italy is increasing sharply despite a lower birth-rate and a higher death-rate than in the South.[20]

Emigration to foreign countries remained a serious problem for Italy until very recent years, and this is borne out by the available statistics (see table 2.2). The main waves of emigration roughly coincide with the industrial expansion in the economy at the turn of the century and with the period of the economic miracle.

Table 2.2   Annual Average Emigration Figures for Persons of Working Age

	Total	*Peasants*
1871–80	98,128	40,144
1881–90	164,969	87,398
1891–1900	242,518	110,214
1901–10	541,079	198,010
1911–20	339,829	94,594
1921–30	225,943	56,789
1931–40	58,021	6,355
1941–50	62,124	13,983
1951–55	232,701	56,654

Source: ISTAT, *Sommario di statistiche*, p. 65.

Since 1955 emigration has lessened. Now the number of unskilled workers leaving the country is approximately equal to those coming into it, and the overall balance has dropped from 60,000 more emigrants than immigrants in 1967, to little more than 9000 in 1970, to only 3600 in 1972.[21]

Emigration to South America has dropped because since the end of the Second World War Italy's own economy has shown the higher per capita income margin of the two areas. With the creation of the Common Market, emigration towards France has also declined in favour of the richer countries of the continent, especially Germany and Switzerland.[22] Figures supplied by the Ministry of Foreign Affairs indicate that during the last fifteen years 2,340,384 Italians have resided abroad, 1,449,650 of these being in Common Market countries and 554,166 in Switzerland.

In the late 1960s and early 1970s Italians were still streaming out of the country, but most of them were no more than temporary emigrants[23] – going for little more than a year, if that, to Switzerland and the Common Market countries, and returning home periodically to profit by the chance of seasonal work in their native place. Thus, in recent years emigration has become very much a seasonal and marginal feature of the national life, without any permanent significance, and most members of the family stay put.

If we also consider the migratory movements from one part of Italy to another as emigration, this still provides a faithful picture of the imbalances within the nation's economy. Table 2.3 exhibits the balance of the emigration figures over a twenty-year period for the whole country and the principal regions. Emigration from the South that used to be directed abroad is increasingly in the direction of North Italy. In 1958 as many workers headed for North Italy as went outside the country, while ten years later, when Italy had taken some strides forward in the economic field, the majority were already opting for North Italy as their destination.

Table 2.3   Emigration Balance-sheet for the Main Regions of Italy (thousands)

	1951–61	1961–71
North Italy (industrialized)	+ 616	+ 956
Central Italy (in course of development)	+ 124	+ 205
Southern Italy and Islands (underdeveloped)	−1772	−2318
All Italy	−1032	−1157

The nature of the migration taking place in recent times therefore reflects the economic state of the nation.[24] The actual movement is from poor rural areas into prosperous urban centres,[25] and from Southern poor rural areas via Southern urban centres into Northern towns. Emigration on the whole speeds up the process of urbanization, though the proportion of the population living in towns of more than 100,000 inhabitants is increasing more rapidly in the South than in the North – rising from 15.5 per cent in 1951 to 33.6 per cent in 1971 in the South, and from 28.3 per cent to 32.3 per cent in the North during the same period.[26]

Emigration also has considerable cultural and social implications, as is clear from many inquiries that have been made, including our own referred to in the Introduction (note 1). In Italy schools and the mass media only exercise a slow influence and even then do not always succeed in their efforts to make new models of living popular. Large-scale emigration, on the other hand, especially when it is only temporary in nature, brings with it much more rapid changes in consumer habits and cultural attitudes; like tourism and urbanization it is one of the main catalysts of renewal. The movements backwards and forwards between town and countryside, and especially between rural areas in the South and the cities of North Italy and Europe generally, provoke a steady evolutionary change, principally with regard to practical behaviour and habits of consumption, and indirectly in the more stable fields of personal values and social *mores*.

One clear result, as we mentioned, was a massive shift away from agriculture to other sectors of employment. From among the available studies we can refer once more to Sylos Labini's attempt (1973) at calculating the extent to which unskilled labour is drained off into one sector of the economy from another in order to understand the drop in agricultural workers between 1951 and 1970. His results are shown in table 2.4. These figures indicate the way in which workers are moving, but, as the author admits, the scheme is over-simplified. The traffic is really in both directions, and the actual movement is quite complex. We know, for instance, that an unspecified but considerable number of those self-employed in agriculture choose to become wage-earners.

Table 2.4   The Exodus from Agriculture 1951–1970 (millions)

Self-employed in agriculture	−2.4	Office workers	+1.3
		In business (etc.)	+0.7
		Total	+2.0
Hired agricultural labour	−1.5	*Wage-earners:*	
		Building trade	+0.4
		Industry	+0.2
		Other work	+0.9
		Total	+1.5

Quite a lot of agricultural labourers move into the building trade as a first step. This trade takes up the less skilled section of the labour force and, whenever it is in crisis, leaves them without jobs, so that they swell the numbers in the hovels and shanty towns on the outskirts of the large cities, especially from Rome southwards. Other agricultural labourers, though not as many, take up jobs that require rather more skill. Then there are some who fail to get any job at all, but live from hand to mouth on the outskirts of the large industrial cities in the North, until they at last succeed in securing a place in the building trade or elsewhere.

The niches filled by such one-time agricultural workers are left vacant by workers improving their social standing, or else going into retirement once their more qualified children have secured some more favoured occupation, or, alternatively, taking up a newly created position that the advance of technology or the expansion of the tertiary sector has made available.

Some agricultural workers, particularly those who were self-employed as farmers or market-gardeners, become office workers or run a small business.

The situation is a complex one, but workers are certainly leaving agriculture for other sectors at the rate of 250–300,000 per year, and this has been happening for many years, with the number oscillating a little whenever there was some temporary change in the economic situation as a whole.

C. Conclusions

6 In addition to the imbalance and uneven development we have discussed, it will be as well to summarize the changes that have taken place or are still taking place in the vertical structure, and which have their repercussions on the complex of factors that determine both the way in which authority is exercised and the form taken by relationships between classes and the nature of social stratification. The advances made in technology and in the economy as a whole during the first and, to some extent, during the second industrial revolution have left their mark on Italy, giving rise with the passage of time to three main interrelated groups of phenomena, of which the first are already fully realized, while the others continue to unfold before our eyes.

(1) diminishing importance of agriculture within the economy as a whole;
the formation of a working-class;
the dominance of the industrial or secondary sector of the economy over the primary or agricultural sector and the tertiary or service sector.
(2) diminishing importance not only of agriculture but also of industry in favour of the tertiary sector;
changes in social stratification within the industrial sector where high status attaches to new roles and forms of activity (we shall develop this point when we discuss the horizontal structure of Italian society).

(3) the increase in automation with the introduction of more advanced forms of mechanization, which seems to be among the factors triggering-off the boom in the tertiary sector;
the clear dominance of science and technology within the social system, giving society a new character, and determining its specific stratification and power structure (as we shall see when we examine the pyramid of power).[27]

What we have just said completes our survey of what, for purposes of convenience, we have called the vertical structure of Italian society, though we have included in the discussion some related observations that were more concerned with spatial mobility. We have seen that the trend in Italian society is from the primary to the secondary sector with the tertiary sector growing in importance. There is also a tendency to employ men rather than women in a labour force that is contracting instead of expanding, and that is declining in numbers, in effectiveness, and in its productive capacity, as society becomes increasingly split in two, with an increasing number living in the North, where most of the industry is, and which has become the cultural centre as well as the trend-setter for the whole peninsula.

These developments result partly from historical causes already familiar to the reader, and stem also from certain features of the contemporary social structure which will emerge in what follows. The typical *polarization* within Italy is a dynamic outgrowth from the equally characteristic *imbalance* and *dualism* already present in the social structure when the character of life was more static.[28]

Notes to chapter 2

1. For these data and a more elaborate consideration of the topic see D'Antonio, 1973, p. 59, using ISTAT as primary source.
2. Censis, 1973, II, appendix, p. 43.
3. See ISTAT, *Compendio statistico 1972*.
4. See Saraceno, 1968b, pp. 709–55, especially p. 712.
5. See ISTAT, *Censimento . . . 1951, 1961 and 1971*.
6. See Saraceno, 1968b, p. 737.
7. See Ferrari Bravo and Serafini, 1972, pp. 13ff. Both authors have expanded this point considerably. Also Sylos Labini, 1973.
8. See Donolo, 1972, pp. 101–128, especially p. 104.

9. *Average individual annual incomes in the different professional categories*

	Total	Entre-preneur	Manager	Employee	Self-employed in agriculture	Other-wise self-employed	Without pro-fessional status
	In thousands	*of lire*					
N. Italy	1364	5510	2060	1270	1200	1730	760
Central	1140	2740	1880	1160	1150	1270	590
South and Islands	994	2660	1910	940	960	1050	560
All Italy	1210	4310	1992	1159	1090	1460	660
In indices (*Total* = 100)							
N. Italy	113	455	170	105	99	143	63
Central	94	226	155	96	95	105	49
South and Islands	82	220	158	78	79	87	46
All Italy	100	356	165	96	90	121	55

Sources: ISTAT, *Compendio statistico, 1972*, and other ISTAT sources.

10. See ISTAT, 'Sviluppo della popolazione', pp. 219–22; ISTAT, 1972, *XI censimento, 1971*, vol. 1, 'Primi risultati provinciali e comunali sulla popolazione e sulle abitazione. Dati provvisori', pp. 1 and 5; Braghin, 1973, p. 98. The data in the 1971 census results are provisional and not entirely consistent with previous figures. The overall total is for the active population and not, as in earlier census returns, for those actually employed.

11. Censis, 1973, II p. 43.

12. ISTAT, *XI censimento, 1971*.

13. Meldolesi, 1972, p. 59.

14. Bergonzini, 1973, pp. 50–54.

15. Meldolesi, 1972, p. 57.

16. *Ibid.*, p. 51.

17. ISTAT, *XI censimento, 1971*.

18. Meldolesi, 1972, p. 51.

19. See Censis, 1973, p. 126, where the problem is analysed.

20. *Ibid.*, p. 126.

21. ISTAT figures.

22. Emigration overseas picked up again after the Second World War and during the early fifties. The Government, it should be noted, took this phenomenon into account, organizing and helping it along. See Mottura and Pugliese, 1973, pp. 231–56, especially p. 234.

23. See Mottura and Pugliese, 1973, p. 232.

24. *Ibid.*, p. 235.

25. It seems to us, however, that the favourable economic developments in the late 1950s, which lasted into the 1960s, gave a different and more positive tone to large-scale movements of workers, who were no longer merely trying to escape from intolerable conditions, or in a mood to accept pretty well any sort of work and to adjust to any sort of situation in their new homes.

26. ISTAT figures. See also Sylos Labini, 1973.

27. Acquaviva, 1971b, p. 55.

28. Basic inequalities of this kind are common to other industrialized and developing countries, and combine with the fact that a considerable portion of the labour force is tied to backward or relatively non-productive areas, because of the rapidity of the economic development, its concentration in particular zones, and difficulties in the redistribution and rehousing of the labour force, which is disproportionately large in some areas, while elsewhere there is an alarming shortage of suitably qualified men. The problem of manpower is only one aspect of the widespread and even organized waste that forms one of the props of the developing Italian society. Waste is characteristic of advanced societies and came to Italy early, at a point when the new economy had only spread as far as a few regions in the peninsula. This resulted in the paradoxical situation of wealth being squandered in underdeveloped areas.

CHAPTER 3

The Horizontal Structure

A. Preliminary observations: the rationale of Italian social stratification

7   The notion of horizontal structure takes us back to what we said in the preceding chapter about social classification and stratification. We relate the horizontal structure to its economic basis, and so one might expect it to almost coincide with the class-system, while other considerations bring it closer to the notion of social strata.

Because our approach is operational and pragmatic we can be content to define 'horizontal structure', 'class', 'stratum' and *ceto* (see p. 10) in relation to our own particular way of analysing this single specific society, and have no need to decide in favour of either Marx or Dahrendorf, Sweezy or Warner. We are simply trying to unravel the tangled skein of Italian society and to take a close look at it. Our actual use of these technical terms will, therefore, define them implicitly, and will in that sense justify their application to one particular society during a certain period of its history, without having any universal pretentions.

With the passage of time Italian society has acquired an increasingly complex stratification in order to meet the requirements of the economic development that we have already described. For, generally speaking,

> *the more extensive and complex the social organization becomes, the more sophisticated its structure and the greater, at times, the separation between the powerful and the downtrodden, the highly qualified and the untrained,*

so that it becomes increasingly hard to appreciate the justice of the remuneration attached to positions calling for a high degree of expertise. At the same time, there is a collective thrust towards more communication, more education, a higher degree of social democracy.[1]

All this has proved true of Italy, and has led to a whole series of upheavals within the social structure, though we cannot yet go into them as fully as their nature requires. Our own analysis begins with property and control of the means of production, because the developing economic situation, which includes these, is certainly among the factors essentially determining the formation of the horizontal structure. Why this should be so is a legitimate question, but at present we simply note the fact.

It is an obvious but still important truth, for example, that the expansion in the ownership and control of industrial plant and commercial undertakings and the contraction of agricultural holdings has radically changed the horizontal structure of Italian society. This is why we propose to defer till later the usual analysis of social stratification based on the distribution of income, the use made of it, the self-image of members of the different social strata, and their opinion of the stratum to which they belong, as well as of the strata to which they make it seem important not to belong.[2] Before making that analysis we shall examine the relationship between individual incomes and the productive source that supplies them.

Along with the Marxists we reject any definition of stratum that derives merely from income, consumption and related social and cultural behaviour. Furthermore, we understand possession and control of the means of production in a somewhat extended sense, so that it takes in the media of communication such as television and the educational system, as well as the production of any sort of tertiary service.

Moreover, while our operational model treats the horizontal structure that is more closely linked with the means of production as distinct from the power structure, it is obvious that, despite its logical attractions and its value as an explanatory tool, the distinction in practice only holds to a limited extent. There is usually a very close link between the horizontal structure and the power structure, though this is not always or necessarily the case. Some institutions impinge on values, others on behaviour, and yet others on both. Indeed, although they are rare in Italy, there are institutions, including some extreme religious groups, which have neither economic standing nor any recognized legal position, but which nevertheless wield considerable power.

Usually, at any rate, any discussion of the horizontal structure will include a mention of at least some of the factors which have a bearing on the individual's place within or in relation to the power structure. The study of the power structure is conditioned by that of the economy. It influences and is influenced by the way in which the means of production are controlled. The nature and extent of its effective hold on social life need to be examined and understood, and this includes the basis of its claim to legitimacy, its relationship with the means of production, and, more generally, its links with the various sources of wealth.

For the present let us turn to consider the horizontal structure, focussing the main questions regarding it from the point of view of control of the means of production. If we relate our study of contemporary Italy to analyses made by certain Italian economists, we can distinguish the following sorts of income in relationship with the means by which they are produced:

(a)   income from land owned: in the country; in the town.
(b)   income from capital invested in: agriculture; business; industry.
(c)   income in return for work: selling one's own or someone else's labour.
(d)   unsteady income: social outcasts and the lumpenproletariat (whether they sell their labour or not).

A few comments may help.

(a) *Income from land owned.* We take income from land owned in the country and in the town separately because, though some may disagree, it is unrealistic not to do so in the light of the rapid urban development taking place, the conversion of agricultural holdings into property-development sites, speculation in areas of probable development, the power in the hands of those deciding which areas are to be developed, and the way in which such decisions are made.

(b) *Income from capital investment.* Economists usually speak of the profits from agriculture, commerce or industry. Even the more old-fashioned authors also include financiers as a related capitalist sub-group operating the banking system and similar services. Their importance is increased in Italy by the extent to which they are under state control. On the other hand, it is essential in the Italian case to distinguish clearly between the public and private sectors of industry when discussing profits, and this is also true to some extent in the business world.

(c) *Income in return for work.* This is a question of selling one's own or someone else's labour. Although several unsuccessful attempts have been made, it is very hard to classify or stratify individuals on this basis. There are many reasons for this. Obviously, one has to consider separately wages paid to manual and non-manual workers, salaries paid to middle management, salaries paid to technical staff and the salaries of the directors and general managers. The salaries of those in the last group, and often of those in the last two groups are somewhat mixed in nature, since they vary to some extent in proportion to the year's takings in the business as a whole; such earnings often defy exact calculation even by authorized official investigators. They vary considerably between sectors and within each sector, depending on whether the work is under private control or state ownership, and also on the nature of the work itself – heavy engineering, the chemical industry, etc.[3]

Equal incomes often carry with them membership of differing social groups and even of different social strata, so that equality in earnings does not necessarily correspond with equality in status and power. Someone in an administrative job, especially within the civil service, is far differently placed from a teacher or nurse.

Then, to add to the complications, there are people with part-time jobs who also earn money as self-employed persons, either as craftsmen or in some other way, such as small-scale farming and gardening.

(d) *Unsteady income.* The lumpenproletariat includes many people, especially in the South, whose incomes are intermittent and often quite irregular. In cities such as Naples, Palermo and Catania their number is relatively stable, being more or less inversely proportional to that of the active population. They often give a city its specific atmosphere and special colour, keeping alive an Italy that is fast disappearing but has not yet lost its importance. We shall return to this point.

8   The scheme we have proposed refers in the first place to the different sources of income, but it obviously has to take into account other factors that help to determine an individual's social standing, such as:

(1) nature and presence or absence of direct or indirect control of or dependence upon the capital or property which is the source of the individual's income;

(2) way in which this income is obtained and how reliable it is – whether the work is manual, intellectual, etc.;

(3) amount of one's earnings, which may depend on the factors mentioned under (1) and (2) and on the nature of the capital investment (agricultural, industrial, etc.).

A more complex and more fully articulated consideration of the relevant factors results from taking note of the grounds on which the individual is allocated to a particular social stratum:

(1) whether one's work is in the public or private sector of the economy;

(2) the ability and opportunity of exercising administrative and political control over the sources of income and over the way in which profits are made and shared out;

(3) contractual rights over the exercise of individual skill granted the opportunity of its being used;

(4) the allocation of different jobs and positions among those on the pay-roll;

(5) the nature and extent of the division of labour within the sector in which one is working;

(6) with what degree of flexibility and autonomy one can carry out one's work.

B. Schematic view of Italian social strata

9 On the basis of the three factors together with the six additional ones proposed in our theoretical model, let us now reconsider the horizontal structure in relation to actually existing social strata. Something like the following classification seems to be required.

(a) *The upper stratum* will comprise:

Those who derive an income from their ownership of land in the town or country, and sometimes also possess other immoveable goods.

Those who have capital invested in finance, commerce or industry from which they derive their income.

Those who exercise some degree of control over the means of production and receive an adequate income as directors or general managers of privately-owned or state-controlled businesses or industrial concerns, so that they can afford to live the style of life the upper-stratum condition demands.

Leading and other well-placed professional workers able to accumulate wealth rapidly and steadily by pursuing their chosen activity alone or as members of a small group, even if only at the local level.

Heads of government departments whose income allows them to live life at upper-stratum standards, and who can be accepted into it because they control the machinery of government which ensures the survival of society as a whole and allows production to take place within a framework of security.

Men of science, heads of research laboratories and university professors, whose position, independently of the salary attached to it, allows them many opportunities of making a living in other directions as editors, by taking out patents on their inventions, being called in as consultants, etc.

Other persons, such as established authors and those in control of the mass media, who exercise an influence that is in some respects similar to that of the members of the preceding categories. They enjoy membership of the upper stratum for a variety of reasons, but must be able to secure a regularly high income, and to accumulate capital quite rapidly.

(b) *The upper middle stratum* will comprise:

The less affluent bourgeoisie of more or less independent means, whose income comes from their control of the means of production, though they themselves may do some work as well, but whose total earnings are not much different from those of regular office workers.

Office workers whose earnings depend on their working for or at least under the control of members of the upper stratum and who thus constitute the labour force of the owners of public or private agricultural, commercial or industrial capital. Their earnings may not be much higher than a worker's average wage, but are paid as a monthly salary.

Their rate of pay justifies our including in this category such intermediate groupings as non-commissioned officers in the army, rural deans, parish priests of large parishes and lower-grade police officers, etc.

(c) *The lower middle stratum* will comprise:

Factory workers and the like who, like office workers, depend for their living on work for or under the control of members of the upper stratum. They sell their labour to the owners of public or private agricultural, commercial or industrial capital.

There is no clear distinction in levels of earnings between the upper middle and lower middle strata, but the latter do manual work for the most part, while the former are mainly clerical workers.

(d) *The lower stratum* will comprise:

The lumpenproletariat whose main earnings are usually less than those of other workers, and are obtained in ways that do not fit into the administrative and productive structures of Italian society today. Because of their importance in the national life and their special characteristics, it seems as well to explain their position in more detail.

Like their opposite numbers in other industrialized societies, they fall outside the bounds of the contemporary capitalist technostructure. However, they are distinguished by the fact that they are (a) more numerous and (b) related by their values and life-style to the fast-vanishing social structures of a now outmoded Italian society. They are a throw-back to the period of underdevelopment, living relics of the past left behind by the accelerating developments in society at large. Their influence is dwindling in extent, and lies mainly in the South. Leaving their home territories or cultural enclaves increasingly deserted, they are moving into the larger Southern cities and, less rapidly, into the industrial centres of the North.

These historical elements at the core of the Italian lumpenproletariat are being joined today by those who for other reasons do not feel at home in the conventional social structures. The school-leaving age has been raised, but, especially in Southern Italy, truancy drives many towards the fringes of society. The earlier retirement age also brings into existence a further band of alienated souls, living outside the mainstream of society, but at the same time providing a reserve labour force that can be called upon whenever there is some special need – just as the housewives can buttress the economy by working part-time outside the home, or taking on occasional full-time jobs.

The implication is that modern Italian society eliminates the problem of unemployment as such by encouraging and, as it were.

institutionalizing this reserve labour force of persons estranged from its main structures. However, old-age pensioners, housewives, students, etc. are not the real lumpenproletariat. This remains as we first described it with the addition of new elements whose position has not been institutionalized. Membership of the lumpenproletariat depends in the main on the way in which a person earns his living. Income obtained outside the mainstream of the national economy of production and services and administration, or obtained surreptitiously or deviously, is obviously not the same sort of thing as the wage-packet of the production-line worker, or the regular old-age pension.

Such, then, is our proposed classification into strata. It is flexible and adapted to the actual Italian situation. It is a simple division into four strata, without making complicated distinctions that are hard to justify in practice. Possibly a division into six, eight or ten strata might have been more accurate, but it would have been hard to show this in an introductory study, or to provide any statistics or other detailed information corresponding to such a division. Our four social strata suffice to indicate the nature of the Italian social problem accurately enough for present purposes. As the analysis proceeds, we shall make some further distinctions whenever this seems useful.

There are limitations to our classification, of course, quite apart from the choice of a restricted number of social strata. After all, the society to which it is being applied is a single society only in name. The various regions have, at least to some extent, their own peculiar and quite self-contained stratification systems, which could only have been illustrated by using some alternative model. Furthermore, Italy as a whole is split in two, so that it might be better to think of it in terms of two separate but interrelated stratification systems, corresponding to two societies that coexist in some sort of symbiosis but never attain total integration.

To the extent that the distinctions between strata have been left rather vague and imprecise, the scheme we have proposed may seem excessively open-ended and pragmatic. On the other hand, in relationship to the dualism present in Italian society, it can appear too rigid. In other words, it is a compromise.

C. The reality behind the scheme

10   There are both qualitative and quantitative considerations to be made – how many people belong to each stratum, what characterizes each stratum, and how one lives as a member of it.

We shall begin with a bird's-eye view. Then we shall consider each aspect in more detail. The final synthesis we shall reserve for our concluding section.

Quantitative considerations

11   The available data, even when supplied by the Central Institute of Statistics, are for the most part unreliable, and the analyses already made by economists and sociologists are far from complete, and do not suffice for our purposes. A few years ago, however, the economist Paolo Sylos Labini did reach some reliable, even if only approximate conclusions.[4] He distinguished five strata, and table 3.1 (in which we have replaced numbers by percentages) shows their progress from 1881 to the population census of 1971. These approximations by Sylos Labini often do not agree with the official census returns.

The table, while comprehensive in its own way, fails to correspond with our own system of classification, and it insufficient for our purposes. The upper stratum, or what Sylos Labini calls the bourgeoisie, is restricted to 500,000 members, which probably is far below the real figure. This is certainly the case if the upper stratum is re-defined along the lines we ourselves have suggested. Moreover, the table says nothing about the lumpenproletariat, which Sylos Labini is careful to treat separately in conjunction with casual labourers.[5] (See table 3.2.) Despite this, table 3.1 does on the whole describe quite well the social stratification of the active members of the population.

Another table also sheds light on the incomes of the various groups in 1971.[6] Sylos Labini notes, for instance, that:

> *rich families (with a net income in excess of 800,000 lire a month) are 3% of the whole (500,000 families or about 1,400,000 persons), while poor, including extremely poor families (with a total family income of less than 80,000 lire*

Table 3.1   Social Stratification of Active and Inactive Population (percentages)

	1881	1901	1921	1951	1961	1971
I *Bourgeoisie*	2.25	1.84	1.98	2.02	2.04	2.56
1. Owners, contractors and managers	1.32	—	1.13	1.26	1.02	1.02
2. Professional people	0.92	—	0.85	0.75	1.01	1.53
II *The Middle-Classes*	50.72	48.46	50.28	50.00	47.44	48.71
(a) Small bourgeois office workers:	2.31	2.76	2.95	9.09	11.22	15.89
1. in the private sector	0.66	0.92	0.90	4.04	5.10	9.23
2. in the public sector[1]	1.65	1.84	2.04	5.05	6.12	6.66
(b) Small bourgeoisie of more or less independent means:	44.03	41.71	43.18	36.86	31.63	28.71
1. Farmers and market-gardeners[2]	30.46	30.67	31.25	24.24	17.85	12.30
2. Craftsmen[2]	8.60	5.52	5.68	5.55	5.10	5.64
3. Businessmen and shopkeepers	2.98	4.29	5.11	5.55	7.14	8.71
4. Transport workers and others in the service sector	1.98	1.22	1.13	1.51	1.53	2.05
(c) Special categories:	4.37	3.98	4.14	4.04	4.59	4.10
1. Soldiers	1.05	1.22	2.04	1.46	1.68	1.79
2. Monks, priests and nuns	0.86	0.79	0.68	0.60	0.61	0.76
3. Others[3]	2.45	1.96	1.42	1.96	2.29	1.53
III *The Working-Class* (working for a wage)	49.00	49.69	47.72	47.97	50.51	48.71
1. agriculture	26.49	26.38	22.15	13.63	10.71	6.15
2. industry	16.55	17.17	18.75	20.70	21.93	22.05
3. building-trade	3.31	3.68	3.97	6.56	10.20	8.71
4. business and commerce	0.66	0.61	0.56	3.03	3.06	3.58
5. transport and special services	1.98	1.84	2.27	4.04	4.59	8.20
Population: active percentage	51.70	48.00	46.50	41.70	39.10	35.50

1. Workers in the public sector include soldiers (IIc1), working-class state employees (III5), and number as many as 1,750,000, in addition to those monks, priests and nuns (IIc2) who also receive an income from the state.

2. Here are included small contractors and sub-contractors; share-croppers have been reckoned with the other cultivators; small professional people have been put with craftsmen, for whom the 1881 figures include those working in their own homes.

3. Domestic servants, porters, sacristans, etc.

Table 3.2   **Lumpenproletariat and Casual Workers in the late 1960s (millions)**

		Casual workers[1]		Lumpenproletariat[2]	
Agriculture	North	0.3	Country		0.5
	South	0.6			
	Total	0.9	Town: 'in industry'		0.5
				other activity	0.5
Industry	North	0.6	Total		1.5
	South	1.4			
	Total	2.0			
Other activities	North	0.2			
	South	0.6			
	Total	0.8			
Total	North	1.1			
	South	2.6			
	Total	3.7			

1. Casual workers were also included in Table 3.1 in such categories as crafts-men, sub-contractors, businessmen, agricultural workers and those in the building trade. They are concentrated in the South, which accounts for 70 per cent of them, or proportionally twice as many of them as in Italy as a whole.

2. The lumpenproletariat has been estimated very approximately, and if it were taken to include certain persons actively holding down some sort of odd job might be double the one we have given. Agricultural workers hired and paid on a day-to-day basis are very poor and have been grouped with the lumpenproletariat, along with some who work in their own homes or in unregistered workshops on a commission basis, or live as unlicensed commercial travellers.

a month) account for 15–20% of the total figure (3 million families or about 9 million persons). The 'rich' include top management in both private and public sectors (200,000), contractors (100,000), professional people (100,000) and rentiers (100,000). The 'poor' include 2 million wage-earners, comprising first of all agricultural day-labourers, some special categories of workers (IIc), 300,000 small tradesmen, counting travelling salesmen, 500,000 peasants with small holdings, 400,000 small-scale craftsmen, and various independent workers. Assistants to workers in agriculture, commerce or some particular craft have especially low individual incomes, but these are usually only an additional contribution to a larger family income. Casual workers and, above all, the lumpenprole-tarian element are reckoned as belonging to the category of very poor workers.

(*'Poor'* and *'very poor'* families include some comprising only one or two elderly folk, usually on a pension, living in the country, and in a position to have home-grown fruit and vegetables or their own farm produce, as well as receiving help from relatives. Their position is better than that of their opposite numbers who live inside a town.) Finally, it should not be forgotten that quite a lot of office workers, farmers, market-gardeners, agricultural labourers and specialized workmen also have some extra work on the side, which never shows up in the statistics – just as many women have some part-time occupation that is not included in official figures.[7]

Typical features of the different strata

12   Clearly this distribution of incomes depends on the factors we have mentioned as well as on other less important ones.[8] We began by indicating the connection between control of the means of production and social stratification, worked out a classification system, and then provided an approximate idea of the numbers in the various categories, while stressing that they were only approximate. It remains for us to consider their qualitative aspect, describing briefly the distinguishing features of the various strata within the horizontal structure of Italian society.

(a) *The upper stratum.* A few decades ago it was easy to define the upper crust within Italian society. It comprised a small, restricted élite circle of intellectuals, bankers, industrialists and land-owners, with a culture that was Catholic or free-thinking or both, and only to a limited extent favourably disposed to Fascism.

Since the war, and particularly in the last few years, the situation has become much more fluid. The state bureaucracy has expanded considerably, and so has the welfare state. Top officials in this state apparatus form a single élite circle with the army and the police, but their status within the country as a whole is not very high.

Rather more importance attaches to the rise of the management class in both the public and private sectors of industry. They, too, are now an élite group with a culture and characteristics of their own, and their own way of exercising the power that is now theirs.

The development of these new élite groups is linked to that of the government, industrial and other bureaucracies that increasingly typify the new Italian society, permeating the educational and social service organizations, etc. Each of these bureaucratic structures has its own hierarchy, and competition is keen, especially in the industrial situation.

In Italy, as elsewhere, industrialization has meant the arrival on the scene of vast complexes, one-time national ones like Pirelli (rubber) and Fiat (cars and heavy engineering), international ones such as the large oil-companies, and these all have their own close-knit bureaucracies and their pyramids of power. 'The rapid development of productive networks has demanded an equally rapid expansion within the administration, and from the early stages of the industrial revolution until now the rhythm of its advance seems to have been in geometrical progression.'[9]

The rapid rise in production that we have observed has, of course, called for an increasing number of experts to plan and draw up programmes for individual companies, whole sectors of the economy, and the nation as a whole. This has meant the emergence of a more complex management system within privately-owned as well as in state-controlled industries, and also in the government departments concerned with the country's economic development. In this way there has come into being a structure of power at the top that is entirely different from the traditionally accepted one; it is based on skill, specialized knowledge, control of the means of production, without being necessarily related to ownership at all.

In the context of this sort of bureaucracy the executives, and in particular the general managers, employed by the larger companies have assumed considerable importance in the life of the nation as a whole. They are earning their living in a way that assures them a certain social status, and this in turn increases their personal freedom and general prestige.

The upper stratum of yesterday is thrown into disarray – their position also depended on economic factors in the background to justify it indirectly, but sprang much more obviously from traditions going back for generations. Members of the new élite are often drawn from quite humble origins, and have made a career for themselves for purely personal reasons or in order to expand their horizons. Their arrival on the scene changes the whole tone of society, modifies the overall culture, and alters the balance of power at the top.

The organization of the new managers coupled with their social status and economic power has diminished the effective influence of rich people investing their capital in industry or the service sector. The relationships between those who own the means of production and those who actually control them are no longer what they were, and prestige increasingly attaches to those who are in control. This is particularly true of nationalized industries, and these are expanding all the time. Such expansion increases the prestige of the management, while, in the private sector too, managers grow in numbers and status. Mere ownership of the means of production begins to seem something rather faceless and impersonal, and in Italy now has little to do with their management and control, which alone seems important.

There has also been, as we shall see, an incomplete attempt to rationalize the whole life of society. This has involved the coming into being of a whole variety of public and semi-public organizations and associations, such as the government's economic development programme advisory committee and the bodies responsible for improving the economy of Southern Italy. In each of these the management class enjoy considerable power and prestige.

However, membership of the upper stratum is not restricted to the *ceti* traditionally within it in company with the new management élites. We must also mention certain professional figures operating in the tertiary sector. In post-industrial Italy their number and influence is growing. As well as such established figures as the doctor with an important practice or the famous lawyer, several other personalities must be mentioned. There are, for instance, the television and film directors, who manipulate the overall culture, men in charge of advertising or information services, doctors in charge of hospitals, and a thousand and one people in charge of one or other new organized undertaking in our modern society. Just think how many writers there now are working in every field, whether technical, scientific or cultural, and making quite a lot of money out of their profession.

Thus, there exists a new upper stratum as a result of a change that has been steady, even if at times it passed unnoticed. The power structure itself is now different, precisely because this stratum is pluralist in its values and in its potentialities. In due course, when discussing the pyramid of power, we shall examine how this renewal and transformation of the upper stratum has affected the power system.

Before concluding, we can mention that the new rich, who make up a fair proportion of the upper stratum, probably because of the rapidity with which they have achieved their new position, seldom have a more than average level of culture, but are rather conservative and narrow-minded, more concerned to defend their own immediate interests than to take a long-range view of life or work out some overall strategy for themselves.

The scientists and top technicians within the upper stratum do spread their own pragmatic and vaguely liberal outlook towards life, but so far their influence on the way in which power is exercised and on the general life of the country is negligible.

In the course of the post-war industrial revolution there has also developed a further social stratum, which we include with the upper stratum, but whose exact position falls mid-way between it and the upper middle stratum. This comprises a fairly affluent group of independent middle bourgeois, which has developed since 1945. Alongside the large-scale industries, but quite independently of them, a very large number of small and medium-sized industries have come into being, especially in the North. The vast Po valley, which holds almost half the total population of the country, is packed with industries of this kind, which are to be found in every town and village. It is a vast network. Sometimes a thousand small concerns are concentrated in quite a small area and cluster round some large-scale industry. A similar situation holds true of the neighbourhood of Milan and the mainland sections of Venice. Here industrialization has cut right through the previously existing social structures, and given rise to entirely new centres of population with quite a different style of living. For the most part, however, these thousands of factories have been fitted into the established pattern, and have adapted themselves to it without necessitating any social changes in the short term. Accordingly, they have not made any great difference to people's politics or to their basic values.

Nevertheless, a new social stratum has come into being, unless we simply say the earlier one has changed its character. Most of these small industrialists (*padroncini* they are called in Italian) have a working-class or peasant background, with a political and social outlook that tends to be rather traditional and conservative. In

Veneto and Lombardy many of them were at one time farmers or market-gardeners, and it is there that they are most numerous, but in many areas they have come to represent the backbone of the Catholic party, which is also favoured by present-day cultivators.

These small industries, as we have already suggested, depend for their survival on the large-scale enterprises, which, at least initially, they supply with spare parts, tools, gadgets, services and the like. Everything is done cheaply, because they operate on narrow profit margins and find it easier to escape taxation. These industries, then, are complementary to the large-scale ones.

There are others, however, which manufacture for direct supply to the consumer totally new products that have never previously been on the market. Some *padroncini*, such as those concerned with washing-machines, fridges and other electrically powered domestic appliances, for a long time, until the recent contraction of the vertical structure, displayed a great spirit of business initiative, which marks them out as men for whom the old Italian value-system is over and done with. They start off as workmen, soon become craftsmen, and suddenly find themselves industrial magnates with orders coming in from all over Europe. There are so many of these people that some believe their activity is the main reason behind Italy's development within the last fifty years.

Tourism is another area in which people are quickly moving out of the upper middle stratum and swelling the ranks of the upper stratum. Peasants, lifeguards, office workers, and waiters are opening hotels and restaurants by the thousand, and very often these are quickly transformed into a whole chain of large-scale holdings. In many cases this has meant that hundreds of miles of coastline in a previously mainly agricultural area have been developed in a way that has pushed the area into the tertiary sector of the economy, without its having ever been industrialized at all. As a large-scale phenomenon this sort of thing has been restricted to Italy and Spain, though it is true to a lesser extent of France, Germany and Yugoslavia. This social and economic upheaval on the Italian coasts has considerable, if unforeseen boomerang effects on specific sectors of the economy, including long-term ones on those places near the coast that produce tourist souvenirs.

In keeping with the Marxist truism, then, the traditional small crafts are in recession because they could not meet the challenge of industrial competition. However, many of the craftsmen of a generation ago proved to be the industrialists of the 1950s and 1960s, and there has also arisen a new range of crafts, often artistic, fanciful and even whimsical in the way both in which the goods are designed, and in which they are put on the market – their inventors never seem to tire of devising new ones, always in the Italian style, which pave the way for their later industrial production and sale.

Thus, it is well known how fashions start a trend in shoes and clothing, and so create a need for industry to supply. Italian designs for car-bodies have been sold and used throughout Europe by the leading car manufacturers. Small craftsmen complement large-scale industry either directly by working for it, or indirectly by inventing new products and opening up new markets that larger industries take over at a later stage.

Such innovations come more easily to those small business undertakings which, although up to date, are rooted in the traditional culture and value-system. In the 1950s, for instance, Italian women's fashions, sexually appealing but self-consciously modest, corresponded accurately enough with the image of herself that the Italian woman was trying to project in society, in which there was a concern to be sexually attractive, and at the some time an equal concern to defend her position as lady of the house. To be in fashion one had to look sexy without seeming a flirt. A few years later this fashion was replaced by others copied from Britain and America, which later still were re-expressed somewhat laboriously in the Mediterranean idiom. One thinks of stiletto heels as indicative of a sex that is 'inhibited and reserved'.

To conclude, the upper stratum has been strengthened and the mobility between strata has been increased by some strictly economic factors, by the new spirit of enterprise and initiative, and by the osmosis between the old and new values and patterns of behaviour. The fundamentally conservative policies and culture of the upper stratum have made it possible for the country to be run along quite moderate lines.

It would not be at all hard to show that this upper stratum divides into two distinct groups, with their own clearly defined characteristics. On the basis of the classification made earlier, we could, for example, distinguish between:

the owners of large tracts of land in town or country and those with holdings of a more moderate size – numerically the numbers involved are small, and we don't dwell on this distinction;

large-scale, moderately rich, and small businessmen and industrialists – we have already clarified this distinction;

the managers and directors of large, medium-sized and small
privately-owned or state-controlled industrial or commercial undertakings;

the very successful and prosperous and the moderately successful
and not so well-off professional people;

the very top managers in government offices, those who have
some real influence, and the rest.

Similar distinctions hold good of men of science, etc.

It is enough for us to have mentioned the possibility, and we feel
no need to go into detail. We merely mention in passing that this
rather shapeless upper stratum divides not just into two parts, but
into at least five main categories of persons, and of these we shall
have something to say in more detail when we turn to consider
the structure of power at the top.

(b) *The upper middle stratum.* In the North, social stratification
does mean a class-system in the classical meaning of that expression, and it operates in the context of the large-scale, medium-sized
and small industries that we have mentioned. In Central and
Southern Italy, on the other hand, *ceti* are rising to prominence
connected with a developing bureaucratic structure that feeds para-
sitically on the rest of the economy.

In the North, then, there is an upper middle stratum of small
bourgeois office workers who feel themselves close to the workers
and the rest of the lower middle stratum, and are at home in the
technostructures of production. In the South, however, the bourgeois elements belong to the administrative part of the tertiary
sector of the economy. These two bourgeois groups are associated
with two upper-middle-strata sub-groups of freelance workers, related to them in much the same way as the *padroncini* are related to
the leading industrialists. Let us consider them a little more closely.

Classes in the classical sense result from straightforward economic self-interest and reflect the way the market operates – at least
this is a respectable opinion. The *ceti*, such as those we mentioned,
tend instead to acquire a monopoly in the satisfying of some need
within the group.

When the class-system operates, incomes are related directly to
the process of production, and derive from successful market-

operations by the enterprise concerned. The lower-grade worker sells his working hours to an organization that produces wealth by transforming work into merchandise, and is, in any event, set up in such a way that his working hours acquire market value.

On the other hand, the *ceti* have only an indirect relationship with the market, enjoy the protection of their own organization and special procedures in any dealings with it, and don't have to worry much about productivity and efficiency as such: they do things 'the Italian way' and that is enough! Per capita incomes in such *ceti* are not in proportion to individual effectiveness, but are connected with jealous distinctions in social rank, different ways of exploiting one's position, varying styles and qualities of life. In this way arise closed social circles with a strong sense of esprit-de-corps.[10]

Those capacities for inventiveness and safeguarding one's own interests which proved such positive factors in the industrial development of Northern Italy have manifested their worst side in the South, and especially Rome. As industry made more and more profits, particularly in the North, the bureaucratic machinery devised more and more ways of diverting these profits towards the *ceti* parasitic on the social body. Taxation became the means of assuring an increasingly high standard of living to an increasingly numerous group of social parasites, and was not re-invested in production or used to create better social and economic infrastructures.

Power within the state passed for the most part out of the hands of the wealthy capitalist class into those of politically and administratively relatively self-sufficient *ceti* of parasites, and these displayed a remarkable capacity for reproducing themselves quite spontaneously. This was because they were a natural outgrowth from the value-system of underdevelopment still accepted in the South. All bureaucrats belonged, as it were, to one big, happy family, and had to look after their family interests before all else, and take care of their clients (just like the Mafia). This system of *ceti* within the administrative machine is merely a modern form of the traditional Italian system of closure and underdevelopment, with all its attendant corruption. There is a family with clients, and the state is a servant to be abused, an enemy to be outwitted, a rival that can and must be corrupted. There is no concern at all for the common good as such.

Meanwhile, in the North, and in industrialized pockets in the

South, the vicious circle of depression is being broken, and real progress is taking place.

Thus, *underdevelopment* means a lot of social parasites with no respect for the nation and no concern for the community. They thrive because they have control of much of the administrative machinery. *Development* means a booming economy thanks to the industrial development that has taken place in the North.

Changes are taking place both in the horizontal and vertical structures because of industrial development, increased mechanization, the rationalization of the production cycle, and the introduction of automation. These changes in structure bring in more specialists and new sorts of workers. Eventually the whole bureaucratic system within the industrial sector has to be changed as well. Specialists, who began by rising to power within industrial concerns, gradually extend their influence to the country at large. Similar things take place in every industrial society. Their importance in the Italian situation is heightened by the backward condition of the economy immediately prior to the present developments, and by the rapidity with which these have taken place. This has increased the tension, and even brought about many head-on collisions between the inefficient machinery of government and the demands of other social groups that production-interests be effectively served by adequate supporting social structures. The storm-centre for the conflict is the upper middle *ceto*, since the upper strata above these have reached some sort of compromise that helps keep them all in power, while the lower *strata* are united on an equally self-centred class basis.

Still, in practice, from unification times right up to the present day the fact that these Southern-born middle and upper *ceti* control the country has meant that even reforms 'motivated by collective interests (in which the middle *ceti* are not the only bodies to have their fingers) often end up wasting even more money than before, since the reforms undertaken are those opportune only in very rich countries, ones which benefit skilled administrators rather than improving the available industrial plant or the tertiary services to the community. Basic problems are meanwhile left unsolved for lack of funds, such as the industrialization of the South, the development of backward areas, and the reform of agriculture.'[11]

Thus, reforms initiated at the top are made ineffective by the incompetence and corruption of the upper middle groups, who either fail to carry them out, or do so badly or too late. As Italy becomes increasingly organized in favour of such parasites, so the *ceti* increase, appearing not only in the national, regional, provincial and urban administrations, but also in the organizations running works of social assistance, universities, hospitals, and countless more or less useless corporate bodies. Such upper- and upper-middle-strata groups place their 'family' interests before everything else, and are a constant source of scandal and disedification to the whole community; they don't even try to make a secret of it.

To sum up, we might join A. Ardigò in his assertion that

> *as well as having a fairly small middle class in the classical sense, which identifies itself partly with working-class interests and is much less numerous than its French counterpart, there are a growing number of dependent and independent middle* ceti *pursuing a variety of interests but all increasing their influence throughout Italy, and apparently striving to control the whole machinery of government. To the extent that their corporate nature affords the State a greater measure of moral support than do members of the other social 'classes', these* ceti *are seen as politically worthwhile. Hence, the government is inclined to pay attention to and show favour towards those social* ceti *and strata which join it in strengthening the machinery of government. Only yesterday such* ceti *enjoyed only nominal independence, but today their autonomy vis-à-vis the powerful and up-to-date capitalist organizations in the northern industrial triangle has only increased their sense of their own power and strength.*[12]

Government employees and people on the pay-roll of these non-productive public or semi-public bodies, even when they do not themselves control the state machine, are in general better placed to make sure that they receive quite a thick slice of the nation's income, usually quite out of proportion to their alleged service to the community.

There is a whole mass of more or less useless organizations linked up with the central political system, and these are used by the various parties to provide jobs for their 'friends'. Since they are not expected actually to produce anything, their inefficiency is not too blatant. They accomodate a considerable number of people who live on other people's earnings. Someone or other has calculated that there are 60,000 such organizations in Italy. This figure is, in fact, misleading, since, according to government sources, it includes 12,928 provinces, communes and associated bodies and corporations, 17,639 communal bodies for social welfare and other similar institutions, and 14,038 charitable and educational organizations. However, even if all these bodies do really exist, they are often only very slow-moving in their operations, inconsistent in their policies, out of date, non-productive or even harmful, like certain of the old educational charities.

The linking of this division of labour with a situation of industrial development has actually had the curious effect of increasing the proportion of the 'pseudo-active' or parasitic population, persons with occupations that are indefinite, carry no responsibility, and produce no result, but which are nevertheless more or less part of the contemporary technostructure. In the industrial sector of the economy work has become increasingly specialized and diversified; in the rest of society it has been reduced to a trivial pastime. Technicians and bureaucrats have developed side by side and are still on the increase. Technicians are needed to provide some sort of integration for the manifold subsystems that go to make up a modern industrial concern. Bureaucrats are needed to prevent industry taking over the rest of the country.

Thus, new technical skills and new information are being increasingly exploited in production, social welfare, education, and so forth. In this way knowledge is used to make society more efficient. However, there exists knowledge of another sort, and its only purpose is to keep the system going. Individuals are trained not to do something definite and useful with their lives, but merely to identify with the system itself. Thus, in the examinations which have to be passed before one can work in certain branches of the civil service, the whole emphasis is on the laws and the constitution, and the candidate must show his familiarity with the organizational patterns laid down for the department in which he hopes to be employed; he need not offer any proof of ability to get results.

For a variety of reasons, then, minor officials have increased in numbers all over the place or, as we say in Italy, the undergrowth of power has thickened. This undergrowth is the useless Southern counterpart to the small industries that multiplied in the North during the years of the economic miracle. To exaggerate and simplify the situation we might say: what industry produces, bureaucracy consumes.[13]

The introduction of automation and the mechanization of both factories and workshops has, of course, required some development of bureaucratic structures within industry itself, and has turned the scales of the balance of industrial power in favour of drawing-office technicians rather than production-line workers, but the way in which the *ceti* have mushroomed in the tertiary sector has been much more prodigious.

Civil servants are more numerous in the South than in the North, precisely because the Mafia spirit, the political pressures, and the family feeling get stronger as one moves further and further South. The greater the social and political pressures, the more urgent the need to find useless jobs for one's 'friends'.

It is the political situation that gives rise to this phenomenon in the upper middle *ceto* to begin with, but there is something analogous at each of the lower levels of the social scale, with each stratum polarizing around two opposed ways of maintaining its identity and preserving its independence of the *ceto* immediately above it. Italian society, after all, was dualistic from the start, and while industrialization broke the vicious circle of depression it did not put an end to this two-way split. The family spirit and the fear of work, which originally motivated the dualism, are masked over today and even their real features may have changed, but society still runs on two parallel lines that show no sign of intersecting.

While it is more obvious in the ranks of the upper middle *ceti*, the bipolarity is within the whole social stratification, and colours every aspect of life, lending its own ambiguity to the social significance of every change and development that takes place. To develop this point more would oblige us to consider several strata at once, and this we prefer to avoid. For lack of data it is hard to offer any statistics about the distinction of the general run of the upper middle stratum from those chosen few who enjoy considerable power and prestige, and whose income is something of an unknown quantity.

The distinction itself is not clear cut. For instance, as we have mentioned, there are contractors with small incomes who also do part-time work for an employer, and employees who do additional work on a family basis, etc. Moreover, there are considerable variations in the rate of pay of different employees, since their abilities and duties vary, even if none of them own or directly control any means of production.

Individual abilities become increasingly important when jobs are less cut-and-dried and leave room for initiative, when the requirements of management are more flexible, and when the organizational structures themselves are less rigid. Variations in personal talent have little bearing on the wage-earning capacity of the ordinary office worker, but an author's income depends very much on his individual ability and the personal prestige attached to it.

The amount of one's income and the range within which it varies both increase with the importance of one's position, sector of employment, as well as depending on the nature of the particular job. Depending on the sort of firm one is working for and the job one is doing for it there are varying basic rates of pay (see table 3.3) and different possibilities of securing a rise.[14] Of course, the variations between sectors are not confined to those shown in the table, and which can be easily explained by the widespread presence of parasites in the public sector. The job flexibility is also different. Thus, in the public sector, the possible approaches to any task are fairly closely defined by a whole series of procedural norms that have evolved over a long period of time, and there is little incentive given to creative innovation. In the private sector, however, entrepreneurs make earnings depend increasingly on personal flair as they rise to positions of greater responsibility.

Another significant factor is the social division of labour. This is slight or non-existent when the structures of production are relatively unsophisticated, as in the traditional crafts, or when we consider the sorts of activity undertaken by the lumpenproletariat. However, it has considerable weight and seems quite rigid in the intermediate strata of society. At higher levels still it flattens out or entirely disappears, it being a matter of policy to concentrate several functions in a single person as one moves up the scale.

One's standard of education also obviously makes some difference, however indirect, and this depends on various social mechanisms, some of them common to every developed country, others being peculiar to Italy.

All these factors conspire to produce the variegated upper middle stratum situation that some have called the 'earnings jungle', because how much each one earns seems to depend, for one reason or another, not on the value of one's work, but on sheer luck, on the negotiating strength of one's particular group, or on the thrust of one's own personality.

Table 3.3 Differences in Earnings of Employees in Different Sectors of the Economy (lowest rate of pay in each category = 100)

	Occupational category				
Type of work	Ordinary worker	Special-ized worker	Ordinary office worker	Office worker with special job responsi-bility	Office worker with some manage-ment responsi-bility
Private sector:					
Agriculture	100	100	124	128	—
Manufacturing industry	131	123	127	148	109
Construction industry	128	126	138	166	150
Commerce	138	121	100	100	100
Banking	—	225	231	195	198
Public sector:					
Civil service	186	176	129	123	113
Telephone service	—	—	236	195	135
Other state-controlled companies	215	201	140	144	—
Concerns of national interest	241	230	174	170	156
Public sector compared with private sector (private sector = 100)	173	172	139	117	112

Note: These differences decrease as one rises up the scale, so that while the variation between the public and private sectors is 17 per cent for office workers with job responsibility, it is only 12 per cent for those with some degree of management responsibility.

The expansion of the middle stratum by an increasing number of *ceti* and parasitic groups affects the distribution of earnings and profits in ways we know very little about, but which are reflected in a few recent surveys, and can be roughly gauged by analysing the results. Here are a few figures to show the absurdity within the present wage-distribution situation. It is worthwhile including a comparison of upper middle and lower middle stratum earnings.

At the bottom of the scale, quoting the 1971 figures, are those earning between 80 and 150,000 lire a month. These include some groups of farmers, market-gardeners, unskilled workers and agricultural labourers. Intermediate groups include postmen (200,000), dustmen (217,000), door-keepers, for example those working for the telephone service (221,000), primary school teachers (231,000), secondary school teachers (336,000), etc. Higher up the scale we find judges (870,000) and doctors in charge of large hospitals (1,600,000).[15] Negotiating power obviously has an effect on salary, and so does being in close touch with the government agencies (as judges are). In general, those on higher pay work shorter hours and have more say in how these hours are distributed.

Some of these figures taken from Gorrieri seem questionable. Workingmen's wages, for example, as is well known, vary so much that one man may earn twice or even three times as much as another doing just as much work – which means a fluctuation between 80 and 500,000 lire. All the same, the most productive workers are in proportion the least well paid, and in the upper middle stratum those in the tertiary sector carve out for themselves the lion's share of the national income, as we have seen. Therefore, working-class families, and even more so the other members of the middle strata send their children to university to study, hoping they will find employment in the tertiary sector.

Today, then, and probably even more so tomorrow 'the wealth produced by a minority of productive workers is channelled away from them and diverted towards the maintenance of a constantly expanding intellectualist bureaucratic structure, instead of being used to solve the underlying problems that beset the economy and the nation.'[16] Italian society, in other words, is swarming with parasites, and it seems probable that their number will increase. The tertiary sector is booming and office workers are swelling their ranks. The fact that manual workers' wages are rising more rapidly than those of office workers does no more than sugar the pill. (Taking the 1914 wages as 100, manual workers earned 287 in effective purchasing power in 1971 and office workers 160.)[17]

It is also difficult to say whether this change represents an overall increase in earnings, or merely an increase in the proportion of individuals now holding down higher-paid posts. The number of unskilled manual workers is certainly less, and a greater number of workers (not only in factories, but also in offices – though not in all sectors of the economy, nor to the same extent as in the industrial sector) now occupy fairly high-paid posts within their particular sector.

Nevertheless, the most important thing happening is the dispro-portionate expansion of the upper middle stratum, which has come to mean with the passage of time a multiplication of social parasites on the one hand, and, on the other, the political and social stability needed for the small bourgeois office workers to consolidate their position. Their social behaviour apes that of the upper classes, and it is only very slowly that they do anything at all to alter current fashions. Their increase means that the working-class stratum becomes less numerous, or else is assimilated into the bourgeoisie. Indeed, new members of this stratum derive for the most part from working-class or peasant backgrounds, and when all is said and done, even workers in marginal positions adopt the behaviour patterns of this new stratum, if only because of the os-mosis within the domestic circle between members of different social strata. Very many families comprise both manual workers and office workers, and contain members with widely differing standards of education, and so forth.

The mass media are not as important in Italy as some people seem to think. Information, opinions and life-styles are handed down from the higher reaches to the lower levels of society rather like this: the élite in power in Italy are closely linked with the upper middle stratum and provide a standard to which they can refer their own behaviour and way of thinking. Communication has few closed doors to break through, because the family spirit and the client system of the traditional society of underdevelopment con-tinue to function, and bring the two groups together. Once the upper middle stratum has come in this way to take some idea or fashion over from the upper stratum, the lower middle stratum takes it over from them, so that in no time at all the lower middle stratum is modelling itself on the behaviour of higher social strata. With minor exceptions the new Italian working-class is very far removed from the political pretentions and the aggressive spirit of the work-ing-class of a bare ten or twenty years ago. When Italian workers vote communist, they are perhaps only voting for the social demo-crats – in due course we shall see to what extent this assertion holds water.

The whole of Italian society is flattening out culturally and socially. It is coming more and more to take over the cultural patterns, the *ceti* and, in some measure, the political attitudes of the upper bourgeoisie, which the upper middle strata and the better-placed workers merely relay and amplify. The upper middle stratum in one way and another serves as a buffer to absorb all shocks and at the same time anaesthetizes any itch for reform. In this way it guarantees the relative stability of the political and social system. The tensions and controversies of twenty years ago (when the development was getting under way) are now no more than a memory.

(c) *The lower middle stratum.* Perhaps we had better begin by linking our analysis of the lower middle stratum with that of the lower stratum. Note, first of all, that the lower middle stratum comprises a hard core of highly qualified workers, a satellite group of less qualified and lower-paid workers in other and less important sectors of the economy, and a floating population of manual workers earning a living wherever they can.

The hard core of the working-class is found in dockyards, metal-workshops, engineering works, car factories, oil installations, chemical laboratories, weaving sheds, etc. Pay is relatively high, conditions of work are fairly good, the trade unions are firmly established, but these workers are still terribly exploited by the capitalist organizations they serve. These workers, we may assume, wish:

to be sure they are not going to be left without work;
to secure rises in pay in keeping with the firm's improved productivity and that of the industry as a whole;
to make some sort of career for themselves or at least to reap the benefits of their increasing seniority within the firm;
to avoid becoming incapable of work through lack of up-to-date training and qualifications;
to avoid overwork or the effects of industrial pollution (never their main concern).

These aims arise from actual experience of the factory situation and can be a bone of contention between workers and management, or else form part of the terms of employment. Some of them are expressed in positive terms as desires to profit by opportunities that seem available, others in negative terms as an attempt to minimize the less pleasant side of modern industrial life.

These workers, however, also have other objectives which relate not to the factories in which they work, but to the towns in which they live. Their demands are then addressed to the local authorities. They wish:

to avoid losing status by dropping down into a lower income-group, and are trying instead to better their family's standing, at least indirectly, by sending their children to good schools;
to escape an excessively narrow life, and so want a better home, improved social services, and a number of reforms.[18]

The satellite group within this class owes its importance to its drawing attention to certain differences that still exist, but that will in all likelihood disappear as the still evolving economy enters on its next phase of development. The group comprises certain workers in the building trade, in firms doing contract work, in small and medium-sized industries that concentrate on regional markets, concerns of marginal importance that muddle through because they enjoy the favour of someone in the government, or simply thrive on brinkmanship. The members of this group wish:

to make their jobs as secure as possible and receive some guaranteed minimum annual income (and so they feel obliged to take on additional part-time work, or try to supplement their earnings by some form of social assistance);
to qualify for a higher rate of pay in order to meet the increased cost of living, and this independently of any increase in productivity, because they are anxious that their position should not become even worse than it already is when compared with that of the higher-paid stratum within the working-class.

All their other aims are subordinated to these first ones, but they place increasing stress on the fact that they refuse to drop down to the level of the floating population of manual workers, and also on their need of homes and essential social services (without worrying too much about the quality of these).[19]

Next let us consider the main characteristics of the remaining floating population of manual workers in order to grasp more clearly the distinction between this lower middle stratum and the lower stratum – in other words between the proletariat and the lumpenproletariat or, which comes to the same thing, between the masses within the technostructure and those still alienated from and largely outside it.

This floating population, being short of work, seeks some form of employment in small industries, in workshops, or in the tertiary sector, but not, as a rule, in the larger factories. They wish:

to make sure of an income to tide them over the immediate future, and don't care whether it comes from work, public assistance, donations from 'friends', as a return for services rendered, or by some other devious route;
eventually to secure a post that will make them members of their immediately superior satellite group.

It is hard to go into more detail about their objectives, because their very insecurity obliges them to be ready to adapt themselves to the prevailing situation, and to devise a sub-culture that makes life tolerable and meaningful within it.

Reviewing these three sections of the proletariat, we conclude that the hard core of the working-class is interested in obtaining a higher degree of participation in the benefits of economic development at a lower (physical, psychological and social) cost to themselves; the satellite group is concerned with securing steady jobs and wages somewhat above subsistence level (relative to their cultural standard); the remaining floating population wish to guarantee at least their own survival.[20]

For quite some time now this lower middle stratum has been drawn in the main from the agricultural sector. As the labour force abandon agriculture they are drifting into industry. Most manual workers leaving agriculture go into the secondary sector of the economy, and especially into manufacturing industries, but a certain proportion also find work in the tertiary sector. The urbanization of the Southern provincial capitals has made them the focal point for this development, and there is also a steady influx into Northern industrial towns. Manual workers, in other words, concentrate on the nerve-centres of industrial development, and in this way they give the contemporary economic scene its characteristically Italian tone, and determine the life-style of the working-class as a whole.

The metal and engineering industries attract a lot of them, and so does light industry in general. In one way or another such industries have been especially significant in the recent economic expansion. The building trade, too, must not be overlooked, and provides work for manual workers throughout the country. The primitive way in which such work is organized, the diminutive size of the individual firms engaged in it, and the very slight amount of mechanical skill required, all make it particularly attractive to these manual workers.[21]

In the metal and engineering industries, of course, we find quite a different picture – mechanization, organization, advanced technology, and emphasis on efficiency mean that working conditions are different, the worker needs a certain amount of skill, and while pay is better, there are unions to contend with, political attitudes to consider, a more elaborate division of labour, and even more elaborate cultural requirements to be met.

Industrialization came to Italy recently and rapidly. Hence, to begin with the workers come mainly from an agricultural background and are not really qualified for their new job.

> *The transition from a peasant-style occupation to integration in modern urban industrial life typically includes a number of phases. Initially the worker divides his time between industry and agriculture, working only casually in industry, often alongside women, in some small factory in a recently industrialized area, perhaps even working at home, or else on a building-site. Such workers still depend on an agricultural economy, and live in an agricultural zone, sometimes in boarding-houses attached to peasant families that are making a little more money for themselves in this way ... Often they seem to turn their hand to a thousand and one different things.*[22]

However, whether the new workers in this group are still giving some of their time to agriculture, or simply living in the country while working in the town, or even living in the town and doing only industrial work, the fact remains that their mentality and background are agricultural, and it is only very slowly that this situation can be changed, principally by younger workers coming to the industrial scene straight from school.

The new skills and training required of the contemporary industrial worker make a great difference to the culture of the masses, despite their agricultural origins. They feel obliged to break away completely from their agricultural past, and can no longer learn their trade from daily and close contact with their parents while on the job. Thus, the traditional apprenticeship system has become obsolete, even in those old-fashioned factories where it once produced highly qualified men.[23] Still, whatever the importance of the gap between the old-time training and skills of the agricultural worker and the contemporary modes of industrial employment, it is the cultural and psychological differences that are the hardest to face – and here the newcomer from a family tradition of skilled craftsmanship is no better placed than the man with a peasant background.

How can we sum up the situation of the lower middle stratum? Clearly, there are a number of different problems, and they each have their separate history, as we have seen, and are connected with the central question of class assimilation as such. Basically, the problems would seem to be: changes within the working-class culture; changes in the sort of skill and training required; changes in the standard to be reached; changes in the actual jobs to be done. We shall examine these problems a little more closely, but still in very general terms.

The peasant-class culture has been thrown into crisis after crisis by changes in society and changes in education. Obviously, environmental changes are very important: a modern factory is not an old-fashioned workshop. The up-to-date organization of labour and developments in the actual methods of working have compelled Italians, like everyone else, to say goodbye to old-fashioned ideas and ways of working.

At one time a factory worker wished to be recognized as possessing just as much skill as an individual craftsman, and so he took a certain personal pride in his specific contribution to production. Today, however, there is nothing remotely craftsmanlike about the working ability and skill required of either the industrial worker or anyone else employed on the modern economic scene, because each job is increasingly fragmented by the modern division of labour. Personal skill becomes a prisoner of the capitalist structures that organize modern labour in a way that makes it irrelevant.[24]

To prepare oneself for this situation it is not enough to come into a factory and learn on the job; one needs to be prepared beforehand. This is not merely a question of moving into a town and breathing in the 'atmosphere'. There is an increasing need today for the worker to have an adequate cultural preparation for his post, and education is the key to this. Highly qualified workers in the past were often self-educated to quite a good standard, but their numbers were few.[25] The schools today have to bring culture to the masses in a measure adequate to their needs in the work situation. As the schools have grown in importance and various forms of adult education have supplemented the overall preparation of the working-classes for their position in life, education has become a central element in qualifying for employment and in improving one's place in any profession.

Curiously enough, this scholastic preparation for one's working life seems to have the effect of isolating men from their fellow workers, since the old hands no longer spend their time in telling and showing newcomers how things are done in the firm nor pass on to them their home-spun philosophy of life. Traditionally the highly qualified Italian worker played a most important role in the factory, and was surrounded by large numbers of still unqualified operatives eager to learn more and become qualified themselves. Thus, the expert had a great ascendancy over the novice, and gave him his professional training.[26]

Today the situation has changed. Specialists more or less corresponding to the highly qualified figures of the past are now to be found in every factory, however small it is, because the production of prototypes of new models for the market, if nothing else, requires their skill. Hence, not even automation does away with the need for this category of worker.[27]

The workers' culture, both general and professional, is tending to disappear as a specific, self-sufficient, independent phenomenon, and professional training now takes place at school, while a man's general culture is also catered for by the mass media. Today the workers' professional and political solidarity focusses on specific issues, and no longer exercises much influence on the general cultural life of the masses, as it once did.

The culture of the present-day working-class is geared to the consumer society and workers now expect even their free time to be organized for them, with the mass media keeping them abreast of what is going on and also showing them how to live. Social life in this way becomes fragmented, traditional cultural models wither away, and the hypnotic influence of urban industrialism casts its spell over the masses. The process is by now well known. The break-up and reshaping of culture along lines that reduce the individual to the status of an anonymous unit in a shapeless mass has proved the bane of the lower middle stratum, and is infecting the whole of society.

Increased social mobility within and between strata accelerates this process, which is linked with the present-day cultural and educational situation. Manual workers move in large numbers from place to place, as we have seen already, and such migrations lead to all kinds of developments. Moreover, within the lower ranks of workers the importance of the more highly qualified man is not as great as it was, and this increases the bargaining power of workers negotiating en masse. Developments in industry in the last ten years and at the time of the economic miracle have increased the demand for better educated manual workers, so that, as a group, they now belong to the technical part of the productive process, sense their negotiating strength is greater than before, and want to be acknowledged as full participants in the business as a whole. Their mentality is new, and they are losing the sense of their old identity as inferior, exploited workers who were unable to come together in defence of their own interests.

Higher educational standards speed up this development. With the school-leaving age raised to fourteen and an increasing number putting in more years of further studies, there is a drop in the number of manual workers available, and this increases their bargaining power with the management. For the same reasons, more of the labour force is made up of relatively well-prepared workers, whose culture and technical knowledge is not far below that of the upper middle stratum. It is in this way that the Italian working-class has grown increasingly bourgeois in its outlook.

The specific problems of the modern workers' qualifications and of their real position in the industrial structure are special aspects of this same question. Changes in qualifications and occupation continue to be both the effect and the cause of other changes in the workers' overall situation.

Initially industrial development lessened the emphasis on being qualified for one's job. New firms had to take on who they could get, and the available labour force in the cities and the North usually came from the countryside and the South. Subsequently, however, one had to be qualified in order to get work. The reorganization of labour in modern industry called for more and more specialized workers of one kind and another. However, these still need to be supplemented by a minority of manual workers with no specific training.

The specialized workers, then, are of different kinds, doing a variety of specific tasks within a complex, mechanized and scientifically organized production process. Commonly, they need to be mentally alert, with steady nerves, and quite nimble. They require 'a basic cultural preparation enabling them to adjust rapidly to changing social situations and to fulfil different functions in industry as changing circumstances dictate'.[28]

It was during the 1960s, when the economic miracle had already had the effect of overturning the traditional economic structures along with the traditional way of life of the lower middle stratum, that the new sort of qualifications required for employment in modern industry became clear on a large scale.[29] Retraining was slow to get under way, and began with the lower rungs of the industrial ladder, the years 1961–70 being of particular importance.[30]

While the standard of qualifications has in general increased, this is more true of some sectors than others. Thus, it is particularly noteworthy in the iron and steel industries (10.6 per cent specialized workers in 1961, 20.2 per cent in 1970), the chemical industry (16.5 per cent increasing to 27.1 per cent), and in the petrol industry (26.8 per cent growing to 55.9 per cent). Similarly, although the phenomenon concerns the whole of Italy, it particularly involves certain regions.[31]

While during the decade 1961–70 there was this rise in the training standards of lower-grade workers, there was at the same time a drop in the overall level of the qualifications of general office workers in industry. Such employees became in many ways similar to the general run of qualified workers, and the result was that the unions began to press for them to be considered and treated as a single category.

It needs to be noted, however, that this development within the industrial sector has not extended to other sectors of the economy, and is certainly not true of the tertiary sector. Mechanization and automation are here less important, the work is different, the size of individual concerns is different, and so the whole situation is different.

The working-class as a whole is nevertheless, as we have already said, becoming increasingly bourgeois, and in this connection it is interesting to observe that wages are, in real terms, increasing more than salaries, the former rising from 57 points in 1880 to 287 points in 1971 while the latter rose from 95 to 160 (1914 = 100).[32]

As Italian society is changing its structure, then, the working-classes are changing their image and along with the rest of the lower middle stratum are stabilizing around the central strata of the social scale in terms of income, culture and technical qualification for their jobs. The outward sign of this transformation within the economy is the restructuring of the various jobs themselves, so that the division of labour which immediately followed the industrial revolution has, in Italy as elsewhere, proved unsatisfactory, and has had to be abandoned. The working man, in other words, is more qualified, better paid (having improved his position more than the office worker), and more highly educated. As a result he is no longer happy doing work which is merely the meaningless fragment of a process outside his control.

The lower middle stratum has completely changed its nature. Workers are differently trained, fulfil a different function, and are integrated in a different way into the structures of production. The modern labour force, therefore, must of necessity come up to a certain standard.

> *The progress of capitalist technology has largely abolished the traditional division of labour into carefully defined specialized functions. What is increasingly needed is the general ability to adapt oneself to the work to be done, to follow through the different cycle of operations within a single phase of production, or to turn one's attention from one phase to another, appreciating the whole productive process in which one is being asked to participate. The workers now need, in other words, some degree of culture, and without it could not play their part in the collective task of keeping the wheels of production turning.*[33]

The lower middle stratum may still be called, if we wish, by the same name as before, but like the working-class in other countries it has changed its nature profoundly, occupies a different position within society, and has changed its attitude towards the lower stratum, which has instead retained many of the traditional features of the working-class, and remains, quite self-consciously, an unfairly exploited and marginal group alienated from the rest of society.

(d) *The lower stratum.* Though far from homogeneous in composition the lower stratum still has its own definite characteristics, chief of which, of course, is the fact of its estrangement from the technostructures of contemporary industrial society, into which it is inserted in a rather insecure, precarious and even intermittent fashion. The lower stratum is even alienated to some degree from the working-class, and differences of interest can even give rise to conflict between them. The lower and more important segment of the lower stratum, or lumpenproletariat, lives in the town, but feels excluded from the mainstream of its life.

There is a regrettable shortage of both facts and theories about this lowest stratum of the population. Some experts consider the lumpenproletariat as a stagnant and almost submerged stratum within society made up of people whose connection with work is spasmodic or insecure, certainly only temporary, so that they are either unemployed or only part-employed, as well as being unduly exploited and underpaid – working inconvenient hours, earning low wages, and having unjust conditions of employment. The submerged section of this stratum comprises in the main people who in theory are self-employed: poor peasants, craftsmen and small tradespeople. The stagnant section, on the other hand, consists of those who depend on others for work, have no control of the means of production, and so are related to the proletariat in the strict sense of the term. The varying estimates of people in part-time employment are arrived at by taking various cross-sections through these two categories.

Marx foresaw their existence, but today they are associated with three additional categories of daily increasing proportions. In the Italian situation in particular the lot of these categories on the labour market is such that most of them feel they are being squeezed out of it, prevented from participating in production, or at least that job-hunting takes up so much time that they become discouraged.[34] Different authors have studied this problem under one heading or another.[35] In C. Donolo's opinion the categories chiefly comprise:

(1) Discouraged female would-be workers who resign themselves to being housewives. Obviously this does not mean every woman of working age, but those who would offer their services on the labour market if they felt they could obtain a moderately well-paid job with adequate social services (such as provisions for looking after their children, transport to and from work, the possibility of work near home, etc.).

(2) Discouraged young people out of a job. These are students or

have recently been students. Commitment to a further course of study is often a way of fending off the threat of unemployment, comes after a certain interval spent in actively looking for a job, or is something to do while waiting for an opening to be created for them in the family business, or until the examination results are published.

(3)   Old people, whether on a pension or not, who would willingly work for even less than an average wage if suitable working conditions were available.

These three groups are a whole mass of people out of work, but who could work if conditions changed.

The lower stratum, therefore, embraces the not yet employed, the half-employed, the under-employed and the no longer employed.[36]

Nevertheless, it would be wrong to think that all the members of these different groups formed part of the lumpenproletariat. The size of his pension obviously makes a difference to a pensioner's social standing; the husband's income has a bearing on that of a wife; and so forth. Various shades of difference mark the transition from the lumpenproletarian labour force still awaiting a job of their own, to the reserve labour force of pensioners with small pensions, and thence to the *ceti* of social parasites with enormous pensions, like certain civil servants who retire very early at pensions twice as high as the wages they earned when officially employed, or could earn if they remained on the employed list.

As can be gathered from these brief remarks, the situation is enough to take one's breath away.

Any analysis of it is complicated by the need to draw a distinction between the lumpenproletariat as traditionally defined, and its reality on the contemporary urban and industrial scene. The marginal position of some workers results from situations of underdevelopment; that of others from the capitalist nature of the development itself.

> *Alienation and exclusion from the nation's economic life was the lot of some at the moment of Italy's unification and it developed in extent throughout the history of her industrial progress. As the market became nationwide and an end was made to fragmentation and the tariff barriers that divided the country, some regional markets lost their importance, came to depend on some predominant central*

*market for a whole series of things, and the consumption
of local produce was thereby restricted. In this way the
local community became jobless. Their present marginal
position results historically, then, from the fact that
economic development took place elsewhere, at the centre,
and that at the same time it influenced them sufficiently to
destroy their very existence as a self-supporting community. The only response open to this challenge was
emigration, in other words the movement towards centres
of economic development of workers threatened with
redundancy. To remain in a marginal position was to
condemn oneself to increasing destitution.*[37]

Recently in industrial centres a new sort of lumpenproletariat has
emerged, comprising workers with an agricultural background who
have never really identified with the new technostructures. Such
marginal elements are particularly common in towns in the South,
where agricultural labourers have always been rather unsure of
work and the available employment has been insufficient to go
round. Today their numbers are increased by the presence of middle
ceti of peasants, tradespeople and craftsmen who have fallen on
hard times, having been rejected by modern society and assigned
to the proletariat when the new technostructures made their contribution superfluous.[38]

As groups of such elements flow into the suburbs of large towns
and live in the slums and hovels they gradually evolve a sub-culture
of their own which is specific to these outlying zones and to the
other squalid parts of the city. These become cultural ghettoes
where wage-earners are scarcely to be found. They often seal
themselves off from what goes on in the rest of the town, and take a
hostile view of the rest of society. As G. Salierno has said, on the
outskirts of an industrial town a state of rebellion is endemic.[39]

We have noticed already that changing educational standards as
well as the nature of city life tend to push the lumpenproletariat
even further towards the margin of society. The unfavourable
conditions in which they live and the peculiarities of their cultural
attitude cause lumpenproletarian children either to avoid school
altogether or else never to rise far above the bottom of the class, so
that their education is never continued beyond the statutory school-
leaving age.

In very large cities a most serious problem has been created by the steady large-scale influx of such elements in recent years. The population of Rome rose from 2,200,000 in 1961 to 2,700,000 in 1969. This means an average annual increase of 70,000 poorly schooled peasants with no professional qualifications, of largely Southern origin. The Mayor of Rome estimates that 12,000 families are living in 10,000 hovels, and that 50,000 families are subletting or sharing accomodation, while 45,000 families live in squalor in the centre of the old city, half of them in property that has been condemned.[40]

The mass of the lumpenproletariat cannot be defined; its characteristics vary, and the occupations and incomes of its members are as astonishing as they are varied. To some extent only, as we have already mentioned, we can associate with them at least three further categories: pensioners; those who work at home; and women unable to find jobs to their liking – distinguishing between those who, while not actually unemployed, are always changing job, and those who regularly perform low-paid domestic duties.

Recently there has been an increase in the number of pensioners, and the proportion of people on small pensions in the lumpenproletariat who try to supplement their income by seeking some casual work has risen steadily. Between 1959 and 1968 the numbers receiving a pension in Italy rose impressively from 2,836,000 to 5,839,000.[41] Obviously many pensioners, home-workers and women are *not* lumpenproletarians.

We have classified home-workers as belonging to the lumpenproletariat if their work is insecure and intermittent. Nevertheless, what they actually produce is very often directly relevant to modern industrial life. There is quite a lot of work being done at home, which is sometimes referred to as 'black' labour.

There are not and cannot be any fully reliable statistics about work done at home, since this escapes controlled observation, and still remains the main form of 'black' labour, or employment not subject to trade-union conditions, sanitary and safety regulations, or regular taxation, save in exceptional circumstances. One interesting survey suggested that in Lombardy 230,000 were working at home – this would represent a considerable proportion amounting to 15 per cent of the number of factory workers. In some regions, such as Piedmont and Liguria, the proportion may be less, but in others, including Emilia, Tuscany, the Marches, Campania and Puglie, it is definitely higher, perhaps much higher. In some provinces in Emilia the number working at home is more than 50 per cent of the total number of industrial workers. It is, therefore, quite reasonable to believe that about a million work at home, the vast majority of these being women.[42]

Garavini estimates the number of home-workers to be as high as 1,500,000. As to the nature of their employment,

while the sort of work done at home varies, it falls in the main into two categories. One sort of job is mostly done with a machine ... the other is principally manual work or work requiring only some simple tool. The assembling of simple parts for some firm of light engineers will usually be done by hand; the relatively economical domestic sewing-machine will be used at home in preference to its industrial counterpart ... The arrangement that certain jobs can be done ouside the factory does not always mean a step back into the past. The modern factory simply transfers to the home or to some subsidiary workshop a chosen segment of the productive cycle, which takes place there just as effectively as it would in the factory itself. Thus, the different departments of production become so many groups working at home and organized by an agent, the gruppista, *who is a new sort of foreman ... Acceptance of work in such conditions depends partly on a woman's finding it hard within the capitalist society to get away from her home surroundings, and so doing a little productive work in the house itself ... Another factor is the difference this makes to costs and profits. There is no formal contract of employment, and wages may be reduced by as much as 50 or 70 per cent, because there is no retirement benefit, no Christmas bonus, no holiday pay, no employers' contributions to be made towards national insurance schemes, and quite a lot of tax evasion.*

The next main category is that of women who are housewives, in domestic service, working full-time at home, or partly at home and partly outside the home, changing their jobs time and time again, and finding only intermittent employment. We have emphasized already that housewives as such need not be lumpenproletarians and are, in our view, already part of the labour force, and there is no need to repeat here what we said about the characteristics of women's occupations when discussing the vertical structure of Italian society.

Thus, we have distinguished:

(a) the marginal position of the historically conditioned lumpenproletariat found mainly on the outskirts of the Southern cities, including Rome – a huge mass of potential workers living on the fringe of society as if Italy still remained an underdeveloped country from both the cultural and economic points of view.

(b) the marginal fraction of the population in large industrial towns that express something of the capitalist structure of life in modern Italy. As well as the lumpenproletariat in the strict sense, this group also comprises the three categories of: certain pensioners; certain women who are housewives, or in insecure jobs, or working only part-time, etc; and men and women working in their own homes for an agent.

The existence of these categories increases the mobility of the labour market and permits the contemporary technostructures to enjoy the services of a cheap labour force that can be called upon whenever necessary and rapidly assembled wherever the work needs to be done. This labour force is, as we have explained, the lowest stratum within the horizontal structure of society, but may very well be essential to the successful functioning of the Italian economy, which is capitalist, unevenly developed, split in two, and polarized in the unbalanced ways that we have already described, and shall have occasion to discuss in more detail later.

Concluding Remarks

13   We would like to conclude this survey of the horizontal structure of Italian society by offering some sort of evaluation of the overall situation. We find ourselves obliged to arrive at no more than a few tentative and provisional conclusions, because the situation remains fluid, and in a number of ways the social strata are still in process of change.

Indeed, the superficial observer could be forgiven for thinking that the social strata that used to exist in Italy were being fragmented to the point of atomization. The distinction between those in power and in control of the means of production and the rest of the population is no longer obvious. There is a considerable levelling out with regard to individual incomes. Cultural values and behaviour patterns have all gone into the melting-pot with the expansion of the upper middle stratum and the more affluent portion of the lower middle stratum, which now set the tone for the whole of society, while in the past one could speak of a peasant society and of a society of businessmen and workers.

The analysis we have made of the horizontal structure and the social strata on the basis of ownership and control of the means of production retains its validity, but it would be absurdly dogmatic to omit to mention the other factors that help to determine an individual's social position.

Cultural and behavioural factors have already been mentioned. Within the horizontal structure, strata and individuals are set apart from one another by a variety of different elements, some of them seemingly devoid of importance and unconnected with the basic value-system. These include style of dress, the moral courage to voice a personal opinion, the effective freedom to do or refrain from doing certain things, etc. For a long time Italy has been in this sense a world apart, a 'closed' society. The code of morality was detailed and quite strict, and to comply with or to reject its requirements was tantamount to increasing or lessening if not one's social status at least one's personal prestige. In some places the situation has not changed. Style of dress, too, often showed that an individual was out of step with the rest of society. The expression of certain political views might also count against one, so that one was made to feel uncomfortable or even to suffer material loss. The 'communist' often found it harder to find work and was excluded from the higher reaches of his chosen profession.

The situation changed slowly, with new trends gathering momentum about the time of the Second Vatican Council and the 1968 youth movements, which were inspired by and modelled on the May rebellion in France, the riots in Berkeley, and similar demonstrations elsewhere. In Italy such restlessness lasted until the end of 1972, and often expressed itself quite exuberantly with sudden explosions of violence.

This sketch of the horizontal structure of Italian society would not be complete without a brief description of the recent changes in patterns of behaviour, in social values, and in the degree of tolerance shown to minorities. However, these remarks will be restricted to what has a direct bearing on the horizontal structure as a whole, and our eventual evaluation of its present shape. At a later stage we shall examine the power-system and the value-system more directly.

We have said that the Second Vatican Council and the student uprisings of 1968–72 made a considerable difference to the horizontal structure. In what sense is this true?

Certainly these manifestations have had more social importance in Italy than elsewhere. The other countries of Europe were prepared to respond to such events, because their industrial development was of sufficiently long standing for their level of tolerance to be high and their social mores already pluralist in outlook. In Italy, on the other hand, even the industrial part of the country still lay under the incubus of the traditional behaviour patterns and the social code of an underdeveloped nation wedded to a closed system of values. For instance, changes in sexual behaviour and the social emancipation of women, which were already taken for granted in other countries, were unleashed on Italy quite literally overnight, and between the new generation of women and their elders there often exists quite a wide gap – the psychology, the way of thinking, the actual behaviour are totally different. The economic development of Italy in the last twenty years, which has rapidly made a developed nation out of an underdeveloped country, accelerated even more the pace of social change, and recent events have speeded up the whole process even further.

As well as industrialization and the 1968–72 youth movements, the Second Vatican Council speeded up the secularization process within Italian society, and oriented it increasingly in the direction of religious agnosticism. The Council gave a new image and direction to the Roman Catholic Church, brought about a sharp drop in religious observance, caused many to leave the priesthood and few to choose it as a possible way of life, lessened interest in religious questions generally, and so severed the connection between altar and throne, between the Church and political authority, thereby releasing the general run of Italian workers from their religious bonds. As a result, the Church became distinct and separate from Italian society as such; more Catholics including a portion of the clergy moved towards the left, individuals increasingly regarded their own conscience as the deciding factor in moral issues rather than following social custom or accepting some authoritative directive.

Changes of this kind obviously did not take place everywhere at the same time or influence each social category to the same degree, and neither did they abolish distinctions of stratum overnight or make social stratification immediately much more flexible. The first places to be affected by the changes were the large cities, especially the better educated groups, and from these they spread to the small towns, the villages, affecting even the lumpenproletariat.

The rigidities of Italian society also depended on other ideologies that served to buttress its stratification system or presented it with a permanent challenge it was constantly on its guard against. These, too, have lost much of their hold. The Italian Communist Party, for example, and Marxism in general have lost much of their credibility and fascination and no longer seem the Church of anti-Christ. The charismatic leaders of yesterday, the intellectual giants, the experts in the moral persuasion of the masses, and the cultural trend-setters, or party-political leaders, are increasingly regarded by the population as simply posturing and projecting their chosen image on the political chequer-board.

The young especially, but also their elders, no longer view life in black and white terms as Communists against Catholics, good against bad, manual workers against intellectuals, factory-hands against office workers, etc., and Machiavelli is no longer regarded as the key to the understanding of Italian society. There are many reasons for this change – improvements in standards of education, better wages, more variety in job selection with a more functional division of labour, changes in the system of social stratification and in the relationships between the various strata (which in turn reflect the other changes already mentioned), and the ceaseless bombardment of news and information that comes from the mass media.

The social bombshell exploded in the midst of university students and intellectuals; its shock-waves spread to younger students and workers, and then affected other groups and social strata, extending even to the lumpenproletarian element and to women, embracing them in the militant feminist movements and influencing them in other ways, too.

Italian social institutions have not been radically threatened by such manifestations, which have even strengthened them in some ways, as we shall see, but they have brought certain new factors into play.

Any stratification system is a sort of classification, and so it relies on certain external differentiating identification-marks, such as style of dress, mode of speech, eating and drinking habits, ways of making love, and general social conduct. Thus, in an advanced and sophisticated society like the contemporary Italian one it would be extremely crude to attempt to discuss horizontal structure solely in terms of income and one's relationship with the means of production.

Atomization does not exactly disrupt the social strata, but it means that one lives within them in a new way as a result of the transfiguration effected in people's social self-consciousness by the events of 1968 and their aftermath. The dualism within society has simultaneously been modified a little as regards the distribution of incomes and class membership, but this has been for other reasons. Atomization is reflected in individual politics, eating habits, life-styles and attitudes towards death. The external criteria of one's status, the things that show to which *ceto* one belongs, the symbols characterizing one's particular group, the marks of one's individual class have all changed; everyone seems to have changed his status, group, and *ceto*, if not, perhaps, his class as such. Where individuals have stayed in the same group or *ceto*, this seems to have changed its character beyond all recognition, so that to belong to it now means something entirely different, or else nothing at all. In times past one belonged to this *ceto* or that group because it was the expected thing of a person in one's particular situation. Today there is a greater measure of free choice. Economic ties and class differences persist, but in other ways the situation is entirely different.

For a few years after this sort of cultural revolution people seemed to be flitting endlessly from one new group to another, and this was all part of the process of each social stratum (but particularly the middle ones) searching for a new image, as each *ceto* within it sought for a new meaning and relevance. By a process of natural selection the majority opted in the end for membership of what seemed a group of like-minded people, but the criteria of membership were quite varied. Today, for instance, which was certainly not the case before, an architect can join a commune, become a teacher, work in the suburbs, engage in politics, or actually *choose* his profession, instead of thinking it is his only available option, or that he need only involve himself in it to the extent required to cover his cost of living.[43] In the lower strata of society this holds true in a different way, and perhaps not to the same extent.

Whatever one's choice, to choose is to commit oneself to, and in consequence to identify oneself with, the interests of a particular *ceto* or social stratum, and these are no longer what they were in the days when possession of a particular qualification or skill seemed automatically to imply acceptance of a specific code of behaviour. Membership of a particular stratum is something one qualifies for in a different way from in the past, and needs to be differently defined. Even if one can still belong to the upper or lower middle stratum, to 'belong' now means something different. This, as well as being obvious, could have been predicted in the light of the various changes that have taken place throughout Italian society.

Even when collective behaviour arises spontaneously, the options created gradually harden into patterns that classify a particular group as distinct from another. The differentiations within society are often based on political projects, life-styles and individual variations in sensitivity,[44] which find social expression in a revised system of stratification, the symbols of membership of a particular class being largely cultural and behavioural in nature. The contemporary classification system adhered to in Italy is much less rigid and fixed than it used to be, because political, cultural and economic changes, including the rise of the consumer society, have thrown it into confusion, as well as modifying the stratification of which it is the visible expression. Italy is fast becoming a post-industrial society, chaotic, increasingly unpredictable, confused, capable of bending to its will both public and private industrial and administrative structures, even at the cost of reducing their efficiency even more – capable, in short, of changing the essential stratification, transforming the whole way in which society operates. Two illustrations of this may be in order. The upper ranks of the clergy no longer function as moral, religious and political leaders for the general mass of the population, being themselves divided, open to secular values, and more willing to think for themselves than they once were. Meanwhile, those intellectuals who were shaken out of their complacency by the cultural revolution that began in 1968 have published an unending flood of new books and magazines. As a result of this the cultural axis has shifted towards the left, and old-fashioned intellectuals have lost their following to a new generation of writers with considerably different interests, cultural backgrounds and political affiliations. All this can be said without entering into any discussion of the slavish way in which so many once took up more or less orthodox Marxist positions, or followed in the wake of some eminent man of letters, with, for example, Benedetto Croce enjoying almost a monopoly of culture till the end of the Second World War.

The middle ceti *have changed radically and, I would say, anthropologically; their positive values are no longer those of their priests or the Holy Faith, but, though they have yet to put a name to their new-found ideology, they now acknowledge in practice the hedonistic values of the consumer society and consequently have adopted the North American Modernist heresy of universal mutual tolerance. By 'improving' the production of superfluous goods, driving people mad with the urge to consume, and manipulating fashions and the mass media, television especially, the Establishment itself has invoked these new values, and cynically thrown to one side the traditional values and the Catholic Church that symbolized their authority.*

Peasant Italy with all its many industries has collapsed, and lies broken in pieces beyond repair; it has left a void that in all probability will be filled by transforming the country into something completely bourgeois, Americanized, tolerant when it ought not to be, a victim of the Modernist heresy . . .

There is no longer any historical continuity. The 'development' the Establishment wanted just because it seemed expedient has come with a vengeance as an epoch-making event; in the course of a few years it has radically transformed the whole Italian world . . . From an ancient cultural organization based on wealthy middle ceti *of humanists and a population of illiterates the country has turned into an up-to-date mass-cultural organization. This fact is enormous, and really does, I must emphasize, constitute an anthropological 'mutation' . . .*

The consequent cultural levelling-down process affects

everybody alike, the populace and the bourgeoisie, the workers and the lumpenproletariat. The social setting has changed in a way that has meant much more uniformity. All Italians are now cast from the same mould. Real differences no longer exist – unless we count as a difference the empty gestures of going through the lifeless motions of choosing one's political colour – and Italian citizens, Fascist or counter-Fascist, are all alike. They have become interchangeable culturally, psychologically and even, which is quite impressive, physically as well. I repeat that, except at election time or suchlike political occasions, there is nothing in their physical appearance, gesture or routine behaviour that allows one to choose between them.[45]

To sum up then. Italian society is bulging at the centre, with the middle strata accounting for the largest proportion of the total population, as in most industrial societies. This is related to the disappearance of some unskilled sorts of work and the smaller demand for other relatively unskilled workers. The Italian way of life is also becoming standardized around a cultural average, with the direction it takes being determined by a central group who pick up moral, social, political and cultural messages of every kind and from every direction, assimilate them, and eventually regurgitate them, so that they are broadcast throughout society. Society nevertheless retains its different strata, and also its conflicts – between strata, between classes, between high and low, between those who control the means of production and those who don't, between those who uphold a particular morality and ideology and those who favour another or none at all, between those in charge of the mass media and those who cannot gain their attention. And all this against the background of dualism and imbalance that we have emphasized right from the start.

Despite all this, possibly because of this, one can apply to Italy Galileo's dictum: *'Eppur si muove'* (It *is* moving, for all that); it is evolving and changing, but we cannot tell if this movement is towards a radically different sort of society, or merely towards some new expression of the age-old formula.[46]

Notes to chapter 3

1. A. Ardigò, 1975b, p. 31.
2. For these questions as regards Italy see Pagani, 1970, pp. 155–82.
3. E. Gorrieri has dealt with the chaotic inequalities in income distribution in his book *La giungla retributiva* (1973).
4. These are the estimates made by P. Sylos Labini, L. D'Agostini and P. Palano. See Sylos Labini, 1973, pp. 100 and 101.
5. *Ibid.*, p. 110.
6. *Ibid.*, p. 104.
7. *Ibid.*, p. 110.
8. Educational attainment is also important. Taking the 1969 income-scale as our sample, with the illiterate's average 63,000 lire expressed as 100, average incomes vary as follows in relation to scholastic attainment:

Laurea (university degree)	410
Higher secondary Diploma	249
Lower middle-school Licenza	179
Primary school Licenza	144
Attendance at a primary school	116

Consiglio Nazionale dell'economia e del lavoro (1973) *VII Rapporto sulla situazione sociale del paese*, p. 59.
9. Acquaviva, 1969.
10. Ardigò, 1973a, pp. 321–32, especially p. 322.
11. Gorrieri, 1973, p. 260.
12. Ardigò, 1973a, p. 325.
13. In commenting on this situation Sylos Labini has claimed that 'there are now more parasites among the so-called middle-class *ceti* than in the so-called capitalist group'. Sylos Labini, 1973, p. 71.
14. Consiglio Superiore dell'economia e del lavoro (1973) *VII Rapporto sulla situazione economica del paese*, p. 57.
15. See Gorrieri, 1973, in which we find the most realistic analysis of this situation.
16. *Ibid.*, p. 32.
17. See Fuà, 1973, p. 81.
18. Donolo, 1972, pp. 101–28, especially p. 117.
19. *Ibid.*, p. 118.
20. *Ibid.*, p. 118.
21. The labour force employed in the building trade dropped from 1,034,000 in 1963 to 852,000 in 1967. This does not mean the trade is no longer hiring new workers, but that many are seeking work in other sectors, or merely being replaced.
22. Amendola, 1968, p. 43.
23. *Ibid.*, p. 38.
24. Garavini, 1970, pp. 36–52, especially p. 49.
25. See Amendola, 1968, p. 42.
26. *Ibid.*, p. 38.
27. *Ibid.*, p. 39.
28. *Ibid.*, p. 41.
29. Between 1961 and 1971, thanks to the reorganization of labour, there was a sharp rise in production within the larger firms, as is clear if we compare the overall rise in production in industry (61.4 per cent) with the increase in the number of workers employed in industry (1.2 per cent). See

Amendola, 1973, pp. 3–20, especially p. 9. The numerical size of the working-class has not changed much, but its characteristics are different, and its composition is no longer the same, being made up of younger people than before.

30. See Paci, 1972, pp. 3–19, especially p. 8.
31. *Ibid.*, p. 11.
32. Sylos Labini, 1973, p. 111; Fuà, 1973.
33. Garavini, 1970, pp. 47–48.
34. Donolo, 1972, pp. 101–28, especially pp. 109–10.
35. See Meldolesi, 1972; De Meo, 1970; and other sources.
36. Donolo, 1972, p. 110. The imbalances in development and the economic alienation of certain groups no longer sharply divide North and South, but uneven growth is now a much more subtle phenomenon throughout the country in general.
37. A nationwide ISTAT survey of July 1969 showed 111,000 families to be inadequately housed, i.e., in places which could not be regarded as rooms, such as huts or caves, or else in rooms meant for other purposes, such as offices, shops, or store-rooms: ISTAT, *Indagine speciale*, 1970, p. 8.
38. One typical casual job on the outskirts of the town is that of making sure that cars do not get damaged. This is a common occupation in Rome and Naples. G. Salierno reckons it brings in 5–10,000 lire a day. Salierno, 1973, p. 91. Some other jobs are of doubtful morality and veer close to the illegal.
39. Salierno, 1973, pp. 39ff.
40. See the Mayor of Rome's intervention on the question of the *Situazione delle locazioni in Italia*, Sindaco di Roma, 1971, pp. 149ff.
41. See De Meo, 1973, pp. 13–14 and 25–26.
42. Garavini, 1973, p. 6. Garavini believes work at home makes a considerable difference to the structures of production and to the size of the profits. Making a very rough calculation, 20–30 per cent of the annual 5000 million lire made from the manufacture of shoes, clothing and textile goods derives from work done at home.
43. Alberoni and Bonin, 1971. The analyses before and after this observation are based partly on their findings.
44. *Ibid.*, p. 116.
45. When this present volume had already been translated into English prior to its publication in Italian, Pier Paolo Pasolini focused attention on this theme. This merits the long quotation, partly because he is one of very few voices from the Left who join us in making the point that can alone prevent political options from remaining empty gestures, but more especially because his remarks both anticipate and serve as a conclusion to what we shall say in Part Two about the relationships between culture, values and attitudes on the one hand, and the power-system on the other. See Pasolini, 'Gli italiani non sono più quelli' in *Corriere Della Sera*, 10 June 1974, p. 1.
46. Other sorts of classification could also be applied to the social structure, and would equally serve to bring out the sort of changes taking place. It would be possible, for instance, to make a different division of the main sectors of the economy as follows: (1) the modern sector comprising the large-scale industrial complexes and their various subsidiary companies, or companies working for them, together with any small or medium-sized firms that supply technically advanced goods to the national or international market; (2) the competitive sector which provides less specialized goods to the local market, or simple manufactured articles, footwear and clothing for

the international market; (3) the politically favoured sector which comprises small and medium-sized firms with a low rate of production that survive on their political credit, obtaining orders on political grounds, and having a working agreement with the political and other administrative authorities, but not making their own way on the market; (4) the competitive service sector doing work on tender, finding the going hard and mere survival problematic – depending very much on steady contracts from larger firms, or on managing to secure a local monopoly of some particular type of work. Donolo, 1972, p. 119.

PART TWO

The Pyramid of Power – Power-systems and Value-systems

CHAPTER 4

How Power is Legitimated

A. The break-down of the traditional scheme of things

1   Our analysis of Italy's economic development and social stratification would remain incomplete if we failed to relate it to the pyramid of social power considered both in itself, and in its associated *ceti* and strata. In endeavouring to achieve this, we shall also need to pay attention to the social atmosphere surrounding the life of the system; this is made up of the value-system and of Italy's political and cultural traditions.

The cultural and political traditions of any country exercise a considerable influence on the process of its development. Like Birnbaum, we understand by cultural, political (and religious) traditions

> *an instinctive awareness of, and also a particular way of thinking about the operation of the machinery of government and its various ramifications throughout and manifestations within society; we are thinking, then, of the psychological attitudes that incline the government to regard particular modes of operation as likely to produce results while, in a country with different traditions, other institutions would have to be invoked in order to attain an identical objective.*[1]

To make Birnbaum's point somewhat differently, we could say that one significant element in the Italian scene was the absence or at least the extreme weakness of the average man's awareness of the operation of the machinery of government, which he hardly gave any thought to. In the early stages of economic development this

93

meant that the Italian mainly relied on individual initiative or on some makeshift form of organization. This attitude seemed at first to stimulate economic expansion and social change, but retarded them considerably once Italy grew into a capitalist technostructure, with public and private sectors.

It is clear at any rate that the prevailing value-system always influences all the other structures of society either positively or negatively, so that, whether it favours the power-system or comes into conflict with it, it is never without some bearing on the structures within which authority is exercised. If values are invoked to justify the existence of structures in general, they seem to have more than ordinary relevance to the structure of power at the top.

We have already made some preliminary attempts to understand the relationships between the value-system, the power structure, and the other overall structures within Italian society during the period of its development. It is now time to re-examine this question from two other points of view. Briefly, we shall see precisely how the earlier scheme of things was thrown into a crisis, and we shall take a look at the set of values which either validate the new system or direct its progress along the road to some further change.

2   We know already that structural changes within the economy have a critical effect on male-dominated, family-centred societies (and vice-versa), that they disrupt the pattern of adaptation to a situation of shortage (and vice-versa), and that they oblige the government to accept the responsibility of promoting economic and social development along lines it had never envisaged. Similarly, they oblige the government to do this within the context of a society whose members have as yet not really come to terms with the new-style behaviour, nor with the hard-headed and pragmatic emphasis suddenly placed on higher education – the social and economic change-over has been so precipitate that the existing institutions, and in particular the family, have been taken by surprise and found quite unprepared. The gap between the new-style society and the earlier male-dominated, family-centred, anti-social and anti-legal model has been too great. The changes and developments that actually have taken within Italian society are, therefore, not so much the result of the organized efforts of its members acting in unison, but rather the fruit of the independent and sometimes contrasting initiatives of individuals and small groups who, for the most part, have been looking to their own private interests, and hardly ever had much concern for society as a whole.

As time passed, however, the overall impact of such individual efforts became increasingly less, and by the 1960s it was becoming abundantly clear that some overall organization was called for, if the progress made in the economy was to have any beneficial effect on society at large. In this way the question of the social function of government came into prominence.

The value-system and thus the way in which authority was justified within society was changing, and the reshaping of society seemed to call for some different division and organization of labour. Progress towards this goal was held back by the continuing survival of the old, traditional value-system and by the Italians' dislike of organized work.

As things worked out, a sudden upsurge in the economy precipitated important changes, bringing about an acknowledgement of new values, and a consequent redefinition of the goals society should promote. The following diagram schematically expresses this process:

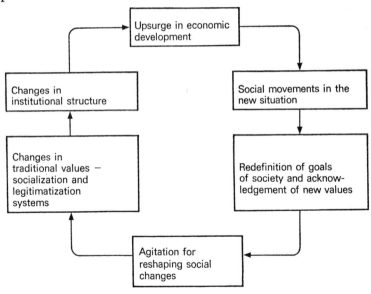

FIG. 2

B. From underdevelopment as an institution to development as a goal

3   We stated in our opening chapter that we would put forward two principal theoretical models to explain the structure of Italy together with a further subsidiary model specifically regarding the power-system.

The first of these was the structural model we have already considered (p. 21), and which is crucial to the understanding of the dynamic process that is taking Italy out of its state of institutionalized underdevelopment and towards the goal of increasing development. It is time to examine now a bipolar model of development and underdevelopment as these influence the dynamics of Italian culture. This model comprises criteria of legitimacy, a socialization system and an institutional system. Our understanding of it will enable us later to come to a closer appreciation of the country's overall power-system.

By *criteria of legitimacy* we mean the various elements comprising the system of values that justifies, validates, legitimates and so lends moral support to the social and economic system, and in particular to the sort of hierarchy it introduces into social stratification and class participation in the pyramid of power. Such are the factors that impart to any society its moral cohesion, lend colour to its claim to exist by right, protect it from the encroachments of any eventual alternative society, and so slow down the pace of change.

The *socialization system* is the mechanism designed to integrate individuals into a society, which it teaches them to accept, inclining them either to subordinate themselves to its requirements or, alternatively, to react violently against it, criticizing and even rejecting it out of hand. Depending on the specific society, such socialization is the task of the family in the first place or else of the schools, and is mainly concerned with group values, but also, as in Italy, with individual ones, and occasionally with the rejection of all values. This latter alternative springs more from the way in which a particular socialization system operates in practice, than from the intentions of those who maintain it in being.

The *institutional system* holds everything together, and comprises the bureaucracy, the army, the police, the prison service, etc. It relies on the first two of these to justify its existence, and does, indeed, help them to maintain their position. In due course we shall examine the implications of a chronically weak system, since Italy has never succeeded in breaking loose from the economy typical of a nation at subsistence level and from the institutional system of a country as yet underdeveloped.

We have, then, a system of values furnishing criteria of legitimacy, a socialization system serving to assimilate individuals into society, and an institutional system that lends order to society and underpins the social distribution of power, and all of these both condition and are conditioned by the economic system. Thus, the systems are mutually interdependent for their functioning, and any change in one implies some change in the others.

4   We mentioned in the Introduction that in nineteenth-century Italy the basic economic system upholding the other three was simply an economy of subsistence, with the result that the institutional, socialization and legitimacy systems supposed a state of material deprivation, and took that condition into their calculations. Because of the way in which the economy was arranged and labour was distributed this was even more true in Northern Italy than in the South.

In an economy, or more generally in a society of subsistence the collective objective is little more than the aggregate of the main aims of the families of which that society is composed, i.e. the drive of each family to secure its own survival and maintain its own identity. In the last century, and especially in the South, Italian society was a family-based society, and family requirements are mirrored in the culture, the education and legal systems, in the religious outlook, and the use of political power.

> *The family, to sum up the situation, satisfies each individual's psychological needs so completely that his sense of belonging to any larger national, regional or even local community, and his active interest in its life, is much less than elsewhere.*[2]

Of course, a society that used to be family-based, and especially one as male-dominated as Italy was, with all her Mediterranean cultural overtones, was not simply a society that was deprived in the material sense, but one in which a small group kept the few available socially influential roles jealously to themselves. Because the overall structure was uncomplicated, there were not many posts of command, and few ways of exercising responsibility. This also explains why Italy's social structure during the first phase was centralized hierarchically, the basic authority figure of the father and property-owner being complemented by the transcendent fatherhood of the priest. This also underlined the second-class position of women who, unless they belonged to the nobility, had no life of their own, and in particular no economic independence.

We can now sum up these remarks about Italian society as a closed, male-dominated, hierarchical and centralized economy of subsistence in a theoretical model, before amplifying the scheme in detail. Reduced to its simplest terms, with reference to the criteria of legitimacy, the socialization system and the institutional system, the model presents the following characteristics:

A CLOSED SYSTEM

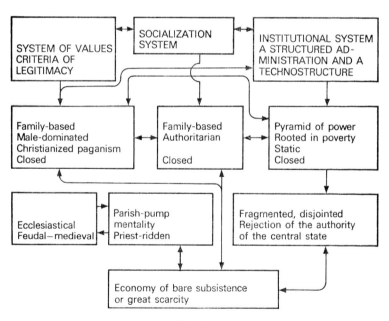

FIG: 3

This diagram shows how the socialization system and the family-based male-dominated value-system in Italian society are intimately related to its half-Christian, pagan and clearly Mediterranean structure. It should never be forgotten that Italian culture was for a long time, and in some ways still is, ruled by magic and religion, the latter being profoundly and unmistakably pagan, with Christianity often no more than lending it a superficial veneer of doctrinal respectability. First and foremost among the pagan elements in the various regional cultures we can mention the cult of the dead, which is quite impressive, and does, indeed, flourish throughout the whole Mediterranean area. Then there are the rituals in connection with the actual consummation of marriage, which serve to emphasize the sexual focus of this whole culture. We are confronted by a society which is in some ways very backward and so makes itself the slave of patterns of behaviour that exert an influence baffling all statistics.

The basic features already described are systematically related to the rest by a series of intermediate links. We can leave anthropologists to examine them in detail, but they boil down to systems of local power, which constitute the grass-roots equivalent of the high-level authority of the Church's hierarchy, of the nobility generally and, in the South, of semi-feudal barons holding sway over their dependants. Religious instruction has been little more than straightforward indoctrination buttressing the official value-system. 'Social sins' are still those which are committed against the authorities or the prevailing social and economic set-up by challenging the position of one's father, husband, lord, manager, etc. Obviously it is implied that a mentality opposed to such 'sins' is a moral asset, and thus attitudes are assimilated and reinforced which make it seem desirable that the actually existing economic, social and cultural systems should be maintained unchanged indefinitely.

The socialization mechanisms in this scheme of things operate to reinforce the status quo. Religious instruction plays its part here, and also woman as teacher of her own children, nurturing in them a sense of subjection, together perhaps with an awareness of personal frustration, and hence breeding in them an attitude of hostile aggression.

5   This model of underdevelopment represents one extreme on the continuous spectrum we mentioned early in Part One, the other

extreme being occupied by the model of development we shall mention in more detail later. The different regions of Italy occupy various positions along this spectrum, depending on the extent to which they have detached themselves from the model of under-development.

Our analysis of the move away from underdevelopment was set out on p. 95 in a theoretical scheme that has been verified empirically on several occasions in field inquiries carried out in the provinces of Puglie, Abruzzo, Veneto and elsewhere. The findings indicate that within areas of underdevelopment change takes place along certain main lines connected with the influence of the mass media, emigration, economic and structural changes.

We now recall this scheme which also summarizes some of what we have just said or mentioned in the Introduction:

A1: The cultural regions of Italy are family-based in their origins.

A2: They still remain family-based to the extent that their economic development has not yet given reality to any proposed changes in values, culture and structure.

B1: Politically they remain closed because of the situation mentioned in A2, i.e.

B1.1: They have a tendency to view with hostility any outside influence.

B1.2: The degree of closure and hostility varies from one part of each region to another and changes in the course of time.

B2: Although developments are taking place the situation mentioned in B1 remains widespread within the various regional structures.

C1: If the parameters of A1 and B1 are acknowledged to be fundamental, then the Southern regions of Italy are for the most part in many ways closed and underdeveloped culturally, religiously, politically and economically.

C2: They are closed societies to the extent that the influence of social communication and of structural factors favouring change has, despite its profound effect, not provoked any real evolution.

D1: The shift away from the model of underdevelopment to that of development, which is obviously stimulated by economic and structural factors, seems to be more rapid when social conditions favour a comparison between the underdeveloped areas of Italy and the developed areas elsewhere in the country or abroad.

D2: This comparison leads the inhabitants of underdeveloped areas to reject or at least revise their previous scale of values.

E1: Communication between developed and underdeveloped areas mainly relies on the mass media and the fact of emigration, and we have seen already that the latter is quite a considerable feature of Italian life.

E2: Thus, even those underdeveloped zones to which industrial development has not penetrated are presented with the model of urban industrial society as a model of something 'better', and to a certain extent they accept it, rather more in its material aspects, but far less in its other cultural characteristics, particularly its values.

Italian society on the whole, when viewed from the outside, looks in some ways like a clearly advanced industrial society, but the details of the situation are more ambiguous. The picture is that of a mosaic formed of elements taken here from the model of underdevelopment and there from that of development, the dominant motifs and rhythms of its design varying from region to region, and even from one zone to another within a region.

Evolution results (a) from transformations induced from the outside by forces within more highly developed areas, such as economic organization and the public development of social organizations; (b) from the impact of the mass media, especially as regards material standards of living; (c) from emigration and face-to-face confrontations which induce a revision of values and can profoundly alter the criteria of legitimacy and public mores generally.

C. The challenging of the role of religious values in society

6   Before turning to consider our theoretical model to explain development, we shall examine the form of the crisis that has faced the traditional model.

It is, of course, obvious that Italy's economic development did involve a crisis situation for the traditional values. However, the earlier stages of renewal seemed to require no more than a reshaping and restructuring of the essentially traditional values to bring them into a form acceptable to the members of the renewed society. In practice the values of Christianity in general and of Catholicism in particular were put forward for acceptance once more, in a somewhat revised form. The goal of development was expressed in terms of an up-dated sort of Christianity, and this was dialectically related to a Marxist sub-culture, which was, by that time, predominant in some of the regions.

This situation proved to be merely the lull before the storm, the grave crisis that was to fall upon the traditional value-system in the 1960s and 1970s, with consequences that we have still to see.

Fascism had presented itself as the guardian of traditional values and had operated a closed society with initiation programmes for the young, male-dominance, jobs for the boys, exaggerated patriotism, a strutting cockiness, and insistence that the Catholic Church was Italian and Roman. With its collapse the other social forces had to redivide the field between them. The Catholic Church tried, at national, provincial and local levels, to use all its resources, including the Catholic party and the Catholic trade unions, in the interests of a belatedly up-dated value-system, in which the Christian values of family-life, hard work, and social concern for others still featured prominently. This revised social model sufficed for Italy in the days of its development, since it gave the sanction of heaven to the process of change.

7   However, a mere twenty years later, the revised value-system itself came under heavy fire, and, at about the same time, the whole structure of the Church was also challenged. Since the structure of Italian society cannot be understood without appreciating all that this crisis meant for every aspect of its life, we had better consider it fairly closely.

The historical background can be filled in quite rapidly. Religious observance throughout Italy was at a very high level at the end of the eighteenth century, with the exception of a few states in the peninsula where religion had never had much hold. It was quite common to have a Sunday Mass attendance of more than 99.5 per cent, and an astonishingly high number of young men chose to become priests (in some places the percentage choosing priesthood was as high as today's percentage for religious observance.[3] The Church, moreover, penetrated every aspect of national life, and was intimately linked with pagan religious attitudes and practices, with the social organization of life, and with the various centres of political authority and other agents of social control.

The French Revolution brought with it a slight but undeniable dropping-off in religious observance. There was no sharp decline in the numbers going to Church, but there was a notable weakening of the spirit of faith, so that deep religious convictions were replaced by rather superficial traditional beliefs. One cannot look at the historical evidence and fail to perceive this change in the religious climate.

A further decline in religious observance, and this time on quite a large scale, resulted from the dismantling of the Papal States and the sequestration of Church lands throughout the peninsula. The French had already made some attacks on the Church's economic and political position, but it had soon recouped its losses, and it was only with the unification of Italy that the rise to power of free-thinking groups deprived the Church of its privileges once and for all. And even this is an exaggeration. At the time of the national unification in 1861 13,946 religious orders were suppressed and their wealth confiscated. A further 1,899 were suppressed in 1866, and 25,080 in 1867. Despite this, the Church as a whole was strong enough to withstand these blows.

However, the real decline in religion did begin round about that time, and it has continued without a break until the present day, with a steady decrease in the Church's cultural, social, economic and political influence and prestige. Its greatest losses came after the Fascist interregnum and at the time of the economic miracle (1953–73).

According to a gallup poll organized by Doxa 54 per cent of Italians still went to Church in 1962, but in the last ten years there has been a further sharp drop in religious observance. A further break-down of the 1962 data gives figures of 60 per cent for communes with less than 10,000 inhabitants, 53 per cent for communes of 10–50,000, and 48 per cent for communes of more than 50,000.[4]

The picture that emerges from later surveys is somewhat more bleak, though the results are incomplete and somewhat tentative. In 1968–69 Burgalassi found that 30–35 per cent of Italians were still going to Mass, about 22 per cent of the people in outlying districts of Milan, and about 30 per cent of the population of Padua and Venice. Doxa's survey in 1972 found 35 per cent of the adult population going regularly to Church, and another 33 per cent going from time to time, but these figures have been challenged, and many feel they are too high. At all events, in some areas religious

observance is almost zero.[5] Then, leaving aside the external ex-
pressions of religious belief, there is also the systematic decline that
has occurred during the last ten years in the way in which these
beliefs are held; this is now confused and often contradictory, and
the appreciation of life as somehow sacred and religious in character
has been largely lost. Moral standards and patterns of behaviour
have departed more and more from Christian values, and the
permissiveness of the consumer society has taken their place, with
more liberal attitudes towards abortion, the social emancipation of
homosexuals, the rise of radical feminist movements, and the
general spread of the consumer society itself.

The severely theological moral standards upheld by the Catholic
Church are being progressively eroded, both from within and
without. The most corrosive attack on them is the work of a
relatively small but very influential group of priests and theologians,
who have made it their business to undermine the traditional
institutions and power structures of their Church, and have even
questioned the dogma of Papal Infallibility, which is, in any case,
according to some recent opinion polls, only subscribed to by a
minority of present-day Catholics.[6]

Thus, the Church no longer has a secure basis in Italian society;
it has lost much of its credibility, and the general run of the Italian
population have drifted further and further away from militant
forms of Catholicism. The Church's credibility, as well as justifying
its own status and authority, somehow served to buttress that of the
Italian political set-up. Thus, the Church's fall from power and loss
of prestige also means that Italy's whole power structure lost much
of its credibility. In due course we shall specify to what extent and
in what sense this has proved to be the case.

The significance of the crisis within the Church is that it under-
mines the very existence of the spirit of comradeship prevailing until
now between the different Catholic organizations throughout the
country. It also makes the Catholic Christian Democrat Party less
subservient to the hierarchy, so that it is now becoming less religious
in its inspiration and more closely resembles the English Conservative Party.

The Church and religion in general are losing their footing in
society. The social structure of Italy is, therefore, being deprived of
one of its main supports, and the country has been obliged to revise
the nature of its claims to be governed by lawful authorities in

accordance with legitimate institutions. Thus, the religious crisis is the central factor in the transformation taking place in Italian society and culture.

The changes in religion itself are changes in quality, quantity, extension and depth.

There is a change in quantity: a decrease in the number of aspects of individual behaviour that can be regarded as religious acts among the social transactions of persons describing themselves as religious.

There is a change in quality: as religion itself is secularized, and seeks some alternative conceptual framework that relates it more closely to the dialectic of praxis in the context of an industrial society and adopts its methodology and values.

There is a change in extension: a different number of people now call themselves religious, and their social and geographical distribution is not the same as it once was.

There is a change in depth: the sense of the sacred is fading, and the value and significance of ascetical and mystical elements in religious experience and behaviour are not appreciated as much as before.[7]

All these changes coincide with changing attitudes towards the Church's institutions and structures. As their sacred meaning is lost sight of and eventually denied, the whole framework of the Catholic Church's authority in Italy is deprived of its justification for existing. Meanwhile, the Church is making laborious efforts to adapt its structures to contemporary industrial society, and the changes have caused a lot of confusion. Furthermore, the members of the Church are losing their sense of their own identity – they no longer trust themselves, and seem fascinated by the life-style of the alternative society and by anything that challenges the system they were brought up in.

If the Church is seen as a legitimatization system or as a power structure, it can be maintained that its greatest enemies are its official supporters. Many feel that the Italian Catholic laity are more conservative than the clergy, who have only taken a few years to destroy the Church's image as something stable and immutable. The Church in Italy was something to be reckoned with, a definite structure one had to take or leave on its own terms, but could not alter. The Church was a fixed, objective reality around which everything else revolved. The clergy, however, have made changes at every level and within every sector of Church life, restructured the whole organization, revised their theology, and entirely re-modelled their actual behaviour.

> *The Catholic Church in Italy has passed unscathed through countless crises, which toppled down civilizations but seemed to do no more harm to her than rain to a window-pane. Now for the first time there is an entirely new situation. The Church is experiencing within herself the birth-pangs of a new world that draws upon her vital energies to nurture its own life, but is so unlike Mother Church in its thrust towards change as to appear as the herald of her own destruction. Thus, the Church finds it increasingly hard to maintain her own identity, and is faced with a battle on two fronts at once. Within her own ranks sophisticated and up-to-date Christians are to be found who give some sort of Christian meaning to every aspect of the contemporary situation, but seem sterile and impotent whenever it is a question of communicating any deep religious experience. This academic Christian culture is sapping the Church of her vital energies. The Christianity now emerging has a certain Hellenic charm about it, and is aesthetically satisfying, but it must not be forgotten that, for the old pagan religions, the Golden Age of Athenian Greece, which stripped them of their sacred auras, was the beginning of the end.*[8]

This is one of the reasons, though there are others, for saying that the most radical changes within Italian society all took place in the course of the twenty years 1950–1970, which seemed the most peaceful period in the country's history. These years witnessed the birth of a new Italy, different from what had gone before, morally, religiously, culturally, socially and, to some extent, politically.

D. The new model

8   This was the first real revolution in contemporary Italy. It was a far-reaching crisis that shook the foundations of Italian habits of moral and religious conformity. The changes meant the end of the old scheme of things.

A new type of religion, of Christianity, of Catholicism and of irreligion emerged from a combination of a number of factors, including on the one hand the industrial revolution and the advances in science and technology, and on the other hand those immediate religious experiences which had been provoked by the break-up of the traditional system. This meant a new way of living or declining to live in the world of religious experience, a different way of thinking about God in the light of science and technology.

In the past, religious experience had related to life in harmony with nature in the context of an Italian society that was predominantly agricultural and kept pace with the cycle of growth in the fields. Today, however, religious experience occurs within the setting of scientific research, advanced technology and the industrial revolution.

The man who lives in this society has a different attitude towards the Church's hierarchical structure, the charismatic leadership of the clergy, and the liturgy itself.[9]

In the recent past the sharp ideological cleavage between Christianity and Marxism and their compromise peaceful co-existence in practice have proved just as unacceptable as the earlier coupling of Christianity with paganism in the traditional Italian social structure of underdevelopment. Italians no longer want either a closed society or one that is only half-open. The overall change

is connected with a whole series of modifications within people's thinking and in their actual behaviour. It can no longer be taken for granted that all Italians accept Catholicism as true. Religious experience is no longer a commonplace and is fast disappearing from the list of experiences that can be shared and enjoyed in common, so that attempts to talk about it resemble a babel of confusion. In proportion as religious experience within the social context becomes increasingly shallow, it is treated more and more as a cultural variable, and the interpretations placed upon it become increasingly diverse.

Today Christian religious experience is becoming something people cannot actually attain. It is no longer

*lived habitually, is becoming rare even as a happening,
and cannot even be proposed as an ideal, because its place
has been taken by sentimental, emotional states.*

The reason for this situation is that

*the official doctrine and ritual of the Catholic Church in
Italy have become colourless and devoid of all impact.
They no longer comprise the essential parts of an individual's initiation into social life, which now depends on
the mass media, on scientific education, on technical training, on adopting the values of the consumer society, on
active participation in the technocracy itself, all integrating
him into the life-style of industrial and post-industrial
society.*[10]

It is hardly surprising that traditional values have lost their hold.
Hard work, family life and love of one's native country are no
longer highly regarded. Less crucial values are in a similar state of
collapse, including civic pride and the special love for one's own
part of the country that once flourished all over Italy.

The crises within religion and within the family are interrelated.
The archetype of the family as guardian of social values seems no
longer relevant. This is not some sort of dissatisfaction with the
traditional family spirit of certain Southern *ceti* that have managed
to survive only as the shadow of their former selves; it is the family
as such that is in crisis.

One indication of this crisis for the traditional Italian family is
the progressive decrease in the actual size of families evident in the
available statistics. The birth rate is falling; an increasing number
of 'families' consist of only one member, and the cohabitation under
one roof of a surviving elderly parent and his/her children, or of
both adult and infant siblings is becoming rare, and tending to
disappear. It is instructive to compare the figures for a typical
industrial region with those for the country as a whole:

	Average number of persons per family		
	1951 Census	1961 Census	1971 Census
Lombardy	3.9	3.4	3.1
Italy	4.2	3.6	3.3

The crisis within the traditional family runs parallel with the
increasing social emancipation of women, though some authors'
emphasis on the declining importance of their role as housewives

fails to consider the countless specialized tasks within the family that the contemporary Italian woman is increasingly called upon to perform. The truth is that developments within Italian society tend

to give a new meaning and attach new functions to the housewife's role. She now has to programme her day and her week. There are various contacts with bodies outside the domestic circle, and to these she may have specific responsibilities to discharge or may need special skills in order to deal with them. In the selection of consumer goods she is faced with complex alternatives, and can to some degree plan the way in which she will make her choice. All this makes being a housewife something of a profession in itself, despite those other and more frequently mentioned developments which have deprived the role of the meaning it once had, and reduced her life to a dull, humdrum routine.

Being a housewife is mainly seen as a woman's full-time job, and exceptions to this rule always mean that both the woman and the rest of the family become physically exhausted, suffer from nervous tension, and feel that their personal needs are being neglected.

Such casting of the housewife in a professional role is particularly noticeable in those families whose male head has quite definitely to be the *breadwinner, and is finding it difficult to make ends meet. It is mainly in this sort of situation that the Italian middle-status-group woman specializes in being a housewife, and plays her role in a way that in any other country would be regarded as exceptionally rigid.*[11]

The changes we have referred to do not mean that the family structure has lost its importance for society, and it has to a considerable degree retained its traditional form. Italian civil law, for example, still assigns important powers and functions to the man who is head of a family. In addition to this, the family as a whole still plays a central role in Italy as elsewhere with regard to a whole series of social obligations that cannot be avoided, such as the paying of taxes and electricity bills, maintaining the required contact with various public officials, filling in forms and questionnaires from time to time, and exercising what is left of such powers, at one time quite extensive, as the husband's authority over his wife, or the parents' right to decide how their children will be educated (where the major decisions are now increasingly made by public bodies or private institutions).

The male-dominant character of Italian society, which derives from the Mediterranean nature of the race and is a very deep-rooted feature of the national way of life, is extremely resistant to change, but is undoubtedly going through some sort of crisis.[12] Its more extreme manifestations are increasingly confined to quite small, relatively isolated zones, and its survival in a more benign form elsewhere is largely limited to the lower middle and lower strata.

Symptomatic of the changed pattern of life are the different attitudes now adopted towards the woman who has committed adultery, the more widespread practice of birth-control, and the discontinued insistence on the pre-marital virginity of one's future wife (though this change may be confined to surface reactions, without any deep change in attitude accompanying it as yet). A new culture is taking shape, a different code of behaviour, a fresh value-system, and Christianity and Marxism alike are coming to terms with the radically new life-styles that are emerging as sub-cultures within the context of Italy's wider and more diversified way of life.

9   At this point it may be useful to sum up what we have said before developing the argument further, and to go back to our initial model of Italian society as a socially and culturally closed and underdeveloped set of structures, in order to compare it with the model that derives from a study of industrial Italy. This will mean comparing and contrasting the legitimatization, systems, the socialization systems, and the institutional and administrative systems.

It will be obvious at a glance that the model we now offer is more complex than the model we presented on page 98, and that it is more pragmatic and empirical in orientation and pluralist in character. In the socialization system the Church and the family are replaced by the family (still partly influenced by the Church), the schools and the mass media. Thus, the socialization system has now come to depend on a number of sub-systems within the culture, and presents a rather provisional and unstable appearance. Religion and abstract idealism give way to the pragmatic mentality of the consumer society, and the common good is made subservient to individual self-interest.

Taken as a whole the Italian system is now fairly typical of the contemporary consumer society, and from this point of view is not at all unique. The need to consume is predominant. The life-style revolves around the prestige attached to what exactly each one consumes, and the quality of life is erected almost into a national

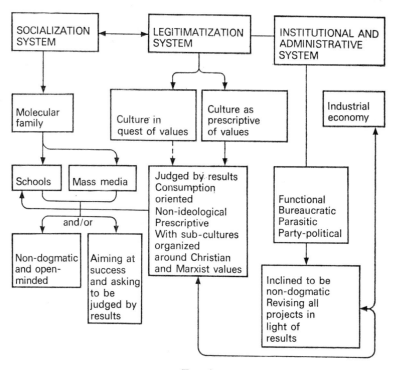

FIG. 4

religion, in which the lip-service still paid to certain traditional values passes almost unnoticed.[13] Society is favourably disposed towards science and increased efficiency, but also towards greater moral permissiveness. In other words, a whole series of contradictions permeates its life-style.

10   To give ourselves a clearer idea of the main features of contemporary Italian culture, we can consider separately and in more detail the socialization system, the legitimatization system and the institutional system.

The national culture in the process of formation revolves around consumption, is deliberately planned, pragmatic, empirically based, pleasure-seeking, scientific and on the whole opposed to ideologies. Although this culture is undoubtedly in the ascendant, it has to come to terms with two sub-cultures, of which the Christian and Catholic one remains the more influential, with the Marxist and Socialist one in second place. Here and there, although they are fast losing ground, one can still find surviving remnants of purely local, male-dominated, family-centred cultures.

The Catholic and Socialist systems are both becoming flexible, often to the point of inconsistency, and there is little difference in practice between the behaviour of Catholics and Socialists, who alike seem content to adjust themselves to the national culture. The time has long since passed when one could think of Marxism as offering a viable alternative value-system to the Catholic model, or as representing the spearhead of progress (and we are not talking about economic policy). In the new situation Marxism seems no more than a step along the road to far more radical reform. It has become clear in recent years that Gramsci's brand of humanism and the cult of science that was associated with Marxism provided no more than a stepping-stone. They helped to break the hold of earlier social systems, but were only a propaedeutic to entirely new post-industrial, cultural models. As time passes we shall learn whether the replacement of the Socialist and Catholic sub-cultures by the new national, or more precisely European, culture represents, as it seems to, a permanent feature of life destined to structure our social behaviour quite firmly.

These cultural transformations have been accompanied by certain changes in the socialization system, the legitimatization system and the institutional system. The family, which has less prestige generally than before, is less important as an agent of socialization, and such influences as the schools and the mass media are now the main ones. As for the legitimatization system, the main thing to notice is that there is less effort than before to inculcate definite values, and that what is being set up in their place is a competitive system in which individuals vie with one another on the basis of ground-rules supplied by the industrial and consumer society with skills derived from their education and from experimentation with new patterns of behaviour. This paves the way for the post-industrial counter-culture which disavows the values of the consumer society and its stress on super-efficiency. This counter-culture already exists to some extent.

In Italy these mutations give rise to more alarm than elsewhere, not so much on account of the more rapidly evolving economy in the background, as because they frequently involve a sudden leap from a male-dominated, family-centred culture and value-system to a post-industrial model, without any intermediate stage to cushion the shock. In some areas, for instance, people who once refused to work because they were living in a closed society, now refuse to work because they are living in a post-industrial one, and have no experience of work in an industrial society. It is consequently hard to decide whether the existence of so many social parasites and the popularity of the hippies' way of life is merely a legacy from Italy's period of underdevelopment or really does express a more modern outlook. A similar observation needs to be made of the political Left – it is not clear whether they are merely passing on the torch of some old traditions of protest, especially in Southern Italy, or are presenting some effective political alternative.

In all probability the real picture is different in different regions, since the impact of the industrial society varied considerably from one part of the country to another and was not felt everywhere at once nor to the same degree. What we can describe conveniently as the urban and industrial style culture first emerged in the old industrial triangle of Milan, Turin and Genoa. It flourished there more than anywhere else, but also spread gradually to the other cities of Northern and Central Italy, to the South, and into rural areas.

The schools and the popular press as well as the radio ensured that at least some of these new values were drawn to the attention of the nation as a whole, but failed to make any great impression. Emigration played a larger part in the diffusion of new values, as various surveys have shown, but was not a nationwide phenomenon.

The schools do modify some aspects of culture, although only very gradually, but in the long run and on the whole they maintain and transmit a traditional outlook; whereas the mass media's influence does bring about changes in external behaviour. The mass media cater for the consumer and only indirectly consider values or the new economic, cultural, and social situation. Emigration has a much more direct effect on values, and in the South, which is the most backward part of Italy, this effect is very great indeed. Here particularly, too, its effect combines with that of the mass media and the improved scholastic situation to produce sudden and considerable leaps forward. The impact of the new knowledge is often direct, violent and immediate.[14]

The male-dominated, family-centred culture vanishes, but very often the progressive Catholic or bourgeois humanist culture is also discarded as obsolete before it has ever been tried.

The dimming if not the total extinction of the humanist ideal marks the rise of a new cultural élite. Inspired by science and technology, their approach is empirical; they ask questions and consider various possibilities, re-interpreting the cultural models of the past in terms of their own particular vision. What they really want is not yet clear, so that it is hard to tell what influence they will exercise in tomorrow's world. Certainly, their interests transcend any boundaries of regional or party-political concern; they are pluralists, interacting with several different value-systems, sub-cultures, social classes, and *ceti*. The new culture brings together widely differing individuals and strata of society. The process is helped along by the boom in paperbacks which in Italy as elsewhere have unified the thinking of people in different walks of life and in different parts of the country as never before. Where Italy differs from the rest of Europe, this is because she entered upon this cultural revolution while still having a plurality of regional cultures and life-styles.

If the largely closed, traditional value-system survives within the Catholic and Socialist sub-cultures,

a series of happenings is in process which increasingly rules out irrational or spontaneous decisions, and requires experts with scientific instruments to collaborate in making society's decisions for it, and in choosing how everybody is to behave.

The logical relationships that hold together the whole fabric of the technostructure, such as the systematic lay-out of machines, organizations, financial arrangements, personal relationships, and social transactions, are closely interwoven, and their development entails a rational structuring of the whole of life to a degree that displaces the earlier culture, and the effect of this increases in rigidity the more one is concerned with the material aspects of life.[15]

Any discussion of the state of individual consciences is out of the question, but as social realities the previously dominant Catholic and Socialist sub-cultures are definitely in retreat, and their place is being taken by the new European culture. Thus, as we must remember when discussing the structure of power at the top, this cultural transformation and the change in the value-system that it brings with it give rise to a crisis for the legitimatization system that has been the dominant one in recent years and has served to validate the institutional system as a whole, the present shape of the structures of production and administration, and the country's social structure. The present system is in crisis because it now seems to be at least to some extent unjustified. A particular institution, such as the Army, now appears much less justified than it did when the general public had no doubts about its practical value, its military function and its effective potential. Moreover the institutions that are still accepted now have to be justified on a new basis and in new ways. The same holds true of socially acceptable behaviour, which is no longer that in step with previous ideas of etiquette nor with the values and customs of the former way of life.

In short, there is a radical change taking place in the value-system that validates the Italian social system. The restructuring of values both reflects and induces changes in the social structure as a whole. It is fascinating to observe the dramatic efforts of Italians to give some new meaning to their lives, to organize the community along fresh lines, and to re-assess the significance or otherwise of life and death. The Mediterranean-type Italian peasant culture has been practically drained of all meaning by industrial development and by the rise of modern culture.

It is still too early to say in what direction things are moving. What has been destroyed we know well enough; we know yesterday's world, and can look back on it with nostalgia or irritation, but the Italy of tomorrow is no more than a vague outline. Undoubtedly, we have lost a lot of our human legacy of friendship and selfishness, of love and blood-lust, but we cannot yet say whether the new things we have got in exchange will lead to a positive or a negative result.

Notes to chapter 4

1. Birnbaum, 1971, p. 64.
2. Acquaviva and Eisermann, 1971, p. 160.
3. See Principe, 1959; Acquaviva and Principe, 1956; and, more generally, Acquaviva, 1971a.
4. Acquaviva, 1976.
5. See Burgalassi, 1967 and 1968; Corbetta and Riccardi, 1972, pp. 27–79, especially p. 55; Scortegagna, 1972, p. 31; 'Partecipazione degli italiani adulti alla vita religiosa'.
6. See Acquaviva and Guizzardi, 1973a, pp. 485–99.
7. Acquaviva, 'Religione e irreligione nell'età postindustriale' in Acquaviva and Guizzardi, 1971, p. 19.
8. *Ibid.*, p. 49.
9. *Ibid.*, p. 43.
10. *Ibid.*, p. 15.
11. Balbo, 1973, p. 18.
12. See Acquaviva and Eisermann, 1971 and 1974.
13. See Acquaviva and Guizzardi, 1973a.
14. See Acquaviva and Eisermann, 1971, for a fuller treatment of this question.
15. Acquaviva, 1971b, p. 86.

CHAPTER 5

The Distribution of Power

11   Fundamental changes in the legitimatization system are involved as well as new values, new social standards and new patterns of behaviour. For, as we have seen, the strength and cohesion of social institutions rise and fall with the varying measure of support they derive from the value-system behind their title to legitimacy. This is particularly true of the system of power at the top, although, as we shall see, its evolution is also conditioned by many other factors.

All that we have said so far is merely a preamble to what we wish to say about the sub-systems between which power is distributed. However, any direct consideration of this question is still premature. As a first approach towards it we shall try to explain the sorts of transformation within the power-system that have accompanied developments in the legitimatization system or basic value-system.

Where, then, are the real nerve-centres of power? It is clear already that today we must speak of a plurality of such centres; it is only by analysing their several natures and relationships that we can hope to form a fairly accurate picture of the Italian way of structuring power at the top.

Theoretically at least, Italy is a parliamentary republic with a multiplicity of political parties. This fact, coupled with the analysis of her changing value-systems, is the context in which to situate whatever we say about the distribution of power.

Let us begin with the sources of income, since to do so is in keeping with the general trend of our argument, and with our distinction between vertical and horizontal structures. Obviously, in analysing the power structure we cannot distinguish merely, or over-precisely or without certain qualifications, between power itself and

117

the sources of income. The distinction is just one we shall make whenever it seems convenient for our purpose, and ignore whenever it gets in the way.

All that we suppose to begin with is that, in fact, and within certain limits that will need to be defined as we go along, the power-system does reflect social stratification and does express the sort of relationships obtaining between the means of production, or more generally between the sources of income (be this great or small) and the vertical and horizontal structures of society as a whole. Furthermore, the power-system reflects the changes taking place in these different aspects of society in the course of its history.

So let us try to pin-point the centres of power within the Italian economic structure and its supporting technostructure. Our preliminary analysis will provide the basis for the rather different and more fully articulated scheme that we shall propose in due course. For the present, something more simple will serve our turn. Within the power-system it seems possible to pick out:

(a) the power of the agricultural sector and the land-owning community;

(b) the power of the public and private sectors of industry and commerce and of those concerned with urban development;

(c) the power of education, the mass media, social services, private and civil administration, the army and police forces, and culture generally;

(d) the political power of the unions, the various parties, and the Church as an institutional structure.

Roughly speaking, sub-system (a) revolves around the agricultural or primary sector of the economy, with the exception of the implications of the ownership of land inside towns or in urban development areas; sub-system (b) mainly concerns the industrial or secondary sector of the economy, with the exception of its commercial component; and sub-system (c) gravitates towards the tertiary sector, which is also the main sector to be influenced by sub-system (d), although this does impinge on the whole economy in one way or another.

This four-fold division follows our earlier model of the horizontal structure fairly closely, except that, for reasons which we shall explain, income from urban development has been detached from that derived from the ownership of land, and placed separately in sub-system (b). By making the two schemes roughly coincide, we have hoped to make the argument itself easier to follow, and it should certainly help to bring out the obvious, direct connections between social stratification and the power-system – in other words, between the horizontal structure and the structure of power at the top.

Thus, if the power-system mirrors the vertical structure in one way, in another it expresses the realities of the horizontal structure, as we shall see. Thus, for instance, such sub-systems of power as the political parties and the trade unions are rooted in the social strata. It is the complex web of relationships between the nerve-centres of power themselves and with the horizontal and vertical structures, that makes up the structure of the fabric of contemporary Italian society, within the framework of the legitimatization and socialization systems already referred to.

A. The agricultural sector and the land-owning community

12 The first thing to remember in discussing the income derived from the ownership of land and the power associated with it is that for a very long time in Italy all power, whether economic or political, whether civil or ecclesiastical, was bound up with the land. Anyone who wished to challenge the power of the Church sought to deprive it of its lands. When the nineteenth-century bourgeoisie were trying to increase their power, their main efforts were directed towards the acquiring of land of their own and the accumulation of agricultural capital. Even if they did not always aim deliberately and methodically to make their stake in the power game through land ownership, this was nevertheless the way in which they achieved their success.

The relationship between land and power goes through five stages. First of all the land belonged to the clergy and nobility whose power came from a long tradition, but laws were passed which transferred the control of this land and more besides to the rising new class of free-thinkers, who administered it more closely, and also secured incomes from industry, commerce and banking. This, then, was the second stage, with vast estates and huge farms in the possession of the ruling bourgeoisie, while farm-labourers and the poor or only moderately well-to-do farmers and market-gardeners remained faithful to the Church, and were the basis of its indirect share in the stakes of political power after the Second World War, via the Catholic Christian Democratic Party.

Fascism represents the third stage. Property-owners supported the regime and, indeed, helped it to power, but the regime tried to provide itself with a more popular basis by increasing the number of small land-owners, winning over the peasants' goodwill, and sequestrating a portion of the huge estates.

Stage four followed the Second World War, when the Catholics, and more specifically the Christian Democrat Party, won over the mass of peasants. An association of direct growers was set up, the *Coldiretti*, in which the controlling influence was in the hands of the Catholic majority, who also held the majority position in the *Confagricoltura*, or association of large land-owners.

In a fifth stage we witness the partial demobilization of these political forces, partly because the increase in industrial capital has considerably undermined the position of agriculture, and also because the years 1952–72 witnessed the break-down of the social structure of the Italian countryside, as well as a sharp drop in the number of direct growers and a decline in their importance as an organized political pressure group.

What is the reason for these five stages, and why has the power associated with an income derived from the ownership of land come to mean so little nowadays? How much of this power survives today and how does it operate?

The answer to such questions is the history of those developments which pushed agriculture together with its associated organizations and its particular values out of the central position it once occupied within the Italian economic and social system (and, in consequence, within the country's power structure) and displaced it to the outer edge. In the 1930s the agricultural contribution towards the national income was already less than the industrial one, and in recent years it has become quite small (about 10 per cent of the total income, as we have seen), but it was only after the Second World War that the fraction of the active population engaged in agriculture, although it had long been less than the industrial labour force, dropped as low as 18 per cent of the overall figure.

There was also a change in the nature of land ownership. Until after the Second World War there had been a steady increase in the amount of productive land in the hands of direct growers, from 18 per cent in 1931 to 36.6 per cent in 1946. The amount of land leased out to them had also grown from 7.7 per cent to 18 per cent, and that available to share-croppers had risen from 17 per cent to 21.2 per cent. Most of the rest was in the hands of large capitalist landlords. As we have explained, this development resulted from the political programmes of the Fascists and, later, of the Christian Democrats, and was also due to economic factors.[1]

The transformation was made much easier by the Fascists putting an additional two and a half million acres under cultivation and placing them in the hands of direct growers, whose number rose by about 500,000. A further two and a half million acres were placed under cultivation after the war. Moreover, the twenty years following the war speeded up the change-over with the expropriation of about 1,800,000 acres from rich land-owners and the use of legislation in favour of a more extensive distribution of land among direct growers. All told, about 6,200,000 acres changed hands between 1946 and 1967.[2] Table 5.1 indicates the proportions of the development from 1946 to 1965.[3]

Table 5.1   Forms of Land Cultivation (percentages)

	1946	1965
Direct growers	36.6	49
Tenants	18.0	12
Share-croppers on individual farms	15.0	
Share-croppers with a third-party interest	6.2	
Cultivated by farm-labourers	24.2	
Cultivated by employees and/or part shareholders		34
Other forms		5

Expressed in relation to the land-area under cultivation and the sort of tenancy enjoyed, the development between the 1961 and 1971 censuses was as shown in table 5.2.[4] Such changes in their financial position reduced the status of the investors in agriculture and lessened their economic prestige. The relationships existing between the larger and small land-owners were transformed, and incomes from agricultural holdings no longer formed a large source of capital investment in the rest of the Italian economy. This becomes clear if we remember that during the golden years of the economic miracle agricultural incomes rose by 12 per cent whereas the overall increase in incomes was one of 53 per cent.

Table 5.2   **Surface Areas of Farms and Sort of Tenancy Enjoyed**

	Variation 1961–1970	
Tenancy	*Farms*	*Acreage*
Direct growers	−343,360	+3,719,678
Wage-earners and/or part shareholders	−51,925	−1,588,883
Farming colony	−185,901	−4,635,128
Other forms	−91,939	−1,196,653
Total	−673,125	−3,700,986

The control of land was important in the beginning, because immediately after the national unification the power-system of the ruling-class was directly related to land ownership. At a later stage, however, even the presentation of a united front by the whole body of Italian peasants did not count for very much. After the Second World War the peasants allied themselves with the moderately progressive Catholic Christian Democratic Party, rather than with the conservative forces of liberalism and fascism. In its moderate rule over the nation this party relied on the peasants not so much as an economic force, but because their votes in the ballot-box could bring into parliament scores of Christian Democrat members to represent them, who would exert their influence on politics for quite a long time.

For quite a long period developments affecting land ownership and the agricultural labour force favoured the direct growers. However, the *Coldiretti* was thrown into crisis by a further reshaping of agriculture involving a reduction in the number of farm-labourers and a measure of larger-scale capital investment in agricultural development. Between 1961 and 1971 the number of farms tenanted by direct growers dropped by 343,360 (about 10 per cent).[5]

We have noted the decrease in the number of farms. There has, therefore, been a drop in the number of direct growers, and thus in their social and political influence. This trend needs to be added to a far more serious weakening of the peasants' overall position: already in 1968 58.5 per cent of direct growers' families had no active male member less than 49 years old. Nobody will fail to grasp the political and social implications of this state of affairs. It means that it has taken only ten years (1961–71) to reverse the increase in the number of small-holdings for which the conservative, and later the moderately progressive groups had to labour so long.

Table 5.3   Structure of the Agricultural Labour Force 1871–1970 (percentages)

	Self-employed		Hired labour	Others
	Individually	*Collectively*		
1871	25.7	17.0	56.9	0.4
1881	24.7	13.7	61.2	0.4
1901	33.4	19.8	46.4	0.4
1911	27.6	18.7	53.3	0.4
1921	39.6	15.4	44.7	0.3
1936	51.3	20.0	28.4	0.3
1959	75.7		24.3	—
1970	66.6		33.4	—

Sources: Serpieri, 1947, p. 123; and (for 1959 and 1970) ISTAT, *Rilevazione nazionale delle forze di lavoro.*

The reshaping of agriculture along capitalist lines has played an important role. Thus, the 45,000 tractors of 1951 had become 700,000 in 1971. There are also other factors that we have not mentioned, but it is certain that the main reason for agricultural incomes' ceasing to be a source and a form of power is that so many have left agriculture and gone elsewhere. Between the 1961 and 1971 censuses the South lost some 2,300,000 inhabitants.[6] In some regions the losses were colossal. Sicily, with 4,667,316 inhabitants in 1971, had lost 440,000 of its former number; Calabria with 1,962,000 had lost 390,000; etc. If we recall that most of those emigrating were previously actively engaged in agriculture, the implications are clear – in certain small towns in the South it is now hard to find any males between the ages of 18 and 45.

Various authors have discussed these figures for one reason or another, but we shall not enter here into a technical discussion that would be alien to our main theme. Suffice it to note that one author has concluded that during the twenty years of the economic miracle (1952–72), Southern Italy lost 6 million inhabitants – an exodus of truly biblical proportions.

The number engaged in agriculture was on the decrease nation-wide. It dropped by 43 per cent between 1961 and 1971, and had dropped by 31.1 per cent in the preceding decade. The proportion of the population actively engaged in agriculture dropped from 42.2 per cent in 1951 to 29.1 per cent in 1961 and 17.3 per cent in 1971, and the last few years have witnessed a further decrease. This steady overall decrease conceals some quite varied movements of the overall labour force.[7]

The fact remains that between 1961 and 1971 agriculture once more took on a capitalist structure, though those administering it and the conditions under which they did so had vastly changed. While the emphasis used to be on large estates and huge-scale farms, today the stress is on the industrialization of agricultural production, and industrial capital is being invested in agriculture. Farms are now run along quite different lines. Both in its actual running and in its relationship with the power structure, agriculture now tends to be absorbed into the industrial sector of the economy, and the old traditions of the country estates have almost vanished. Yet not quite, Despite all the modernization, there is still an old-fashioned side to agriculture. As well as the up-to-date farms with full-time employment for all and a hardly perceptible increase in the workers' average age, one still finds the economically inferior small farms that barely manage to survive with part-time hands and elderly workers.

There are about 50–60,000 large or intensively cultivated farms today with a high degree of capital investment, and a further 200–300,000 medium-sized farms in the hands of either direct growers or share-croppers with capitalist backing.[8] There must also be about 3 million small and sometimes very poor farms, often little more than scraps of land, owned by pensioners who work on them for a few hours a week to supplement their pension, or by industrial workers and others who work on the land part-time – sometimes they are looked after by family friends on the non-active list, or kept merely as a hobby. Nor can we omit to mention the really poor peasants, and there are plenty of these. Their existence, like the way in which the earth is now being used, symbolizes the general decline in agriculture and its near extinction.

Only the farms that have attracted capital investment are prospering, increasing from 7.6 per cent of cultivated areas in 1947 to 20 per cent towards the end of the 1960s.[9]

The power-system within Italian society was conditioned by agriculture for a long time. A study of the country's economic development and of the changing circumstances of the labour force tends to confirm the existence of a five-fold division, along the lines we initially suggested, in the history of the relationships between the overall power structure and the sub-system of power deriving from agriculture and enjoyed by the land-owning community. At this point we need not go back to the very beginning, but can restrict our attention to a consideration of those forces which are still relevant to the present-day ongoing situation. Very briefly, then, we can distinguish three stages: first, the dominance of very large farms supported by conservative *ceti* (and by the Fascists, 1920–43) – here the *Confagricoltura* was influential, and also earlier organizations of rich land-owners, one of which went back to the start of the century; second, the dominance of small- and medium-scale farmers and direct growers, with moderate political views, suitable related organizations affiliated to the Christian Democrat Party, and a mutually beneficial relationship with the Catholic Church; and third, the collapse of agriculture – against the background of the crisis in politics, in the national value-system, and in the Catholic Church. There is also a new-style agriculture on industrial lines, but this shares the political stance of industry as a whole, and its leaders are like any other industrialists.

To these three stages there correspond three groups still exercising political power: the rich owners of agricultural land who have almost disappeared as a class; the direct growers whose small-holdings are very much in recession; and the new-style agriculturalists who are best seen as belonging to the industrial sector. Meanwhile, as the old rural proletariat disappears, a new-style agricultural worker is also emerging, whose political and cultural attitudes, value-system, income, and union membership make him increasingly resemble his fellow industrial workers in the towns.

B. The sectors of industry and commerce, including land-investment in connection with urban development

13   We have seen that the development both of the commercial and banking system and of the industrial system coincided with the rise of a national bourgeoisie, the unification of Italy, and its first wave of economic expansion.

The ideas and influence of such bourgeois elements constituted the mentality, the outlook and the relatively unlimited power of the ruling-class. A closed *ceto* of entrepreneurs consolidated their position by bribery, corruption and steady pressure. They achieved a tremendous ascendancy over the working-classes, and for a long time both political and economic considerations made it quite out of the question that these should even think of negotiating about their conditions of employment or lay claim to any legal rights.[10]

Yet the economy these entrepreneurs administered was fragile and based on narrow-minded even though quite traditional thinking. The economy was weak. The entrepreneurs were few. Their ideas were also few – but their power was great. Tariff-barriers and social legislation favoured the entrepreneurs, and the electoral laws enfranchised only the comparatively rich.

As the industrial economy made headway, the closed *ceto* of entrepreneurs steadily strengthened their own position, and these industrial magnates became truly a class apart. It was with their help that Fascism came to power after the First World War in 1922. Nevertheless, it was during these Fascist days that the entrepreneur-class met their first setback: the 1929 economic crisis led to the setting up of a solidly structured nationalized industrial complex, and this strengthened its own position as time went by.

Yet, by the end of the Second World War it was political and social rather than economic factors that had contributed most to damage the image of the entrepreneurs in the private sector. Their collaboration with the Fascists had compromised their credibility. They found themselves unable to improve their cultural and political standing, and produced neither an up-to-date and consistent social and economic policy, nor a cultural programme, nor even a political party of significance. They remained fossilized in their outmoded traditions, or alternatively, aware of the weakening of agricultural associations of entrepreneurs and of their own threatened isolation, they joined forces with the Catholic Party, which was eventually able to speak for entrepreneurs in the public sector itself. The class conflicts of the final phase of industrial development directed the main brunt of their attack against private capitalism, and this was considerably weakened as a result.[11]

The entrepreneur-class might very well have been able to recover its position, but for the fact that the strategy it adopted was utterly mistaken. After the reconstruction period, and while there was a boom in the economy because of the war in Korea, they concentrated on pushing the economy forwards towards the economic miracle, but left others (mainly the Catholic politicians) to deal with politics, while the nationalized sector was allowed to take the lion's share of heavy industry.

Private capital has no strong organization today, and, from the political point of view, occupies an inferior position in the power structure, which rests on such focal points as the central administrations of the state, of the political parties, of the corporations running the mass media, together with the management in charge of state enterprises, including the national banking system, and the managing bodies of insurance and social welfare associations, universities, or high-level cultural institutions, etc. Private enterprise has become small, devoid of prestige, power or any decisive voice in the orientation of Italy's future economic development – though an exception must be made for some specific sectors, such as the oil companies and one or two others, which are mainly controlled by international private enterprise.

Round about 1957, as the Common Market was getting under way, the Italian economy still hinged on about twenty large enterprises, some of which were mainly or entirely state-owned, while the rest were mainly or entirely private in nature.[12] In addition to these there were many large concerns (and there are more today) which did not control the market, but might be dominant in a particular region, and had their headquarters away from either Rome or Milan. There were also a certain number of groups, mainly foreign ones with special interests in petrol, heavy engineering, electronics, food or the pharmaceutical industry. Certain firms, too, had special international connections, such as those linked with the Vatican.

There have been no great changes since 1957, save that electricity has been nationalized and a single national grid established, while the chemical industry has witnessed the rise of a few really powerful groups. Otherwise, the power structure of heavy industry is much as it was. On the other hand, small and medium-sized industries have expanded rapidly during this period.

A cross-section of Italian industrial turnover is provided in an existing analysis of the fifteen major concerns.[13] In 1967, 74.3 per cent of the nominal capital invested in shares was invested in 2.47 per cent or 1015 companies out of a total of 41,120. Of this 74.3 per cent, 51.9 per cent was invested in 113 companies with a capital of about 10 billion lire.[14] To complete this picture we give the 1972 list of the twenty-four main companies in table 5.4.[15] These companies have a turnover of 9326 billions and employ 642,507 workers; *at least* fourteen of them (marked with an asterisk) are under state control.

Table 5.4   Monopolies in Italy in 1972

	Turnover (billions of lire)	No. of employees
FIAT (cars and engineering)	2127	184,091
Montedison* (mainly chemicals)	823	55,800
Italsider* (metals and engineering)	720	46,609
AGIP* (petrol and its by-products)	694	7,215
SIP* (telephones)	678	57,894
Magazzini Standa (department stores)	364	21,161
La Rinascente* (department stores)	295	15,487
Alitalia* (air-traffic)	285	14,706
Alfa Romeo* (cars)	282	24,518
Olivetti (typewriters and adding machines)	255	32,729
Pirelli (rubber)	253	27,950
Shell italiana* (controlled by Agip)	249	3,876
SNIA Viscosa (chemicals)	242	24,304
SNAM* (chemical preparations)	241	5,187
IBM italiana (distribution and service)	239	7,067
ANIC* (chemicals)	230	12,516
Montefibre* (chemicals)	196	18,629
Chevron oil italiana (petrol and its by-products)	188	853
RAI* (broadcasting – radio and TV)	183	11,630
Zanussi (fridges and washing-machines)	170	20,000
API (petrol)	161	1,067
Dalmine* (metals and engineering)	158	13,289
Italcantieri* (shipyards and engineering)	152	12,356
Siemens (electricals)	141	23,573
Total	9326	642,507

There is an even greater concentration within the main industrial groups (see table 5.5). The three largest ones, IRI, ENI and Montedison are under state control, and these account for more than two-thirds of the turnover and three-quarters of the employment-roll of all groups in the field. Moreover, the state exercises some sort of control over at least two other groups. The nature of this concentration, therefore, supports what we have said about the decline in the power of private enterprise. During the thirty years 1943–73 the state increased its dominance in the heavy industrial sector, and two successive policies orientated the exercise of such industrial power.

Initially, until about 1963, the state industries were the close allies of private enterprise. This was reflected in the existence of protective tariff-barriers and in the way in which economic expansion was stimulated and encouraged. Latterly, however, with at least tacit government approval the state enterprises have severed their connections with the private sector quite considerably, and have set up their own production networks. Prior to 1963 the government rarely

Table 5.5   The Ten Main Industrial Groups

	Turnover (in billions of lire)	No. of employees
IRI	4678	449,800
Montedison	2100	168,000
ENI	1604	75,500
Assicurazioni generali	742	72,273
Olivetti	548	8,800
Riunione adriatica di sicurtà	421	43,484
SNIA Viscosa	411	3,415
INA	257	7,520
Società italiana resine	206	8,333
Industria Buitoni Perugia	155	8,594
Total	11,122	845,719

interfered with the running of the state industries, and only when this seemed absolutely necessary. It since seems to have become definite policy to replace state control systematically for private enterprise, especially in key industries but also in large-scale industries generally. The alliance between the Socialists and the Catholics (who include a number of entrepreneurs in the public sector) has made politicians aware of the clash between public interest and private enterprise in production arising from the competition that exists (even if unplanned) between public money and private investment. Private investors are now also disengaging themselves from state enterprises and placing themselves, to some degree, in opposition to them.[16]

Although the changes in the entrepreneur-class, the transformation of industrial power, and the growth of the state industries have been continuous, the development was particularly rapid in times of crisis. Both the major crises that occurred between 1962 and 1972, and particularly that of 1963–4, found the private sector weak for want of reserve capital of its own to fall back on, and because of the harsh line adopted by the state-controlled banks. Precisely at such times, however, partly to give a boost to the economy, more money was poured by the state into the public sector of industry, which grew quickly in importance and increased its hold over the economy.

Although such state action did not reflect deliberate policy, it created it, and made a tremendous difference to the Italian power-system and to the stratification of Italian society. What the final outcome will be it is still too early to say, but the last few years have sufficed to show that the thrust of public investment into the economy tends to give it a boost generally.

For example, consider the growth of investments in state-owned or partly state-owned enterprises, and compare it with the growth of investment in the private sector (table 5.6). The table omits the years after 1970, which would have required a more complex treatment. (Their inclusion would, however, have left the overall picture unchanged.)[17] During the last three years investment in state industries has accounted for more than 40 per cent of industrial investment.[18]

Table 5.6   Growth of Industrial Investment

	Public Enterprise		Private Enterprise	Total growth
	State-owned	State has shares		
1967	+7.1	+0.8	+16.3	+13.1
1968	+11.1	+14.2	+10.4	+10.7
1969	+16.8	+24.9	+5.0	+11.0
1970	+17.8	+19.2	+7.5	+12.8

The power of the state is clear not only from the size of the investments, but also from the number and importance of the sectors under state control. These include practically all electricity production, almost all the iron and steel industry, 80 per cent of the chemical industry, 80 per cent of banking, and possibly 80 per cent of the pharmaceutical industry. The state is also rapidly gaining ground in such sectors as cars, supermarkets, food-stuffs and textiles. It has the major interest in the railways, airways and shipping services. The only check to its advance is the presence of international investment, and this itself is often an unstable factor. The state, for instance, now controls the major interest in Shell italiana.

Thus, we can no longer consider the Italian economy as a private-enterprise system. If all the economies of Europe, from the most favourable to free-trade and private enterprise to the most socialist and state-dominated, were arranged in a continuous series, ranging from West Germany to the Soviet Union, the Italian economy would be somewhere in the middle, but it is moving slowly towards the Soviet Union.

Following Alberoni we can provide this synthesis of the economic position of public and private enterprise, and of their power in the country:

(a) *Private capitalism has lost so much ground as a national force as no longer to have any real political bite.*

(b) *State capitalism has arrived on the scene in the meanwhile, and its position requires clarification.*

(c) *International capitalism is important in the sales sector, but not particularly influential in the field of production.*[19]

14 The situation, therefore, is changing rapidly, and a new class of entrepreneurs is emerging. We can assess their numerical strength, specify their culture, and give some idea of their political programme and power. However, before doing so, we would like to return to a few questions that touch upon the economic basis of their position. The development has been, as we have seen, in the industrial and commercial sectors, but these are also affected by incomes accruing from the ownership of land in towns and development areas, and these in turn cannot be considered separately but are strictly related to the state of the building trade, as well as to all (or almost all) the rest of the power structure. It needs to be noted, too, that money invested in such land has often been previously withdrawn from the private sector of industry.

It is possibly more important to fix our attention on investment in urban development than on commerce because, with the exception of a few chains of supermarkets partly or entirely under state control, this is broken up into a series of small enterprises in the hands of the upper middle stratum – it is only the directors of the *Confcommercio* (national confederation of businessmen) who have a place in the power-system, and even that is far less influential than the agricultural and industrial organizations, or the peasants' associations.

Investors in urban-development land are, however, a considerable force in the power-system. Their importance has been increased by the high rate of migration throughout Italy and by the large-scale urban development that followed the Second World War. Investment in the building sector has climbed steeply, particularly with the 1950–57 upsurge in the economy. Interest rose from 3 per cent just after the war to 6–7 per cent. The buying and selling of sites and large-scale speculation in building eventually brought about an increase in the proportion of privately-owned houses – from 40 per cent in 1951 to 51.5 per cent in 1966. All who can manage it are investing in land and speculating on development areas: public and private bodies, political parties, industrialists, owners of large estates, and, of course, builders.

The opportunities for speculation on building-sites, and for speculators to corrupt public bodies, thanks to their influence in the power-system, mean that this sector of the Italian economy is fast becoming a systematic pilferer of public funds on a large scale. In medium-sized as well as in large towns there is the repeated instance of land designated as a public park or earmarked for some other social purpose being parcelled out as building-sites. Whole forests go the same way, often common land which has been declared private by some legal quibble or just in sheer defiance of the law. Hundreds and even thousands of kilometres of coastline are ruined and changed into private building-sites. Residential villages have even been constructed in national parks – in Abruzzo, for instance. Woods with preservation orders on them are set on fire, in the hope that planning permission will then be obtained. And so it goes on: in the North much more than in the South, but anywhere at all when speculators in building feel it worth their while to bring pressure to bear.[20]

The power associated with investment in urban building-land and the speculation that accompanies its use are text-book cases of how power structures operate, but we shall not dwell on them since a comprehensive treatment would take us outside the limits of sociology. They involve the linking of economic and political power, the corruption of the administration, and other such factors.

However, certain aspects of the proceedings are typically Italian, such as the institutionalization of corruption in the political parties. There seem to be several political parties speculating systematically in the competition for contracts to construct motorways or other public works. The firms wishing to secure the contracts regularly pay a certain percentage to each of the political parties with an 'interest'. This is no secret, and parliament itself has even been involved.

Speculation in building and in city funds is the most obvious present-day version of the behaviour common among rich people in the days of the closed, underdeveloped Italy and of their method of making use of their power. The practice is more in evidence where urban development has been particularly rapid, and where the ties with the Southern culture of underdevelopment are closer. Thus, it is common in towns which have never known industrialization, but have become post-industrial overnight.

The outstanding example is Rome which, from being a pre-industrial city, was transformed into a city of tertiary services without having ever been industrialized at all. It is crowded to overflowing with hovels and shanties mid-way in style between slums and South-American *favelas*. In 1969 69,000 families were sharing accommodation. 16,000 families were living in the so-called *borghetti*, townships on the outskirts which have grown spontaneously as best they could. The suburbs of Rome have no public parks, but have been entirely built up by land speculators and house 900,000 people, with hardly any social services at all.

> *What is being born and growing in this way is a city split in two, a huge ghetto on the outskirts that contrasts with new houses let at a high rent, hovels alongside residences in perfect taste miles away from the city-centre and devoid not only of the usual services, but even of any centre of their own, so that the whole development area is fast becoming an 'archeological island' of rich tenants in a sea of squalor.*[21]

In Rome there are some almost invisible but very strong political, economic and social forces influencing the course of urban development and speculation on building-sites. They corrupt the experts or at least find ways of bringing them round to their point of view. In Italy's capital city even the public parks are changing hands on the private market.[22]

There seems little chance of stopping this parcelling out of land against the public interest for houses and flats, and sites earmarked for parks, roads, schools, low-priced hostels, or university buildings continue to be sold to private developers.[23] City authorities seem impotent to cope with this speculation, and in the last few years more than 2500 acres have been wrongly allocated in this way.

Such speculation belongs to the private sector, but is quite closely related to the power of people in public positions. It is as if private investors have turned their backs on industry to concentrate on urban development. 'The cities are the backbone of Italy, and what is happening to them shows that development has got quite out of control; that nobody is able to make any real difference to the way in which group situations evolve once they have gathered momentum. It is not yet clear whether such inability merely reflects our lack of adequate technical and scientific knowledge, or stems from some deep-seated prejudice that prevents our using properly the means already at our disposal.'[24]

So far, then, we have indicated two basic variables. On the one hand, the growth of state capitalism has hit private capitalism badly; it now has less money and less power as well as less political influence. On the other hand, what money remains is being used for speculation in urban development in general and spent by preference on the purchase of building-land. This is the magnet that lures all those who either cannot or do not wish to invest in industry. The net result of such large-scale speculation is growing social and economic chaos.

15   The factors we have mentioned, including the decline in the power of private enterprise, the increase in urban development investment, and the expansion of public industrial investment have transformed the power structure. In particular, since the end of the Second World War Italy's economic development has been noteworthy for the continuing emergence of a new class of entrepreneurs and managers in the public employ. Entrepreneurs in the public sector have developed enormously in the post-war period (1945–55) from a nucleus of new men who owed their powers of political leadership to their place in the resistance movement (1943–45), and used their political enthusiasm to help state industries expand – very often independently of the state itself. As time passed, however, the power of these men was overshadowed by new faces in key positions in state industries. These were, of course, friends, or at least friends of friends of the family; in other words, the favourite clients of influential figures in one or other of the Italian political parties. As usual, it was jobs for the boys. The push towards further expansion in the state industries may have lessened, but the political importance of these entrepreneurs in the public sector has certainly increased.

As a class, however, it must be admitted that for many years they worked well. Many of them had war-time records in the Catholic resistance groups. Their politics were flexible and open to a variety of solutions to Italy's economic problems: nationalization, control of industry by local authorities, government acquisition of a controlling or major interest in the shares of companies still privately-owned and administered, etc. Such policies reflected the Catholic background of men in this entrepreneur class. The Church itself had always been careful to allow some degree of flexibility in its own internal structures. Economically the Church has its own Vatican financial system, some straightforward capitalist enterprises, cooperative ventures for consumers to participate in production, Renaissance banks, up-to-date banks, and a whole series of commercial set-ups that exemplify all the many possibilities provided for in the Italian code of civil law. This is the basis of the Church's ability to adapt itself quite easily to changing economic, social and political situations, and at the same time to preserve certain features of capitalist society whilst orientating society towards something quite close to state socialism.

Entrepreneurs in the public sector, however corrupt they may be as a result of the system of taking a friendly interest in the parasitic members of their family, do manage to combine consideration for the wishes of their political sponsors with attention to the requirements of the industry for which they are responsible. In times of crisis, certainly, the political parties and the entrepreneurs in charge of the public sector of industry, while respecting the latter's autonomy, have never taken very long to come to an understanding about the day-to-day running of affairs.

In any case, for these entrepreneurs to produce, to run a business, and to play politics is all of a piece. Progress is not merely their economic ambition, but their political aspiration, their ideal, and, very often, their religious vocation. What Max Weber said about the link between Protestantism and the origins of capitalism finds in contemporary Italy its modified and somewhat paradoxical application. What are now being linked together are the development of state industries and the Catholic–Socialist ideals of the entrepreneur class engaged in the public sector.

To sum up, the entrepreneur class brings together three typically different power-groups:

(a) Private enterprise in banking, commerce and industry. This is losing its hold because, after the Fascist period, it failed to adopt some flexible policy in view of Italy's changed social and political situation. There are also economic reasons for its loss of power.

(b) Entrepreneurs in the public sector. These are moving up and becoming stronger, partly because the economic policy favours them, partly because of their political shrewdness, partly because they contrive to be in close contact with influential politicians whom they use (and by whom they are used), and partly because of their mainly militant-Catholic background and connections.

(c) Investors in urban-development sites. Such sites attract capital and financial know-how from the private industrial sector, from agriculture, from political groups, etc. Social parasites are particularly active in this sector where there are plenty of rich pickings. Rapid expansion here does not help the economy as a whole, and indeed withdraws capital from areas that badly need it, preventing the long-overdue creation of social and cultural infrastructures to improve living conditions in large urban centres.

The power of these three interrelated groups is linked with the rest of the power structure, but has particularly close connections with the state administration and with the political power of the trade unions.

C. The structures of social administration

General observations – the state bureaucracy

16 So far we have considered the bureaucratic structures of power connected with the buying and selling of land in both town and country, and with privately-owned or state-run industrial and business concerns. In due course we shall talk about the power of the political parties and the trade unions, but to complete this survey of the technostructure we must also say a word about the public administration. This comprises two major divisions: (a) administrative bodies; (b) organizations of manipulation and socialization.

Administrative bodies include the civil service and the administrative sections of regional, provincial and local governments, as well as such repressive organisms as the army, the police force, and the tax inspectorate.

Organizations of manipulation and socialization can also be repressive (like prisons and psychiatric hospitals), but may simply cater for people outside the system (like old-people's homes), or seek to make them come to terms with it (as do schools, children's nurseries, radio and television services).

We have no intention of probing into all these sub-systems, since such an analysis would not throw very much light on the overall structure of Italian society, which is the object of our study. Instead, we shall confine our attention to the more important sub-systems, and attempt to see what sort of pattern they fit into, and how they help to give the general structure of society its special character. We shall try to see with which strata these organisms are mainly concerned, and whose interests they really serve – which groups prosper as a result of their efforts, and which suffer.

Obviously, the whole of society stands in a general way to gain from the possession of an efficient bureaucratic technostructure. Economic development has introduced differences in mentality, economic interest, political outlook and general culture into the new working-class, the new middle and upper middle strata, and the new cultural élite, but all alike feel it is an advantage to have an efficient administration.

The one they actually have has shot up like a mushroom, and has spread throughout the whole of society. It is always chaotic and often inconsistent. The characteristics it has now developed were not wished by any group, any class, or any body of the élite – but there they are. From unification days right up to the present the economy has made progress, slowly at first and then quite quickly, but, with the exception of the first few years, no ruling or administrative class has ever emerged capable of dealing responsibly with the consequences, and of setting up an administrative system that could effectively keep pace with developments.

The number employed in public administration has undoubtedly

Table 5.7   Increase in Employment in the State Administration 1881–1962
(to nearest 1000)

	Population		Employed		Employed in state administration	
	No.	%	No.	%	No.	%
1881–1882	28,951,000	100	452,000	100	98,000	100
1911–1912	36,900,000	127	693,000	153	263,000	268
1961–1962	50,600,000	174	2,734,000	604	1,340,000	1362

increased even more rapidly than those working in any other sector. Personnel increased steadily from 1882 to 1915. The coming of Fascism applied a temporary brake, but with the adoption in 1931 of a policy of general and even territorial expansion, the rise in administrative employment figures started once more. By 1943 the state was employing 1,430,060 people. The figures were lower just after the war, but very soon began to rise again. Table 5.7 summarizes the three main waves of expansion.[25] This increase continued throughout the 1960s and has given rise to a certain amount of concern, as is mentioned in one report on the social condition of the nation:

> On the one hand there has been in the ten-year period 1961–71 an increase of about 12 per cent in the number of administrative workers in the private sector, and this has not resulted in any sharp variation in the distribution of workers among the various sub-sectors. There has been a very slight falling-off in commerce, with tiny increases in transport departments, communications, insurance, and money-lending employment figures, together with small decreases in other areas.
>
> Meanwhile, employment in the public sector has not only increased more rapidly, but with a constant acceleration. There was an increase of 33.5 per cent between 1964 and 1971. In the last two years the annual increase of employees in public services and administration has been between 100,000 and 150,000.
>
> ... Thus, a bureaucratic take-over in the tertiary sector unparalleled in Europe seems to characterize this period. We may have already passed and are certainly not far short of the situation in which public-service personnel

*account for 30 per cent of employees in the whole tertiary
sector. If this figure is compared with that of 18.9 per cent
in West Germany, 12.9 per cent in 'Napoleonic' France,
and 14 per cent in Belgium, the situation begins to seem
somewhat obscene.*[26]

What are the reasons for and the practical implications of this
expansion? How did Italy reach such a situation of bureaucratic
stalemate, for that is what the figures and percentages show it
to be?

There are different sorts of reasons. Some of them are historical
and go back to the original foundations of the Italian bureaucratic
system, in which power was highly centralized. The historical
development of Italian society has also included a limited but
increasing transfer of power to the South. Other factors stem from
the imbalance and dualism within society, which we have already
had frequent occasion to mention. Thus, some of the historical
reasons concern the origins of the system.

The Italian bureaucracy is French in inspiration, but its technical
structure partly follows the Belgian model, which was of partly Dutch
origin, having been inherited by Belgium after the war of Belgian
independence. The Italian system was devised by Piedmontese and
Franco-Italians employed by the Kingdom of Sardinia which
brought about the country's unification. For a long time its efficiency
reflected its origins.[27] In 1861, at the time of the unification, Piedmontese law was extended to all the small states of which the political mosaic of the Italian peninsula was composed. Turin, the capital
of the Kingdom of Sardinia, was under the spell of French culture,
French being spoken almost right up to the city-walls, and having
been adopted by the middle-classes as a second language alongside
the Piedmontese dialect. Sardinia gave the government and administration a French cultural basis and a French spirit.

The bureaucracy was honest, efficient and rapid in operation.
However, once it was transferred to Rome and took on more staff
it became ponderously slow. Among the factors contributing to this
change was the introduction of an extremely complicated system of
regulations. The effect of these was heightened by the fact that the
bureaucracy remained highly centralized. Later, too, the personnel
were ill-prepared for their work, and there was corruption at every
level.

To transfer the capital to Rome was a terrible mistake, and carried with it all the consequences of operating the administration in the Southern style. Bureaucracy became an end in itself. Regulations were multiplied. Efficiency, specialized knowledge, and a high degree of skill became quite irrelevant to a career in administration. A legalistic uniformity in handling all matters, including economic ones, became the norm, and personnel were, as we have seen, selected on the basis of their familiarity with the regulations governing the operation of public administration.[28] The only thing the system preserved of its original character was a negative element: it remained highly centralized and hostile to regional participation in decision-making.

The civil administration has identified itself with this policy of centralization with which it was born, and clings to it even against the express will of successive governments. Pre-fascist democrats, Fascists, and Christian Democrats alike have never had the determination or power to change this situation. At the beginning, this was quite understandable: 'Piedmont had simply transferred an administrative structure from Turin, first to Florence and then to Rome', and had clung on obstinately to its right to nominate the higher-grade personnel in the public administration, the army and the diplomatic corps.[29] However, this does not explain why the bureaucratic structure should remain so centralized and stagnant after it has had such a tremendous internal expansion. It doesn't make any difference in which way things are moving – the system resists all attempts to change it, and manages to accomodate every proposal or demand for its adaptation within the already existing framework, thereby frustrating all efforts.

On the one hand, then, the bureaucracy is still centralized, and prevents other structures making their own decisions, since all projects have to be referred to the centre for approval. On the other hand, the system becomes increasingly unwieldy, preserving the worst aspects of its French and Piedmontese origins, and taking over the worst features of the Southern style.

The appointment of bureaucrats from other regions of Italy has only increased the amount of centralization, inefficiency and parasitic inactivity. The state administration is becoming more and more Southern-minded in its outlook, from top to bottom. In the 1960s about 60 per cent of those employed in public administration were of Southern extraction, and to these we can add the 21 per cent originating in Central Italy, coming mainly from Lazio and especially from Rome, who are very much under Southern influence. In this sense, we can say that the South accounts for about 80 per cent of administrative personnel. The North, by contrast, with 46 per cent of the overall population, supplies less than 15 per cent of higher-grade state officials.[30]

This is, therefore, an additional factor contributing to the imbalance and dualism in Italian society. The North has an increasingly up-to-date advanced industrial structure and an efficient industrial bureaucracy, but this is paralysed by a cumbersome and inefficient state technostructure, which reflects the underdevelopment and the traditional closed culture of the South.

The degree to which the state bureaucracy is influenced by the native culture of the Southerners in charge of it or working for it is hard to say. It is certain, however, that their influence is considerable and entirely negative. We pointed out in the opening chapter that Southern Italians form anti-social *ceti*, distrust and are hostile to the government, and are generally disinclined to involve themselves at all in the official scheme of things. With these ideas, values and traditions, how can Southerners administer the country? It is hard to answer this question in detail, but the overall effect of their cultural background has been catastrophic.

The country's central administration reflects the defects of practically the whole state bureaucracy; the administrative machine is essentially hierarchical in structure, so that work is never organized in collaboration, but all power is concentrated at the top. However, those at the top are incapable of decision, and tend to leave things in suspense. They evade all acceptance of responsibility. Any decisions that are made are arrived at very slowly, then rendered ineffectual by political intervention or undue insistence on red-tape.

Corruption and privileges for the select few are the order of the day. The situation is further blackened by scandal after scandal. For reasons we have mentioned and others too numerous to specify, an advanced industrial society remains saddled with the worst sort of Levantine administration. The family spirit and the Mafia traditions of the underdeveloped parts of Italy have been incorporated into the civil administration, precisely because the majority in its employ come from places where the traditional value-system has retained a certain hold. This is why people get jobs merely because they have friends in high places or can pull political strings, and it explains the vast expansion of the bureaucracy at every level. The trend is strengthened by the fact that bureaucrats have ready access to the central organs of government, and use their favourable negotiating position indiscriminately and without scruple.

17   The traditional Italian (and especially Southern Italian) institution of clients attached to influential families is among the principal reasons behind the inefficiency, the failure to take action, and the corruption of the power-system in general and the administrative machine in particular. The origin of these clients is obscure, but almost certainly goes back to Roman times. In the classical period the client was linked to his master because he depended on him for help. A *cliens* is one who is obedient, but the term also involves the notion of mutual respect: *Patronus si clienti fraudem fecerit saces esto* (loosely: 'master and client must respect one another'), we read in the Law of the Twelve Tables of the Roman Republic. The spirit of this primitive enactment remains the basis of the present-day client–patron relationship.[31] Yet, while this relationship is a personal one, in contemporary Italy it prevails mainly between groups of people with a common interest and one or other section of the public administration.

> *Briefly put, the clientela relationship exists when an interest group for whatever reasons, succeeds in becoming, in the eyes of a given administrative agency, the natural expression and representative of a given social sector which, in turn, constitutes the natural target or reference point for the activity of the administrative agency.*[32]

In such a situation the individual sectors of the public administration sometimes seem like the feudal holdings of a small number of powerful groups within society. Even apart from this cultural institution of ours, convalidated by the moral authority of an ancient value-system that plagues the whole country, the bureaucracy, as already mentioned, has managed to help itself to increasingly large slices of an economic cake to the making of which it has really contributed very little.

In addition to strike action, these bureaucrats, and especially those in high positions, are able to exercise a variety of pressures, because they are in contact with the nerve-centres of power, in the army, the civil service, the educational system, the cultural sphere, government accounts departments and ministerial secretariats. The bureaucracy has stability and is, therefore, able to work steadily in its own interest, to which it sets no limits. They say in Rome: ministers come and go, civil servants remain. They have a simple time-table, but hardly ever keep to it, come to work very late, take frequent breaks with none to gainsay them, and sometimes only put in a few hours a week, like the majority of university professors. Thus they have all the time in the world to look after their own affairs, maintain their social standing, and increase the parasitic condition of the whole state administration.

Ordinary workers and others employed in industry produce the greater part of the national income, and apparently are better equipped to gain the upper hand in any confrontation. Nevertheless, they always seem to fall victim to these non-productive parasites, who really earn no money, but are highly paid for being vaguely occupied during no more than 20 per cent of the time for which their terms of employment require them to work. They work less and less, but skim the cream off the national income for themselves, increase their own salary levels, and multiply their earnings like the loaves and fishes of the Gospel story.

It is easy to provide evidence of this imbalance in the distribution of incomes. Taking the overall average income as 100, in 1972 the average income in agriculture was 50.5, in industry 90.5, in the tertiary sector 112.6 and in public administration 139.5. Between 1961 and 1973 government sources show that average earnings in public administration rose from about 1,500,000 to 4,000,000 lire, in industry from 763,000 to 2,500,000 lire, and in agriculture from 276,000 to 1,300,000 lire.

The situation of the universities after 1968 is a classic illustration of this state of affairs and of the difficulties encountered in trying to do anything about it. The only significant response to the crisis consisted in increasing the salaries of lower-grade personnel without increasing their work-load, granting more extensive privileges to professors and lecturers although these still gave little time to teaching or research and devoted much of their energies to non-university work, and employing additional staff who produced very little and proved of very little use. The staff increases at each level meant that a larger number of persons did more casually and with less effort the very same work that a smaller number had done before. Thus, the number being employed increased, and the amount of public money being spent on them increased considerably, but no other results seemed to be forthcoming.

Figures published by the Supreme Court of Civil Appeal reveal the scandalous fact that while in 1952 120 magistrates pronounced about 3300 sentences a year, it now takes 375 magistrates to give the same result, a reduction in productivity of two-thirds.

18   Similar things happen in every branch of the state administration. A sector expands, its running-costs increase, the work actually done goes down, and both state control and the institution of social parasites tighten their hold on society.

Instead of trying to dissect the details of central administrative costs, we shall consider the administration in the other parts of the country. Communes, provinces and regions all suffer from parasites and mal-functioning in the same way, though the extent to which this holds true increases as one moves further South. In general the revenues of these departments never meet their running-costs, which are increased astronomically by the high wages and salaries they pay their employees. Local and provincial administrations seem continually and increasingly to be overspending and there is no secret about the reason behind this phenomenon.

Larger towns suffer from this situation even more than small communes. Thus, the debts for a single year of communes with more than 500,000 inhabitants show an increase of somewhere between 3.4 and 4.5 billion lire. What is worse, the part of the debt resulting from current expenses rose between 1971 and 1972 from 61.4 per cent to 65.7 per cent of the overall amount.

Government figures put the debts of the communes at 15,784 billion lire on 1 January 1974, and by 1977 the figure is expected to reach 36,000. Rome's debt stood at 2694 billion lire on 30 April 1974, more than that for the whole of Austria; 73 per cent of this debt comes from paying off other debts, interest on loans, and salaries, and only 27 per cent is invested. The situation is worse in Naples, where only 2.3 per cent of the debt results from new investment. The average debt incurred per citizen on 1 January 1974 for the public administration of Turin stood at 335,000 lire; Genoa 427,000; Milan 486,000; Rome 788,000; Palermo 848,000; Naples 855,000. These recent figures confirm the split between North and South.

As might have been expected, communes in the South incur the largest debts, both in absolute terms and as a percentage of the total expenditure.[33] The net result is that they have no funds available at all for projects of civic or social interest.

The same sort of thing is happening in the provinces and, as in the communes, expenses are increasing more rapidly than revenues (see table 5.8).

Table 5.8   Revenue and Expenditure in the Provinces (billions of lire)

	1968	1969	1970	1971*	1972†
Total revenues	428.4	471.1	516.2	573.8	623.2
Total outgoings	520.7	573.1	637.3	748.5	898.2

* provisional figures   † estimated figures

Although the regions are not so long established, developments in them point in the same direction: stagnation, inefficient administration, excessive running-costs.[34]

The situation worsens almost every year. The excess of expenditure over income in local administration rose from 562.5 billions in 1968 to 789.4 billions in 1970. The whole of public administration is in financial difficulties. The social parasites sucking its blood are penetrating deeper and deeper into the system, and the general corruption is steadily increasing.

It is particularly unfortunate that this sort of administration is, although only indirectly, in control of the state industrial system, which is expanding all the time and has a comprehensive plan of economic development. Government planning of this sort arose after the war in an attempt to solve the problems of the South, and put an end to its cultural, social and economic underdevelopment. With the passage of time the government and its administrative organs have intervened more and more in the general development of the economy and of society as a whole. A plan was drawn up in the South and for its advantage. The state set up the necessary machinery. Minds were prepared to accept the new ideas. Technicians were called in. Something was actually being done, although there were all the usual faults and failings of official Italian administration.

Italian society already carried the burden of underdevelopment and a dualistic structure, as we have repeatedly pointed out. The new policy of government planning and intervention imposed additional structures and infrastructures on the South, for the benefit of the more backward areas. The ruling-class adjusted psychologically to these innovations, and so, after using them in the South, extended their application to the rest of the country. From the end of the war till about the early 1960s the South was used to try out and improve upon various institutionalized technical devices devised to further planned growth. The integration of the South into the national economy and economic planning were one and the same thing, and paved the way for large-scale planning on a truly national scale.[35]

This all strengthened the image of the state as entrepreneur, administering a plan of overall development, though allowing the newly created regions varying measures of responsibility for their own part in its implementation. The administrative machinery was the old system with some fresh refinements, at least partly Southern in origin.[36]

It must not be overlooked that planning has given considerable power and responsibility to various ad hoc technical and economic bodies, such as the *Cassa per il Mezzogiorno*, the other state banking institutions set up to finance development, etc. Directly or indirectly, like the state industries, all these bodies depend on the state bureaucracy, and consequently share all its defects and self-contradictions, such as the presence of social parasites, low standards of efficiency, low productivity, high salaries for their employees, and involvement in the family affairs of political clients, etc.

The parasitic nature and the inefficiency of the administrative technostructure is reflected in the associated structures of repression. The most outstanding example is provided by the army which has experienced in miniature all the ups and downs of the general administration. Immediately after the national unification the highly efficient Piedmontese army was integrated with the unwarlike and inefficient armies of the other Italian states,[37] but preserved a certain amount of prestige which Fascism served to enhance.[38] The reputation of the armed forces after the war was lower than ever before, partly because they had lost the war, and partly on account of the general distrust of the whole administration and of the way the country was being run. In any case, there are no grounds for thinking the army is in any way more efficient than the administration.[39] Certainly, the military are not highly thought of in the country at large. Questionnaires about young people's career-preferences always get answered in such a way that soldiers, officers included, come near the bottom of the list. The average Italian is not much interested in patriotism, the Italian reputation abroad, national defence, etc.

There is nothing new about the Italians' lack of interest in warfare – their conduct in the last war is proof enough of that. The army is something to laugh at rather than something one respects or admires.[40] Anything, in fact, that smacks of officialdom is treated as only of slight importance: military parades, the activities of government ministers, the duties of the President of the Republic.

Like the state administrative system, the army suffers from the historical consequences of the value-system accepted in Italy prior to its development. Thus, the man in the street resents the power structure, distrusts officialdom or at least does not care for it, and as well as disliking the administrative technostructure as a whole, is opposed to obligatory military service, and aware of the army's inefficiency because of the experience of those citizens who have served their time in the army.[41]

This is not to say that the army or the police have no real power within the power structure or the technostructure. As in the past, the armed forces remain somewhat aloof from the common people, from parliament, and even from the government. However, the military authorities in Italy are increasing their autonomy because the armed forces are coming more and more to resemble a branch of the technostructure, as is the case in many other countries. The army undoubtedly remains a power in the land, even if this power is rooted in the apathy of the masses towards it, and so in their lack of interest in controlling its activities. Italy, in other words, also has its invisible military government, which comprises officers in the General Staff, élite corps attached to Nato, the police, the carabinieri, and personnel on special duties.

Other bureaucracies in the service sector

19   Negative social attitudes towards them may make little difference to the army or the police, and can hardly worsen the inefficiency and parasitic attitudes of these instruments of control and repression – though they may contribute towards even higher running-costs. However, it is quite another matter when one turns to consider other important social services influenced by the carrying-ons of the public administration.

As examples, we can mention child-care[42] and hospital management. It is quite obvious that children are poorly served and often neglected.

To illustrate this we can take infant mortality. Italy has an infant mortality rate higher than that of any other country that has reached a comparable level of development. This is the result of the defects of the system, and inequalities between the various regional cultures, as well as the lack of effective channels of communication to spread information about recent progress in the prevention and cure of disease – in other words, an inefficient administration coupled with other factors perhaps of less importance. As regards deaths prior to birth or during the first week after birth, Italy's death rate is the second highest in Europe. Statistics gathered from twenty-two different countries place Italy in 18th place for deaths during the first year after birth, i.e. she has one of the *highest* infant mortality rates.[43]

During the period we are considering the infant mortality figures for Italy have fallen much more slowly than in other countries developing at a similar, or even at a more gradual rate. Hardly surprisingly, the figures differ sharply between North and South, being higher in the South. The mortality rate is also higher for illegitimate than for legitimate births, and higher in the lower classes than in the upper ones.[44] In other words, the costs of Italy's development and of the shortcomings of her social administration are having to be paid in human lives. It has been suggested that the contradictions in the development of Italian society and the dualistic character of the industrialization, together with the parasitic nature of the state bureaucracy, have cost the lives of between 35,000 and 150–175,000 babies, who have died needlessly during their first year of life. All these deaths might have been avoided if Italian society had developed differently.

The situation is no better in other sectors where dualism makes its effects felt, such as the quality of economic development, cultural evolution, or the amount of inefficiency within a given organization.[45] Interesting and comprehensive surveys have been made with regard to these various points, and can be usefully consulted.[46]

The running of the education system

20   We must say rather more about the schools situation, since education should be one of the main driving-forces behind cultural, social and economic development, but the educational system is conditioned by the state of the public administration and by the technostructures of the country as a whole.

Twenty years ago in Italy there were few schools and they served only the élite. Education is now available to the masses, principally because the social and economic development of the country in the early 1960s brought with it a demand for more highly qualified workers, and for more people with certificates and degrees. The expansion, however, is still chaotic and uneven, not only because the social structure is still unbalanced, but especially because the educational system is not yet adequately prepared to face the situation – partly it is afraid to.

The Italian educational system was set up to provide the élite with a suitable culture and to teach the rest to read and write. Its foundation years extended from unification times until the earlier part of the present century. Under Fascism and immediately after the war more importance was attached to its function in preparing young people to qualify for good jobs on the labour market. By the 1960s education had become even more relevant to a person's social standing and job capability, and as the lower classes struggled to better their lot, the educational system was regarded, especially after 1968, as a tool with which to transform the social stratification system.

The schools were expected to function as they do in any advanced industrial society, but this brought them into collision with the closed value-system and obsolete structures of underdeveloped Italy, with its traditional way of organizing things and justifying its own existence. In such a situation the schools have to try to achieve almost single-handed a process of re-education and resocialization that theoretically one might expect other agencies to be involved in as well. The school is being required to do the family's job for it.

This is education and socialization in the widest sense. It is quite demanding, and entails educating parents as well as their children. This is something new for the schools, and presents a tremendous challenge at the primary education stage – nursery, kindergarten and elementary school. These new responsibilities that have been thrust upon the schools carry with them a great deal of tension and impose a considerable strain upon the day-to-day working of the traditional Italian education system. As we have already said, its response to this challenge is poor, slow in coming, and even then quite out of date in both method and presentation. Although it is being expected to transform and modernize society, the educational system on the whole serves rather to reinforce and perpetuate the old system of stratification.

When Italian society was so structured that the upper and upper middle classes were relatively small, the education authorities issued few degrees or higher certificates, and most students had to rest content with a chance of qualifying for a certificate at the end of their third or fifth year of elementary schooling. It was not until the 1960s that economic developments made it seem desirable to impose the obligation of attending school for at least eight years, in other words until the end of middle-school, when a further certificate might be obtained. The educational system has never paved the way for nor helped on any change in social stratification. Instead, it has always failed to keep in step with the evolving needs of the rest of society. As society has grown structurally more complex, and as the lower and upper middle classes have increased their ranks, the schools have adapted themselves to the changed situation – but always with a considerable delay and only because economic and social developments left them no alternative.

The reason for this is simply that the education system has a rigidly centralized bureaucratic character copied from the French. It lacks and seems incapable of aquiring the flexibility needed to make it an instrument of development and emancipation within a constantly evolving pluralist society suffering from the tensions between North and South. Even today it frequently happens that pupils come to Italian schools for lessons, while Italian is for them still a foreign language they can hardly understand; they are only familiar with their own far different dialect.

The structure of the Italian educational system is so out of touch with the rest of society that it is almost impossible for it to produce any worthwhile results. It simply takes any pupil who comes along, feeds him into its own private system, and turns him out after standard processing. Unfavourable circumstances that we have already mentioned imposed considerable delays on the implementation of schemes to teach everyone to read and write, and this fact has contributed to the schools remaining so badly out of touch with real social needs. In other words, the uneven social development both reflects and helps to perpetuate an unbalanced educational development, though the situation is at last improving.[47]

Because the schools are still without any up-to-date organization, a few of its traditional institutions still operate in a discriminatory and unfair way that delays social change. We can mention, for instance, the selection process. Economic development has led to changes in social stratification, but the schools not only fail to keep pace with these, but actually place obstacles in the path of their realization. The schools represent and express the culture and language-habits of the middle and upper middle *ceti*, and the selection process they adopt fails to take the individual situations and cultural backgrounds into account.

With the exception of the universities and, to some extent, of the upper forms of secondary schools in recent years, the teachers are bourgeois women from the lower middle or upper middle strata, working to help their family along and to supplement their husband's income. They impart to their pupils their own brand of bourgeois culture, whether they desire it or are likely to benefit from it or not. This way of teaching amounts to a rejection of children from the lower strata, or from the South, or from areas with a closed culture, or whose families are culturally not so well equipped. Hence, they feel alienated.

In Italy, of course, there are countless children who come from backgrounds where the sub-culture still reflects the closed value-system of underdevelopment, and the schools are treating these very badly. Selection works against the children's interests in many different ways that depend upon the schools' out-of-date way of doing things. This is particularly true of the years of compulsory education, and the lumpenproletariat and the proletariat suffer most of all. The running of nursery-schools and kindergartens should help children from these *ceti* to overcome the disadvantages of their background, but, in fact, it does little or nothing to redress the balance, and they remain victims of their immediate social surroundings and family circumstances. Thus, those differences in the children's own culture and in their attitudes towards the rest of society which have been formed independently of the schools and even before going to school at all, are reproduced within the school environment, where selection discriminates against the underprivileged, poorer and less knowledgeable children right from the start.

Selection of this sort is connected only indirectly with social stratification as such, but nevertheless it exerts a steady pressure. There are no reliable statistics for the country as a whole, and from numerous local surveys that have been made we shall cite only that made at Sesto San Giovanni in Lombardy. This is an industrial town near Milan. Elementary school examinations there are failed at least once by 37 per cent of the children of unemployed, pensioned or disabled parents and of children without a father, by 20.8 per cent of the children of manual and general workers, by 11.8 per cent of the children of more qualified workers, and by very few children whose parents belong to higher social strata.[48]

Culture as well as social class is a significant factor. Most children who fail their examinations were born in the South, and the next largest group of failures is made up of children born in Lombardy of Southern parents – 27.5 per cent of elementary school failures, and 45.7 per cent of middle-school failures. The percentage of failures in elementary school examinations for children born in Lombardy of non-Southern immigrant parents is 14.2 per cent, and when their parents are Lombards the figure drops to 13.7 per cent.[49] Failure to obtain the leaving certificate at the conclusion of their compulsory schooling has the further result of making it more difficult for these youngsters to secure jobs to their liking on the labour market.

The actual school enrolment figures are generally high during the eight-year compulsory education period (see table 5.9). Selection, exclusion and truancy are marginal phenomena in the towns, but reach considerable proportions in rural areas, where it is still profitable to provide children with full-time employment. In any case, agricultural schools are few and far between, and seem poorly organized. Of course, selection and discrimination operate in more ways than one. Without a suitable education one cannot qualify for an up-to-date job in production. The modern organization of labour has put an end to the possibility of work in the old traditional trades. The workman of today has to be versatile and ready to adapt himself to a variety of changing requirements. Education is, therefore, absolutely imperative.[50] The education required is also of a new kind, and must mature the personality as well as developing the mind. If a child fails to secure a certificate while attending middle-school, this may spoil his chances of ever improving his position as a worker in later life.[51]

Table 5.9   Percentage School Enrolment: Official Returns 1970–71

Age	6	7	8	9	10	11	12	13	14	15
% enrol-ment	100	100	100	99.9	98.9	96.2	93.0	82.9	66.7	53.1

Source: ISTAT.[52]

Let us turn now to consider more advanced studies. In the past only those with an upper-class background could aspire to higher certificates or degrees, but it is easier nowadays for more students to attend the relevant course of studies. Since actually obtaining the higher certificate or degree opens the door to better jobs, it is clear that the examinations operate as a selection process that makes it harder to change one's social class.

The available data support the view that those who have obtained a higher certificate or a university degree are in a privileged position. On the labour market these privileges mean in practice that those with higher certificates or degrees:

are unemployed rather less frequently than others;
are employed in preference to others in newly created jobs;
are employed in preference to others when existing jobs expand and need additional staff (in 1951–61 33 per cent of new jobs were filled by personnel with only lower certificates, but in 1964–68 the figure was only 19 per cent);
someone with a higher certificate earns on average 33 per cent more than a person without it, and the worker with a degree earns twice as much as one with only a lower certificate.

It is also possible to point to some future trends. Although relatively few have degrees, they are more highly privileged than those with higher certificates: only 0.3 per cent of the former are unemployed, but 9.8 per cent of the latter. In 1969, 4.2 per cent of those with degrees were still looking for their first job, but 35.8 per cent of those with higher certificates were still looking for theirs. On average someone with a degree earns 305,600 lire a month, and someone with a higher certificate 185,000 lire a month.[53]

However, the position of those with degrees is not as privileged as it used to be. The unemployment figure for this category is still relatively low, but it is nevertheless rising, and it is fair to suppose that as the number of persons with degrees in search of work rises in the next few years, their chances of employment will become even less favourable. The growth of the intake into secondary schools and high schools is fairly steady, but the expansion in the university sector is rapidly accelerating.[54] The increase in the number of people with degrees has in recent years resulted in its being harder for them to secure suitable positions and has tended to narrow the gap between their salaries and those of people with higher certificates. In addition to this, there is a tendency for the difference in earnings between industrial employees with higher certificates and other workmen in lower positions to become less noticeable.

On the whole, and as one looks towards the future, it is likely to remain difficult for youngsters with a higher education behind them (in the shape of a higher certificate or degree) to secure suitable employment on the labour market. In the 1950s and 1960s the economy developed at breakneck speed. Since then it has continued to expand, but with some sharp fluctuations. Some figures suggest that the possible expansion of the labour market in favour of graduates is now much less than it was, especially in agriculture and industry, though not in the tertiary sector.[55] A study carried out by the Karl Marx Centre points to the conclusion that it is difficult nowadays to imagine a future in which graduates will actually be out of work: 'What is more likely is that graduates will not be able to secure jobs in production as good as those now available to them, and that the value of the degree will become less.[56]

However, although it is extremely likely that during the next ten years expansion will remain the characteristic of education at all levels, and particularly with regard to higher and university education, there are already available data to suggest that the increase in the numbers of university students has already passed its peak.

For the first time, after many years, we can observe a significant slowing down in the increase of the attendance figures for high schools and in particular for universities. The reduction may very well be due to the shortage of professional openings, since this critical situation possibly disinclines poorly situated members of the population from applying for higher education, though their presence

*would increase the number taking advantage of it very
considerably indeed.*[57]

It must not be forgotten that three main things have happened to
education in the last twenty years:

Primary school attendance over a five-year period has become the
universal practice and the attendance figures are very high indeed.
Compulsory education for eight years is already an effective
reality, though there are gaps still to be filled, especially in the
South.

Far more are taking the higher certificate examination (after 13
years at school) and many more are actually obtaining a
certificate.

More are going to university, and more are obtaining a degree.

During these twenty years education for the masses in Italy came
first at primary school level. In the 1950s it reached middle-school
level. In the 1960s the universities were affected. The results of this
push forward in education have been impressive, and have made a
difference to social stratification and social mobility.

These three stages of development are confirmed by the available
statistics. Higher certificates were granted to 61,000 in 1951, to
104,000 in 1961, and to 228,000 in 1971 – a fourfold increase.[58]
Fewer youngsters are now attending secondary schools with a
classical bias, and more are going to those which provide a commercial, professional or technical training. This is because many are
now studying at school with a view to the job they hope to secure as
soon as they leave.[59]

In the early 1960s people with higher certificates seemed already
two a penny, and as more have taken the examination since, so more
have succeeded in it, and the figures have continued to rise. The
situation is unbalanced. Too many with higher certificates are
applying for the more popular sorts of job, while in other sectors
there is a shortage of qualified applicants.

The picture in the university sector is somewhat similar. A large
number of graduates was 'produced' between 1945 and 1950,
mainly in the wake of the Second World War. There was a fairly
steady stream of new graduates during the 1950s, about 20,000 a
year, which gave only a slight annual increase in the total number of
graduates (about 1.7 per cent).[60] New graduates were 5.7 per cent

of those employed for the first time in 1951, but only 4.5 per cent of those employed in 1961.

The developments in education in the 1960s reflected the expansion that had taken place within the economy. Between 1961 and 1971 the number of graduates rose quickly, and there was a three-fold increase: 19,724 in 1951; 21,886 in 1961; and about 60,651 in 1971.[61] The rise in the numbers attending university was just as notable, especially during the late 1960s (see table 5.10).[62]

Table 5.10   Number of University Students

Year	1966–67	1967–68	1968–69	1969–70	1970–71	1971–72
No. of students	456,476	500,215	549,783	616,898	681,731	759,872

21   We can summarize briefly both the positive and negative aspects of the relationship between the Italian educational system and the general social structure:

Education is expanding rapidly, first at primary, then at secondary and university levels, and the imbalance and defects of this expansion partly stem from the speed with which it has taken place.

The expansion also constitutes the schools' contribution towards a standardized culture for the whole country, and reflects the collapse of the traditional cultures. For the very first time all Italians will be able to start their lives with a few cultural elements in common.

Despite obstacles which are intrinsic to the social structure as such, the improved cultural standards are encouraging and promoting social mobility and enabling people to improve their social position.

Despite such changes, the schools still exercise selection in a way that is damaging to the lower classes and perpetuates their estrangement from the rest of society.

The rapid expansion has not been accompanied by any equally rapid increase in the number of available jobs, and certainly not of good jobs. Many workers are not employed in ways commensurate with the studies they have done, and this gives rise to social and economic unrest.

Although the overall picture is one of expansion it must be stressed that the sort of culture provided by the schools fails in fact to correspond with the new requirements of the masses and the changes that have taken place in the rest of society.

The education service is not very efficient, and shows itself unable to keep abreast of a developing society and its needs. The number of graduates and holders of national diplomas is, on the whole, out of step with the number of posts available on the labour-market, either generally or in the individual sectors. People come to the end of their studies equipped with an out-of-date culture that proves an anomaly in the society in which they have to earn their living. There is insufficient specialization, and the system leaves little room for freedom or more integrated curricula. The obsolete and the chaotic predominate. Professional and technical preparation for a career is inadequate, yet diploma-holders are supposed to be able to function in a factory, as engineers, doctors, social workers, etc. The whole structure is enormously expensive to run but produces little, and if balance-sheets were published as for any other company showing costs and benefits, the balance would be largely negative.

Some conclusions

22   Italy, then, has her own administrative and repressive techno-structure, and we shall provide an overall view of its characteristics in diagram form very shortly, but it cannot be denied that the whole organization is inefficient in a way which almost guarantees that a failure in one sector will lead to a chain of failures throughout the entire system.

Although Italy is now an advanced industrial nation, living conditions remain hard, dramatically so when anybody is sick or family quarrels come to the surface. 'The family situation is characterized by the uncertainties of tomorrow rather than by any actual permanent shortage, by the chaotic and inefficient state of the social services rather than by their total absence, by an unfair exploitation of the labour-potential of fathers of families, women and children under age, rather than by any lack of work as such.'[63] This, however, does not alter the fact that the hardships families have to endure derive to a large extent from the way society is organized with a chaotic, inefficient and parasitic technostructure.

Distrust of the power-system is increased because the courts are so slow and inefficient that quite a large number of persons who will eventually be judged innocent have to spend several years in prison while awaiting trial. On the other hand, there are well-known instances of notorious assassins having been set at liberty without any trial at all after a period of preventive detention, simply because of the slowness and inadequacies of the judicial system. In certain sectors, and we can mention the education system because we have said quite a lot about it, the situation is even worse, because it contaminates the actual future of society. Another grave cause for alarm is the extent to which the inefficiency of the state bureaucratic system paralyses the life of public structures generally and, indeed, of the whole tertiary sector of the economy.

Centralization is the main factor behind this amplification and multiplication throughout the whole social structure of the defects of the central bureaucratic technostructure, and decentralization would, therefore, improve the situation. The situation itself can be represented diagrammatically as follows:

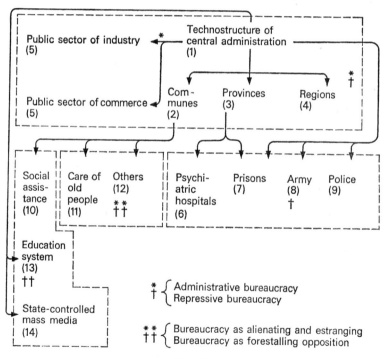

Fig. 5

23 Obviously, this technostructure is not much different from that of any other advanced industrial country, though it contains a few special features, such as the hierarchical division into communes, provinces and regions, and one or two interconnections.

The aspect peculiar to Italy remains invisible: it is the way the structure serves to spread inefficiency, the way it penetrates every nook and cranny of national life, the way blood-sucking social parasites exploit it for their own ends. What the diagram reveals are the positive and negative links between public and private bodies.

In addition to these, we need to notice the linking up of the power of the administrative machine with the whole tertiary sector, where the consequences of the former's inefficiency are simply disastrous. Special attention must be paid to the way in which public superstructures in the tertiary sector are related to certain intermediary bodies, which mediate between them and both the rest of the tertiary sector and other sectors besides. These include a vast assortment of research groups, study organizations, consultative bodies, etc., 'serving' both the public and private sectors of the economy. There has been, in particular, an increased demand for systematic comparative time-and-motion studies. As well as both public and private sectors of industry having set up special associations to carry these out on their behalf, there have come into being various specialized offices for operational research, consultative bureaux to advise on modernization programmes, and these, of course, not only coordinate the various sectors of industry with each other, but bring them into closer contact with the unions and the political parties. This marriage between industry and bureaucracy in all its ramifications (industrial, political, etc.) is one of the new features of Italian society which cannot as yet be neatly labelled and pigeon-holed, but is certainly significant.

In Italy as in other countries it is quite impossible to draw up any accurate and detailed map of the maze of conflicting interests and policies that guide the activities of the various research groups, commissions, parliamentary inquiries, government bodies, and technical and scientific associations. The only clear point to emerge is that science and technology are constantly increasing their effective presence on the political scene, where their power is embodied in specific individuals and organizations who represent their interests and concerns. Education has brought these men to the top of the social ladder: technical experts, specialists, civil engineers.

Even if Italy is not yet a technocracy in the full sense, these men already have a finger in every pie. Such experts have their place in every industrial country, but in Italy they are, as a group, less aware of their political importance, their social responsibilities, their contemporary function; their attitudes are influenced excessively by what their fathers did, because they have not yet had time to formulate views and policies of their own – the industrial development has been too rapid, and they have not yet sufficiently digested its implications.

Nevertheless, even in Italy these groups of specialists and technicians are forming their own associations to represent their interests, and these frequently take up political or socially decisive positions of their own in public, and do not merely echo the opinions of other interest groups.[64] Moreover, the general inefficiency is such that in recommending efficiency (and often achieving it themselves) these groups are frequently swimming against the stream, and opposing the general tide of events.

Politicians within the government and at party headquarters seem devoid of either critical acumen or creative imagination, and tend to rely heavily on the advice of such specialist bodies, whether it is a question of reforming the administration, dealing with the problem of pollution, or improving the environment generally. These specialist bodies thus become, as it were, the voice of applied science.

Neither science nor technology, however, are any longer as important as they were a few years ago to such organizations, however valuable they may remain in themselves. The latter's present concern is now only that of maintaining and transmitting a system – perhaps this was always so.

24   Once economic development really got under way, Italy made it her business to provide herself with an adequate research organization. However, if its operation was not entirely brought to a halt, it undoubtedly suffered considerable set-backs from certain scandals, such as those regarding the pharmaceutical investigations conducted by the Higher Institution for Health, and the proceedings of the National Centre for Nuclear Energy. Add to this failures resulting from lack of funds, commercial support or an up-to-date organization. Thus, Olivetti failed to break effectively into the market for electronic adding-machines. The plans for a large-scale expansion of the state electrical engineering industry failed to materialize. The National Research Council suffered from increasing paralysis, and its activities and plans proved ineffective and bore little fruit. The Centre for Biological Research in Naples had to be dismantled. Eminent scientists were expelled from their posts or compelled to work in isolation because of professional rivalries and the crisis in university life. Some experts, and it will be enough to quote Alberoni,[65] claim that the crisis of scientific research has been so far-reaching that Italy, although economically speaking the seventh or eighth industrial power in the world, is now either an underdeveloped or at best a developing country only.

Other countries with a degree of industrialization equal or a little superior or inferior to that of Italy have scientific research systematically organized as a real force in the nation, but Italy does not. It is quite obvious that research is stagnant and that politicians are largely ignoring it. A few figures are enough to convey some idea of the situation. In Italy 6.0 out of every 10,000 inhabitants are engaged in research, while Belgium has 16.8; Canada 12.6; France 17.9; Germany 18.0; Japan 19.5; Norway 10.4; Holland 25.8; Great Britain 29.4; the United States 35.8; Sweden 21.6; and the Soviet Union 22.1. Lagging behind Italy we find Austria with 4.5; Greece with 1.5 and Spain with 2.1.[66]

The cause of the trouble is the lack of administrative support for research programmes by the various competent bodies. The scientists are there, but the means required to encourage them to produce results are in short supply. A few research establishments actually have real political influence, but either cannot or will not use it in the interests of their own development – even when their political pull is quite considerable. It would be quite easy for research scientists to carry out their own cultural and political campaign. They have at their disposal hundreds of reviews and magazines, both specialized and of a more general nature, some technical and others addressed to a popular audience, which are edited by men of science both inside and independently of research centres. Thus, to take only one example, the National Research Council handles the public side of scientific research, especially that carried out by the universities. It was spawned by the university élite, and all attempts to influence its proceedings from the outside have so far failed, so that, even if it has no scientific policy of its own as yet, it is certainly in a strong enough position to be able to afford one.

Such a policy might seem a superfluous irrelevance if we were discussing pure science, but in the field of applied science it can be of very great importance. However, while the National Research Council cannot be swayed from the outside, its financial allowance can be reduced to a mere pittance so that it can hardly function, and this is what happens.

25   Actually, of course, research and politics are interrelated in countless ways, and the gradual transition from a purely technical scientific organization to a group interested in exercising political pressure precludes our drawing any hard and fast boundary. A very large number of societies conceal their real aims, whether deliberately or not. Each group tries to pass off its own private interests or those of some particular political or economic group as the interests of science, the welfare of the community or the upholding of public morals. It is not for nothing that the Mafia is called an 'honourable society', and that 'honour' is what drives its members into action. It is 'justice' and the 'good' of the community that impel these organizations to apply more or less lawful pressures on politicians, something which, as we have seen, they are in a position to do because of the corrupt state of the administration.

Group interests in Italy are so much to the fore that when the administration or the government does something it is often impossible to know whether this is because they want to, or merely because they have been pushed into it. Italians refer to this control mechanism by means of which subordinate structures determine the nature of higher-level decisions within the power-system as *sottogoverno* (subsidiary government). Even apparently purely consultative work or merely technical research can, once it is carried out in the context of these large organizations, have a very considerable influence on those in a position to make politically important decisions; equally it can itself be affected by such decisions. This is particularly so because the traditional power-system increasingly makes use of such organizations to develop its own plans, and, as the various political parties and power-groups lose their original ideological inspiration, they turn to science and technology for some justification of their choice of political options. However, to understand how these organizations actually fulfil their main task, viz. scientific research, is to be immediately aware of their intrinsic weakness.

26   The inefficiency of the state administration, the intermediary organizations, the scientific research groups, and of those supposed to increase the fund of technical know-how, all tend to weaken the entire tertiary sector, and the whole economic and social structure of Italian society suffers accordingly. There is nothing at all surprising about inefficiency in administration having a bad effect on distribution, or poor technology injuring the whole service sector. In an advanced industrial society one can never make clean distinctions between the public and private sectors of the economy, since their functions are always interrelated and complementary. Thus, the system by which goods and services are distributed, which has been only slightly placed under state control, has broken down and is hindered by the use of a model of the consumer market which is twenty years out of date. The situation has been made even worse by high distribution costs, due to the profits of such middle-men as wholesalers, customs officials, government inspectors, or local supervisory bodies. Furthermore, there is a tendency for the primary and secondary sectors

> to pass their own difficulties on to others, seeking profit-margins in the tertiary sector that are no longer justified by their own growth, especially in the light of rising production costs. In other words, it does not seem fanciful to claim that when those working the market realize the production system allows them only a narrow profit-margin, they are tending more and more to seek out new ways of exploiting the situation in the tertiary sector, either by having recourse to strategies already accepted by public opinion, or in other more devious ways. Thus, major industrial groups both public and private have considered the advantages of their own participation in building programmes for houses, schools and hospitals, or in schemes for improving the environment. Again, several agricultural concerns and large-scale food producers have planned out ways of stock-piling and eventually distributing their goods in order to exploit the potential market as fully as possible. There have also been some rather speculative ventures of even more doubtful morality, such as the way in which certain industrialists work the stock exchange or manipulate their financial resources, or in

*which certain businessmen and agriculturalists speculate
on their own products.*[67]

The commercial part of the tertiary sector is responsible for 30–
40 per cent of earnings in this sector, and when its unbalanced state
is taken in conjunction with the imbalance in the private services
zone, and in state-controlled or state-inspired research organizations,
the whole system is seen to be in a bad way. One official document,
a recent report on the country's social situation, notes that:

> *recently a lot has been said about the need for our society
> to resist its own strong temptation towards Mediterranean
> and/or over-conservative behaviour-patterns under pain
> of compromising its identity as a European and industrial
> nation; it is only too obvious that this temptation originates
> from and develops on account of the way in which the main
> parts of the tertiary sector (distribution services and public
> administration) are developing without adequate guide-
> lines or controls, and acquiring regressive and often
> shameful characteristics – the distribution system was
> never excellent and is now rather dilapidated; many
> divisions within the tertiary sector are increasingly domi-
> nated by bureaucracy; job-opportunity in the public sector
> is dangerously over-privileged; the tendency to model both
> occasional and routine ways of handling affairs in the
> private part of the tertiary sector on the practice of those
> employed in the public part is even more dangerous; some
> cumbersome organizational machinery is being over-
> developed simply in order to provide more jobs; too many
> people are being allowed to run up personal expense
> accounts out of public funds; there are many other extrav-
> agant schemes for making the general public suffer in
> one way or another from problems and tensions that have
> little or nothing to do with the development and promotion
> of a mature economy by a responsible state administration.*
>
> *Thus the race to hand over all difficulties to the tertiary
> sector has been followed by the further evasion of unload-
> ing them on the general public, which is expected to
> accept all the problems and all the double dealing. While,
> in the last few years, Italy has been congratulating herself
> on her cultural and political primacy, public intervention*

and public expenditure in the economy have proved her
soft under-belly open to attacks and pressures from every
side; its existence has made it easy for private individuals
to continue to enjoy their privileges at public expense, and
this continues to be a major factor in the spiral of inflation
that is having such a dramatic effect on our lives and that
we are trying to do something about but finding hard to
eliminate.[68]

The development of this phenomenon has exacerbated tensions in other key sectors of the economy, and meant a further escalation of the problems of social privilege. The multiplication of anomalous situations in which workers in the public sector are favoured and others discriminated against means that the distortions attain such vast and obvious proportions as to compel their adoption by other sectors, resulting in a general lowering of productivity throughout the whole national social and economic system.

The higher reaches of the administrative and bureaucratic substructure are an expression of the system on which they depend and which they serve to operate. They have a tendency to expand at the expense of the other sectors of the national social and economic life. With the expansion of the state technostructure, there is an increase in the numbers of social parasites living off the tertiary sector. The whole expansion is presided over by a power-system that personifies and makes effective this entire process. It seems impossible to put a stop to what is happening, and the causes for it date back to the very origins of the present Italian state. The power-system controlling the tertiary sector extends its links with the political power-system as such, and thus secures its own position even more, as we shall see in the next chapter.

Notes to chapter 5

1. Clough and De Rosa, 1971, p. 135.
2. Esposto, 1970, pp. 237–62, especially p. 241.
3. Acerbo, 1961.
4. ISTAT, *2° Censimento generale dell'agricoltura: 1970*, p. 134.
5. See Mottura and Pugliese, 1971, pp. 3–18, especially p.6. See also D'Anna, 1971.
6. Censis, 1973.
7. Within agriculture social stratification carries with it some considerable

fragmentation of functions. Thus, there are 'proletarian agricultural day-labourers, others on fixed wages (farm-labourers, helpers), semi-proletarians without land of their own (renting a plot in the South or working in small colonies without a farm), peasants with a modest livelihood (owning or holding the lease of a small-holding, share-croppers and colonists in areas of low yield, such as mountains and high hills), fairly well-to-do peasants (the same group, but on gentle slopes or in the plain), capitalist peasants (owning or holding the lease of farms of some size, with some mechanization and hired labour), middle-class and large-scale capitalist land-owners.' Daneo, 1972, p. 87.

8.   See ISTAT, *1° Censimento generale dell'agricoltura: 1961*, p. 25. The recent more specialized and intensive production methods have enabled capitalism to advance despite the shortage of land and the difficulty of securing any large unbroken area. In the course of a century the production of oranges has increased fivefold, milk production is six times what it was, there are three times as many cows and four times as many pigs.

9.   See Daneo, 1972, pp. 14 and 93.

10.   See Morandi, 1959, pp. 157ff.

11.   See Alberoni, 1972, p. 16.

12.   See Ragozzino, 1967.

13.   *Ibid.*

14.   The system the state uses gradually to take control of the Italian economy is that of state participation in the private sector – the majority of the shares pass to public ownership while the company remains a private one in the eyes of the law. In this way the state extends its influence in all directions, takes over whole chains of companies, and invests government funds at far higher interest than a private individual could command. Nationalization is also used to expand the public sector in the more conventional way, the most recent instance being the nationalization of electricity production. The supervisory body in charge of state industries, the IRI, was set up by the Fascists after the 1929 crisis by a law of 23 January 1933. At first its only purpose was to help industrial firms and banks to surmount their financial difficulties. It bought shares with the intention of selling them back later, but then decided to retain all or some of them for good, and to administer them on the state's behalf. In this way, almost by chance, a new sector of the Italian economy came into being.

15.   See *Il Sole – 24 ore*, 18 November 1973.

16.   See Ardigò, 1973a, pp. 322ff.

17.   Sylos Labini, 1972, p. 156.

18.   D'Antonio, 1973, p. 231.

19.   See Alberoni, 1972, p. 11.

20.   The situation is so obvious that even the carefree tourist cannot help but notice it. It is not without good grounds that some continental tourist agencies attract their clientele to Italy with such slogans as: Go to Italy before the Italians destroy it.

21.   Ferrarotti, 1970, p. 16.

22.   *Ibid.*, p. 19.

23.   *Ibid.*, p. 20.

24.   Acquaviva, 1971b, p. 19.

25.   De Marchi, 1965, p. 11.

26.   Consiglio Nazionale dell'economia e del lavoro, 1973, pp. 37ff.

27.   It must not be forgotten that the 'Kingdom' grew out of the Duchy of Savoy, which was originally completely French. Thus, we are discussing

a state that began in France and only very slowly over a period of centuries spread across the Alps and became partly Italian. Until 1860 almost a third of its territory had a predominantly French population, but, save for the Valley d'Aosta (now an independent region within the Italian republic), this part later passed to France in consideration of help given to Italy during the 1859 war. This was Nice and Savoy, which Mussolini quite unreasonably wanted back in 1940. At the time the only part of it inhabited by Italians was a very narrow strip of coastline extending as far as the old town of Nizza. The rest of the population spoke only French, and the Italians were certainly not of pure descent.

28. See Spinetti, 1964, and Benvenuti, 1962.
29. De Marchi, 1965, p. 15.
30. *Ibid.*, p. 91.
31. Ferrabino, 1934, p. 29.
32. La Palombara, 1964, p. 262.
33. See Ministero degli interni, *Direzione generale dell'Amministrazione civile.*
34. For all these bodies see Censis, 1973, p. 438.
35. See Ferrari Bravo and Serafini, 1972.
36. *Ibid.*, p. 123.
37. The army became an integrated force in 1861. Its structure was made definitive at the beginning of this century by two decrees of 1906 and 1908, and the system has stood the test of experience. The Chief of the General Staff and the General Staff in agreement with him command the army in war-time, and have authority for all technical matters, which are to be decided on military and not political grounds, while the Ministry for Defence or the Ministry for War hold the relevant political authority.

Government intervention is mainly directed towards fixing the size of the army budget for defence. From 1862 to 1912 military expenditure amounted to 23.7 per cent of total national expenditure – this period covers the war to take Rome (1860), the third war of independence (1866), the campaign in Eritrea (1882–96), the war in Libya (1911–12). Army expenditure was more than that on education, administration and justice together.

Until the First World War the armed forces were a sort of feudal zone living apart from the rest of the country. See *Il potere militare in Italia*, pp. 49ff.

38. Despite the army's exclusion from political life, it cannot be denied that it played an important role during the Fascist period, both in the coming to power of Fascism and in the Fascists' running of the country. Nevertheless, the army and the Fascist party remained separate; indeed, one might say that the armed forces were never more independent of the political authorities than they were under Fascism. This is also clear from the events of July–September 1943, when, in the absence of any alternative political power on the scene, the armed forces succeeded, however badly, in bringing about the fall of Fascism and the signing of an armistice.

39. The Italian army numbers about 450,000 men, comprising 120,000 regular soldiers, 80,000 civilians in permanent service, and about 250,000 conscripts. Neither in efficiency nor striking force does the army reach the level these numbers would lead one to expect. A few years ago Israel maintained about 330 planes with 17,000 men, while Italy requires an air-force of 74,000 to look after not much more than 400.

To these 450,000 men in the armed forces we should add about 200,000 members of the various police forces.

However, the real armed forces amount to some 50,000 professional officers, both commissioned and non-commissioned, and about 200–220,000 conscripts (not those just existing on paper, which Italy has never been short of, as during the 1940–45 war when she managed to send to Africa whole divisions that hardly existed at all, either in terms of men or of available weapons and equipment).

40.   See Galli, 1972.

41.   The rather small part played by the army is confirmed by their relatively slight allocation in the annual budget. In 1969 they accounted for only 2.9 per cent of the gross national expenditure, contrasting with 3.5 per cent in West Germany, 4.4 per cent in France, 5.1 per cent in Great Britain, 5.6 per cent in Czechoslovakia, 8.5 per cent in the Soviet Union and 8.6 per cent in the United States.

42.   In 1969 only 1.58 per cent of babies under the age of 4 went to a children's nursery, the highest proportion being 2.61 per cent in Emilia Romagna in the North and the lowest 0.70 per cent in Calabria in the South. In practice 'a social provision as important as that of nursery schools hardly exists as yet in Italy'. Berlinguer and Terranova, 1972, p. 154.

43.   *Ibid.*, p. 32. In Italy in 1967 the rate of deaths round about the time of birth was 34.8 per thousand, higher than the figure for any other European country except Portugal with 39.4 per thousand. No figures are available for Spain. The figure is very low indeed for the more developed countries such as Sweden (18.9 per thousand), Denmark (19.6), Finland (20.5), Norway (20.8), Czechoslovakia (21.3), Holland (21.4), Switzerland (22.0), East Germany (23.9), Poland (24.8), Great Britain (25.8), France (27.2) and West Germany (27.2). Lower figures than the Italian one are also found in such non-European countries as New Zealand (21.4 per thousand for the white population and 24.1 for the Maoris), Canada (25.0), the United States (27.1) and even Mexico (31.9). On the other hand, there are higher figures for most underdeveloped countries, and also for the Argentine (39.3 per thousand), Chile (48.5) and the islands of Mauritius (70.3).

Italy is also towards the bottom of the scale among European nations when we consider the infant mortality rate. The Italian figure of 33.2 per thousand is less than that for Spain (34.0), Greece (34.3), Poland (38.1), Portugal (59.2) and Yugoslavia (62.1), but is much higher than that for the more civilized parts of Europe.

These data are taken from Organisation mondiale de la santé, 1967, and Braghin, 1973, p. 384.

44.   A study made in 1968 showed clearly that infant mortality correlates positively with the occupation of the parents.

Still-births per 1000 births in relation to the parents' occupation

	1960–62	1965–67	% *variation*
Agriculture	29.3	24.8	−15.4
Entrepreneurs and managers employed in agriculture	18.1	18.2	+ 0.6
Self-employed in agriculture	26.4	21.0	−20.5
Paid to work in agriculture	31.3	27.4	−12.5
Working on the land in any way at all	29.2	24.9	−14.7
Industrial and tertiary sectors	21.3	17.6	−17.4
Non-professional workers	29.1	28.4	−2.4

Sub-contractors	22.7	19.4	−14.5
Self-employed	20.6	16.6	−19.4
Entrepreneurs and managers employed in industry or in the tertiary sector	17.0	13.2	−22.4
Following the liberal arts or some profession	16.5	12.8	−22.4
Professionally employed in administration, technology or other work	16.9	13.3	−21.3
Working in graphics, installing or supervising machinery, etc.	20.4	16.7	−18.1
Craftsmen and industrial designers	22.0	18.3	−16.8
Commercial art, tradesfolk, various services	24.0	20.3	−15.4
Total	23.4	18.9	−19.2

Source: ISTAT, *Annuario di statistiche demografiche*, various years, and Braghin 1973, p. 369.

45. The dualism and inefficiency of Italian society are also reflected in the prison system. Apart from the fact that for well-known reasons it is easier to be imprisoned if one belongs to the lower classes, or has not had a good education, it does seem that a high proportion of those in prison are of Southern origin. If we consider the birthplace of those in prison, then 3.7 per cent come from abroad, 57.7 per cent from the South, 11.9 per cent from the Centre, and 26.1 per cent from the North, the rest being of unknown origin. This compares with the fact that the South accommodates 34.9 per cent of the total population, the Centre 19.0 per cent and the North 46.1 per cent. See Ricci and Salierno, 1971, p. 66.

46. *Ibid.*

47. According to M. Barbagli: 'In 1950 about 30 per cent of the Italian population had either never learned or else had forgotten how to read and write. Italy had the highest illiteracy rate in Europe. At the same time, however, our country had the highest proportion of university students in its population when compared with Switzerland, Sweden, Germany, France, Great Britain, Holland and Belgium.' Barbagli, 1973, p. 16.

48. For these data see Aymone, 1973, p. 39.

49. *Ibid.*, p. 48. Similar conclusions regarding the operation of the selection process during the years of compulsory education resulted from a study of a sample in Bologna by Catelli, 1973, especially pp. 24ff.

50. See our remarks in the section regarding the lower middle strata.

51. See Balbo and Chiaretti, 1972, p. 28.

52. See 'La selezione nella scuola dell'obbligo', pp. 70–73.

53. Balbo and Chiaretti, 1972, p. 35.

54. The number attending secondary schools rose from 383,906 to 1,552,988 between 1950–51 and 1969–70. Of these 56.4 per cent receive technical or professional education, while 80 per cent of those terminating their period of compulsory education successfully continue with their studies, 70 per cent of these proceeding to university. See Bini, 1971.

55. In general very few graduates are employed in agriculture. Their number dropped by one third between 1960 and 1967. Even if the present stable figure represents a rationalizing of the agricultural sector, it still means graduates have negligible opportunities of employment in it (it occupies a mere 5000).

In recent years the industrial sector does not seem to have done much to increase job-openings for new graduates. In the second half of the 1960s it absorbed some 57,000 or 10.5 per cent of the employed graduates. No rapid expansion can be expected in the 1970s – provisional estimates for 1980 suggest that about 75,000 graduates will be working in industry at that time, an increase far below the likely expansion of the graduate sector of the potential labour force due to developments in university education.

The majority of graduates find posts in the tertiary sector. In the late 1960s it employed about half a million or 90 per cent of working graduates. Its capacity to offer them employment seems to be increasing – 86 per cent in 1951; 87 per cent in 1961; 88 per cent in 1966. The whole tertiary sector is expanding, and by 1980 is expected to offer jobs to about 900,000 graduates. However, in Italy this expansion has been slowed down by the presence within it of social parasitism and meaningless staff increases in certain areas – the tertiary sector in Italy is not go-ahead as it is in other countries. Research suggests that in 1980 the number of graduates seeking work will exceed the posts available to them by some 120,000. Such estimates are only approximate. See Centro K. Marx, 1969, pp. 39, 39–40 and 41–42.

56. *Ibid.*, p. 42.
57. Barbagli (1973) pp. 19 and 21.
58. *Ibid.*, p. 20.
59. *Ibid.*, p. 19.
60. See ISTAT, *Compendio statistico*, 1962, 1972.
61. In recent years the number of graduates has increased as follows: 47,673 in 1969; 56,895 in 1970; 60,651 in 1971. Most students are enrolled for degree courses in the Arts. There has, however, been an increase in the proportion taking Science subjects: 26,497 new students in 1969–70; 28,150 in 1970–71; 32,061 in 1971–72. The overall increase of students in the science faculties is about 10,000 a year, giving 105,802 in 1971–72. See ISTAT *Compendio statistico, 1972*.
62. *Ibid.*, 1968, 1969, 1970, 1971, 1972.
63. Balbo, 1973, p. 24.
64. See Acquaviva, 1962, for a fuller discussion of this point.
65. See Alberoni, 1973.
66. The figures are not very recent. See Avveduto, 1968, pp. 153ff. In recent years the situation has certainly not improved.
67. Consiglio Nazionale dell'economia e del lavoro, 1973, p. 11.
68. *Ibid.*, p. 12.

CHAPTER 6

Political Power in the Strict Sense

A. Preliminary observations

27   It is the political system in the strict sense that coordinates and gives its tone to the various aspects of the power-system we have mentioned: the land-owning community, investors in urban development, industrialists, businessmen, public administrators, organizers, social service directors, military leaders, chiefs of police, research scientists, top technicians, etc. Hence the great importance attaching to the organization of political life, the party-system, the trade unions' organization, the various schools of thought within the different political parties, etc.

Italy to all appearances has a democratic, parliamentary, republican, multi-party, political structure. However, the various political forces in the field are really the expression of a number of different factors in the Italian situation, which we shall examine more closely in the following pages, but propose to mention briefly right away.

(a)   The way in which politics are conducted is influenced all the time by what remains of Italy's closed culture from the days of her underdevelopment. We have noticed already how important this fact is for any proper understanding of the rest of the Italian power-system, and we shall find it is equally significant with regard to the political system itself.

(b)   The new culture is another important element, and cardinal to the thinking of pressure groups and of the technocrats within the political structure.

(c) There is also the Catholic culture that inspires the Christian Democrat Party and is the substance of its search for common ground within its ranks, with its supporters and, to a varying degree, with other parties.

(d) Finally we must not omit the Marxist and Socialist culture, which influences the thinking of the vast majority of the parties on the left, and links them with the trade unions, the cooperative societies, etc.

It is in the soil of these four cultures that we shall find the roots of the ruling-class, the party-political system, electoral campaigns, the political and negotiating strength of the unions, etc. The same cultural soil brings politics into relationship with other sources of power. It links up Italian political life socially, financially, culturally and even morally, and binds together the whole national social structure.

A word first of all, then, not about Italy's closed culture itself, which we have already discussed, but about its influence, and about the structures in which it is, or is not embodied. Traditionally the peasant is hostile to the government. Today's peasants include people who have just moved into the towns, or have been there no more than a generation. They exercise considerable influence on the life-style of the towns, and on the colour of local politics. The main characteristic they bring with them is their hostility to the power-system. As Friedmann expressed it, writing particularly about the world of the Southern Italian peasant: 'this peasant has been educated to consider the government as his worst enemy while expecting that it does everything for him.'[1] Capannari and Moss confirm this when they say that 'A feeling of distrust pervades the attitude of the peasant. He distrusts and fears the distant government in Rome and dislikes the local representatives of civil power. *Governo ladro* (the government is a thief) bespeaks the basic attitude of the peasant toward authority.'[2]

Two attitudes result from this lack of interest in politics and hostility towards authority of the old peasant society which has just been swallowed up in the overcrowded towns. First of all there is apathy towards, lack of interest in and distrust of the power-system, and this brings with it a resigned acceptance of political scandals, a failure to notice which government is in power, and a belief that every government is bad and that politics never have any bearing on social progress, etc. On the other hand, we find modern variations on the age-old family-client theme in a desperate attempt to curry favour with some individual or group in the government or at least with access to a measure of political power. Both at national and local levels the most traditional and widely known ways of organizing such exploitations of power are themselves being transformed. The Mafia is the obvious example. It has been said that not very long ago the Mafia achieved a boom in corruption.

> *Every day the Mafia dies out, and every day it is born again in a new form that guarantees the continuance of its nefarious life and activities: there is ample evidence of its capacity to expand and to follow the example of others' success.*

In Sicily

> *from the end of the war until the 1950s the Mafia supported agriculture, favoured regional autonomy ... gave a helping hand to the liberals and Christian Democrats on the political right, and shot down those who supported the trade unions. A new phase in its life began as soon as Sicily was given its own regional constitution with special powers. Giuliano was liquidated,[3] and the Mafia installed itself in the towns, lobbying party-politicians, public officials, the staff of regional offices, institutes in charge of loans or building permits, people concerned with business, marketing, government aid, or the giving of technical and scientific advice. This was the boom in corruption. Nothing happened that the Mafia did not know about beforehand and have a hand in, and no development escaped its influence.[4]*

In addition to speculation and various rackets connected with agriculture, the Mafia went into politics, and took over such sectors as urban development and the sale of building land. The Mafia also concerned itself with cemeteries, fruit-markets and chemists' shops. Emigration meant that many members of the Mafia moved from Sicily to other parts of Italy, and especially to Rome. Their activity is no more than sporadic in Central Italy, and almost unknown in the North.

The traditional Italian culture was thrown into a crisis by the upheaval in the social and economic system, which had previously supported it. The discarded culture became the life-style of those in charge of the country's administration and political system, and contaminated these with such features as the selling of political support to one's clients, paying political parties to look after the family interest, demanding favours on personal grounds, exercising unfair pressure, etc. Thus, the traditional culture did not vanish without trace, but a vendetta against all opposition to it was perpetuated in the very corridors of political power.

Fortunately, this is not the whole story about the conduct of Italian political affairs. There is also the new, technical, scientific, efficiency-conscious modern culture. The old culture and the Mafia style of life are rooted much more deeply in the South than in the North, and although Rome is heavily contaminated by their influence and is, unfortunately, the centre of most departments of government, the conduct of affairs elsewhere has a more technical basis. In intensely industrialized areas the political system is much less contaminated by the traditional culture. The administration is far less ideologically oriented, takes a pragmatic view of situations, and while considering the feelings of the electorate, usually opts for whatever is technically the sounder policy, so that the basis of decisions lies in a different social stratum than it would in the South.

Which of these two cultures is dominant? Possibly a scientific and technical and certainly a pragmatic, down-to-earth approach characterizes the country as a whole, and as this new culture continually expands Italy draws closer to the rest of Europe, but the official political system is still dominated by the old culture, which is refusing to die. The trouble is that the political parties have their headquarters and their leading men in Rome, which is also the centre of the government administration. Most Italians who do not live in Rome live in the North or the Centre rather than in the South, and the centre of gravity of Italian political life lies towards the North; yet the political leadership is concentrated in the Centre, quite close to the South, in a city dominated by Southern immigrants who have infected it with their mentality and culture.

28   However, it must be remembered that as well as and alongside these two national cultures, the modern and the traditional, Italy supports two further sub-cultures, the Christian–Catholic and the Socialist–Marxist ways of life. While the national cultures colour the whole of political life and determine the level at which it can be carried on, the sub-cultures influence the details of its concrete realization. They are the life-blood of the two main political parties, which we shall consider more closely later, and a number of other smaller parties are constellated around them in various combinations and subject to certain qualifications and reservations.

How did these two parties become dominant, and why are two needed? Each is the expression of an important sub-culture in which it is rooted, with trade unions, cooperative societies and similar associations to give the party a real basis at grass-roots level. For our purposes there is no need to probe more deeply into the ideological content of these sub-cultures than we have done already. However, it will be useful to discover more about their structure and organization.

Let us take a look at the Catholic sub-culture from the political point of view. As political attitudes have matured and the Church's own outlook has broadened, the Catholic party has based itself increasingly on the acknowledgement of a certain pluralism within the Church's structures and associations. A very strong and all-pervading network of relationships has been established. This has been for many years the supporting structure for the political work of the Christian Democrats, who are the Catholic party. A Christian and Catholic political platform rooted in a Christian culture are basic to the whole organization.

It is a militant Christianity, that since the war has committed itself to definite political action, at least since it shook itself free of Fascist influence. For many years the crusade against communism, or against 'the enemies of religion' was the cement that held this culture together and made of it a militantly political union.

The sorts of association linking its supporters together, under the overall direction of the ecclesiastical hierarchy, are extremely varied, ranging from the Catholic Action Association of Italian Workers (ACLI) to the Catholic Action groups of Italian Teenagers (GIAC) and the Italian Catholic Universities Federation (FUCI). A glance at almost any diocesan bulletin brings to light a list of scores of associations that supplement the parish structure and bring together the most varied sorts of people: working-men, intellectuals, professional people, industrialists, managers, farmers, direct growers, etc. This diversity in the interests and aims of the different societies is reflected in political terms in the Christian Democrat Party itself and in the Catholic trade union (CISL), which comprise elements from all these bodies and so necessarily have a rather heterogeneous leadership – each prominent figure having tended, and to some extent still tending to express the interests of the particular organization that is the basis of his political strength and his capacity to win votes in an election. For a long time it was the joint campaign against communism that held all these forces together.

Overarching all these societies was the organization of the Church itself in the various parishes and dioceses with the considerable support of efficiently structured religious orders of priests and nuns. Thus, many societies held their meetings in parish halls, were organized on a parochial basis, and invited a priest to join them as their chaplain and spiritual adviser.

To finance all this colossal organization the Church needed a complex and carefully articulated economic structure, capable of supporting such additional social enterprises as children's nurseries, Church schools, colleges, and social-work organizations. In Italy, it must be remembered, the Church is massively committed in the social field, and has its own hospitals, old-people's homes, children's homes, etc. In addition to this, members of the various religious orders work in a large number of state-run or independent institutions of this kind. Nor, finally, must we forget the influential Catholic University (which has centres both in Milan and Rome), the large number of parish cinemas and Catholic publishing houses, or the Church's commitments in the tourist industry.

All this amounts to a massive political and cultural organization. It does not really do much to deepen or bring up to date the Catholic value-system, but it certainly helps to spread it throughout society, ensuring that the Church is always effectively present among the masses, and is at the same time always assured of at least indirect access to the different centres of influence within the power-system.[5]

Catholic Action provided the fulcrum for this whole organization, so that the whole Catholic position was weakened considerably by the crisis within Catholic Action, from which the leaders of most other Catholic societies had been drawn. In 1956 Italian Catholic Action had 950,000 adult members and 705,000 junior members, who could readily be called upon to participate in any cultural, political, religious or moral campaign, the FUCI playing a particularly prominent part, with ACLI often rallying round in its support. However, round about 1966–7 this organization began to collapse as the Church lost its social and ideological credibility, partly because of events in the Second Vatican Council, and by 1969–70 the disintegration was complete. The present membership is 395,000 adults and 140,000 junior members, which represents only 42 per cent and 20 per cent of the 1956 figures.[6] As an indication of the pattern of cultural and moral shifts within society, it is interesting to note that the smallest drop is in the adult women's membership, while the largest decrease is in the junior girls' membership.

However, it is not only Catholic Action but the whole of the Church's organization that has been thrown into crisis by the new technical and scientific culture, the changing standards of morals and behaviour, the consumer society, the revision of basic values, and the new standards of judgement. The crisis has undermined the Catholic party at grass-roots level, and changes in theology have contributed to a further weakening of the connections between the party and the Church, the unions and the Church, the Catholic Action groups and the Church, and, in consequence, to a weakening of the links between these various Catholic associations themselves. We shall have something to say about the probable consequences of this state of affairs when we consider the Christian Democrat Party in more detail.

Let us turn for the moment to consider the Socialist–Marxist sub-culture. The situation is very similar to that within Catholicism. If Catholicism derived its strength from a single-minded crusade against communism, Socialism's development is rooted in the peasants' traditional hostility to authority, and in opposition to the Church in the form of anti-clericalism. It is well known that it is in Catholic countries that the more extreme forms of Marxism flourish, and this was true in Italy (and to some extent is still true) because the Church had educated people to messianic ideals – politically, culturally and psychologically. The Socialism of the countries of northern Europe is modelled on Protestant pluralism (e.g. in England and Scandinavia), but Catholic countries (e.g. France, Spain and Italy) think of their Socialism as rather like a highly centralized Catholicism, a monolithic influence in society that dominates both the national culture and the individual conscience. This should make it easier to understand the historical and cultural derivation of Italian Socialism.

It originated in the same soil and came to birth in the same cultural climate as the Mazzinian and Republican movements and the other left-wing groups that brought about the unification of Italy.[7] Its roots are sunk in a chaotic swamp in which anarchy, utopianism and republicanism are equally at home. Its nature varies from place to place, depending on the social conditions of its first appearance. In such places as Lombardy and Piedmont it is mainly a working-class phenomenon, while in Umbria, Emilia and Tuscany it attracts the peasants rather more, and has a lot to do with the share-cropping system of employment. Thus, in some areas it is strongest in the city suburbs and in others in the countryside, but always where there is most hostility to the Church and the open-minded members of the ruling class – hostility which is often violently expressed.[8]

With the passage of time the ruling-class that brought about the unification of the country has been shown to be incapable of governing it, and together with the development of the Catholic and Socialist parties and organizations this has promoted the formation of an organized working-class.

Organization in the strict sense, however, came only very gradu-ally. Long after Socialism had spread throughout the rest of Europe, it remained little known in Italy where, nevertheless, the spirit of rebellion was strong, with armed gangs leading insurrec-tions, as well as pursuing a general strategy of terrorism and assassination – the stiletto being a favourite weapon.

As a mass phenomenon Marxist–Socialism dates back only to about 1890, and gave the unions, which had been forbidden prior to that date, their specific shape. In 1891 they set up the first *Camera del lavoro*, or provincial organization of workers, which by 1902 numbered 300,000 members and 80 local offices. The Catholic unions began to spring up in 1898 and developed just as quickly. There was a similar expansion in the many peasants' associations. Particularly at the turn of the century the workers developed their activities with strikes and various other tactics in an attempt to secure better pay and improved working conditions, as well as some degree of political power and better publicity for their own ideas. Developments of this kind continued until the beginning of the First World War.

At the start of the present century the workers also banded together in various cooperative production schemes, of which there were 547 in 1909. Consumer cooperative societies are of much earlier date; in 1883 there were 250 such organizations with 70,000 members; by 1910 there were 1704. Workers' mutual assistance associations numbered 1000 in 1873 and had reached 5000 by 1895. By then we can say that the social basis of the Socialist–Marxist sub-culture was completely laid. There were sufficient grass-roots organizations to ensure adequate contact between the workers and their cultural and political leaders in what was initially the Socialist Party, and later, especially after the Second World War, the Communist Party.

The workers' organizations became stronger still after the First World War. The structure could not compete with that of the Catholic Church in either complexity or power of penetration, but it was certainly quite vigorous. The trade union remained the main line of communication among the masses, 600,000 workers belonging to some organization by 1919; in the following year the figure was almost two million. Thus the workers' organizations were already in a position after the war to take over factories and farmlands – 600,000 workers and 280 large-scale firms.

Fascism brought this process to a halt, and amalgamated in its own orbit various scattered groups outside the two dominant sub-cultures. These included capitalist industrial and agricultural circles, philanthropic associations, the army and navy, and a portion of the less affluent middle-classes.

With the collapse of Fascism the two sub-cultures reasserted the dominance that they had in reality never lost, since Fascism had never constituted an authentic cultural option. During the post-war period (1945–8), apart from the fact that leadership within the Socialist camp had now passed to the Communists, the situation and problems to be faced were much as they had been before Fascism had arrived on the scene. The Catholic and Socialist sub-cultures divided the field between them, and were politically supreme. The eventual outcome of this was the present party-system, with the Christian Democrat and Communist parties in the key positions at the centre of Italian society.

Politically Italian society may be structured into a system of several parties, but the political scene is clearly dominated by the Christian Democrats (DC) and the Communists (PCI) who control the two sub-cultures and occupy the two main political battle-fronts, though there are obviously Catholics and Marxists who vote for other parties, and many non-Catholics who vote for the Christian Democrats. Political life essentially revolves around these two sub-cultures and is conditioned by them. Before going any further it will be as well to take a closer look at these two parties, at the other parties and also at the trade unions which provide the context for their operation and whose historical origins we have already touched upon.

B. The political parties

The Christian Democrat Party

29   After the Second World War no middle-class political group had sufficient hegemony to seize the political leadership itself, and the Catholic, Socialist and Communist forces decided to accept parliamentary democracy, with a view to using it to achieve their own sub-cultural interests and concerns. When Fascism collapsed at the end of the war only the Catholic Church had the structures and organization (dating from the post-Concordat period of Fascism) needed to support any consistent and stable form of administration. This situation favoured the birth and growth of the Christian Democrat Party (DC),[9] which was initially a clerical party because of its Catholic origins.[10]

At this time, it must be noted, the Christian Democrats' influence was mainly used to balance and stabilize the Italian version of capitalism, in an attempt to bring it into line with Catholic social doctrine and a philosophy of the state as the instigator of progress and reform. The Christian Democrats interpret their position as a central one, and desire controlled development without any violent or sudden breaks with previous practice. They serve the interests of the middle *ceti*, safeguard the rights of the private sector of the economy, and regard the state's function as that of promoting development despite the difficulties to be encountered, and of correcting any unhealthy deviations in the economy in order to secure a more balanced growth.

The Christian Democrats pursue this moderate policy under the leadership of a small group of prominent men who represent local interests or specific social categories. These men played a particularly important role within the party during the 1950s. They guaranteed it a certain number of votes and had notable organizing ability. In the South they also belonged to the traditional family network and had their clients. Since the late 1960s this situation has brought about a certain crisis in the party, because of the reshaping of Italian society and the tendency to break away to some extent from narrow and merely local ways of viewing situations.

At all events the position of these leaders became less central in the late 1950s as the party gradually transformed its organization and strengthened its real links with the masses at grass-roots level. It no longer harbours any illusions about being able to enjoy an absolute majority,[11] and has reconciled itself to consolidating the position it has already won, improving its organization, encouraging more of its members to participate actively in its affairs, and making its own contribution towards healthy economic development based on a better managed government strategy. In other words, at every level of the nation's life the DC places the emphasis on stability and prudent planning.[12]

In at least three ways the DC has now become a party for the masses: electorally, as is obvious from its having secured an almost absolute majority of the votes cast in the 1948 general election; because of its large membership; on account of the way it is organized and structured.

A word about each of these three points.[13]

When the Catholic Party had been reconstituted as the DC it secured 35.2 per cent of the votes for the Constituent Assembly in 1946, and 48.4 per cent of the votes in the 1948 general election.[14] It then suffered some severe losses and in 1953 obtained only 40.1 per cent of the votes. Since 1953 there have been no great variations in the DC's electoral returns. There was a slight gain in 1958 – 42.3 per cent of the votes (+2.2 per cent); a loss in 1963 – 38.3 per cent of the votes (−4 per cent), as a result of the first attempt at an opening towards the left; a slight recovery in 1968 – 39.1 per cent of the votes (+0.8 per cent); with little change in the last elections in 1972 – 38.8 per cent of the votes.[15] Thus, since 1953 the DC has accounted for about 40 per cent of the Italian voting population. Existing variations can be attributed to temporary changes in the political outlook and have little or no bearing on the party's policies and influence.

From the point of view of the geographical distribution of its support the DC follows a fairly even course, and maintains its position. Most of its support comes from the South, but it has a considerable following on the islands and in some Northern areas. In the Centre it has rather fewer supporters than its national position might lead one to expect, this being the established stronghold of the Italian Communist Party.[16]

At the present time the distribution of Catholic voters among the various social strata and professions reflects fairly closely the actual class stratification of the Italian social structure. Wage-earners account for 44.8 per cent of the DC vote; the small bourgeois self-employed group for 36 per cent; small bourgeois people receiving a monthly salary for 14.4 per cent; university students and religious 3.2 per cent; entrepreneurs and professional people 1.6 per cent.[17]

Those who vote DC are not all Catholics, and are only partly subject to the influence of Catholic organizations. On the whole its policies are moderate, and most moderate groups give it their support.[18]

The Catholic element is a stronger feature of the party itself than of those who vote for it. The party is also very much concerned with developments in rural areas, though more peasants seem to vote for it than care to become members of the party itself. There is also a smaller percentage of women party-members than of women among those who vote for it. Something similar holds true of the workers voting for the DC in comparison with those actually belonging to the party. On the other hand, the percentage of professional people, entrepreneurs and higher officials in the party is much higher than their percentage in the part of the electorate that supports it.[19]

During the last twenty years social and economic changes, increased social mobility and migration from the country to the towns have not made much difference to the DC's support at the elections. In 1972 those voting for it reflected the same sorts of background and in much the same proportions as the supporters of the Catholic Party of 20 years ago.[20]

During the 1950s the relationship between party-membership and electoral support varied from one area to another, but became rather more evenly distributed in the 1960s. This is an indication of the party's growing ability to wield an effective influence at all levels of society, and shows its relative maturity as a party for the masses and its diminishing dependence on élitist support. The DC sees itself as the party at the centre, the spokesman of the general run of Italian society in all its aspects, even if, as some authorities have pointed out, this fact is seen more clearly in the social distribution of those who vote for it than of those who have opted to become official members of the party as such. At all events, its policies are moderate and tend to draw the various classes together in a common purpose. Thus, it increasingly commands popular support.[21] The growth in DC party-membership is as follows:[22]

Year	1948	1953	1963	1973 (estimate)
Membership	1,127,182	1,146,652	1,621,620	1,900,000

In the North, Lombardy and the area round Venice is the main 'white' or Catholic zone. In 1946 the party was strongest in the North where over half its members were situated. Subsequently the distribution has changed, so that now well over half of the membership is in the South and the Islands.

By occupation, about 20 per cent of DC members are manual workers, another 20 per cent are engaged in agriculture and a further 25 per cent are housewives.[23]

One characteristic to emerge from an analysis of the membership figures for this Catholic party is the positive correlation with the percentages of illiterates throughout society; there is also a negative correlation between the figures and individual income distributions. Although this was always the case, it became more evident in the 1960s. Speaking in general it is possible to maintain that throughout the country, and also within the various regions, 'the number of DC party-members increases in proportion to the rural nature of the environment and along with the illiteracy rate, while it decreases as one moves towards areas where individual incomes are higher.'[24]

In the mid-sixties the DC had 1500 party officials and 150,000 active members;[25] today it has about 800 party officials and 60,000 active members. The party has 13,600 local groups or *sezioni*.

Some estimates put the party's annual expenditure at about 20 billion lire, which is met by anonymous donations and by the normal annual subscriptions. In 1973 the latter amounted to 600 million lire.[26]

A word now about the various factions within the party, which is far from monolithic and has very little internal unity. During the last fifteen years pluralism has been the order of the day, giving rise to many currents or divisions within the party. At the present time there are nine of these altogether. Such factions tend to reflect the main three streams of Italian political life (in which the DC occupies the central position), i.e. the right, the centre and the left. The few studies dealing with this aspect seem to indicate that the factions are not linked with any special geographical area or social stratum, though the presence within a particular area of the leader of one of the factions does exercise a certain influence. Ideological considerations certainly play some part in the attitudes adopted by the various factions, and affect the nature and the extent of the support they command at the elections.[27] The factions cannot be understood without some appreciation of the party's internal organization and of the imbalance we have noted in the country's economic and social development. 'The composition of their membership in the upper echelons of the party is extremely fluid, and within the ruling-class itself it is sometimes hard to decide who belongs to any particular faction.'[28]

Finally, but not by any means a point to be overlooked, in order to understand the structure of this Catholic party and appreciate the extent of its influence, we have to take into account various supporting organizations. To a large extent this means the different organizations within the Catholic Church that support the party structure and help it along in its various activities – strengthening its lines of communication, contributing to its more effective organization, and helping to make the masses politically aware.[29]

Outstanding among such organizations are the Catholic Association of Italian Workers (ACLI) and the Direct Growers' Confederation (*Coldiretti*). In the mid-sixties the ACLI numbered more than a million members, of whom 600,000 were industrial workers, 200,000 were employed in the tertiary sector, and a small proportion were engaged in agriculture.[30] Only 20 per cent of those in the ACLI are members of the Christian Democrat Party, but 25 per cent of them are under 25 years old, so that they have the dynamism of youth. The Association tends to press the party towards left-wing positions.

The *Coldiretti* in the mid-sixties brought together 1,800,000 families or 3,500,000 workers. As a social group direct growers are aging, and the Confederation has aged with them, so that most of its members are over 50. The communist association catering for the same category is the National Alliance of Peasants, which commands no more than 10 per cent of the potential membership, while 90 per cent go to the Catholic confederation.[31]

The existence of such associations and their links with the political parties allow their members to exercise some real influence on the power structure, on the running of the country, on the adminis- tration of government, and on local affairs as well as on the main public bodies. The Christian Democrats are in effective control of the social reality of the country, both because they enjoy the support of these other organizations we have mentioned, and because they are influential in key positions in such important mass media as the press and television.

The DC has its own daily paper, *Il Popolo*, and a magazine of monthly discussions, *la Discussione*. It also has control of some important publishing houses. The party's own cultural outlets are not much developed, however, and it relies heavily on the support of the Catholic world. As a political force the DC is helped by having control (though not too obviously) of about one third of Italian glossy magazines (in terms of the total number of copies printed), and of about 20 or 30 per cent of daily papers. In the publishing field the party has become increasingly well-established and clearly committed since the 1960s, and even has a small publishing house of its own, the *Cinque lune*.

All these connections, however, balance one another, bringing together forces that sometimes agree with one another and at others oppose each other, so that the net result is not very great, and they largely neutralize their own influence. Thus, the party does not serve as an agent of political change, but interprets and expresses the actually existing realities of a many-faceted Italian society. Thanks to this it can keep its balance and preserve some degree of independence without giving way to the monolithic ideological pres- sures of reactionary Catholics or accepting the ultra-progressive policies of communist fellow-travellers beyond the limits of what is acceptable to the electorate as a whole. Thus, the DC is clearly a central and moderate party, open to influences from both left and right in various combinations that exclude all extremism and allow the administration to pursue a policy of moderate reform.

Conservative elements in the Catholic sub-culture exert pressure on the DC and are particularly influential in the government, so that the party finds it very difficult to carry through any programme of reforms, since these can always be criticized as anti-Catholic or lay in inspiration. Events subsequent to the Second Vatican Council have, although only to a certain extent, thrown the rigid schemes of those at the head of affairs into disarray, because the Council emphasized the individual Catholic's right to personal freedom, also in political matters, and this proved something of a crisis for upholders of the Church's traditional social teachings. Thus, it meant an end to the Church's rigidly anti-communist stance, and it was no longer possible to claim that every good Catholic should support the DC.

Briefly, recent years have witnessed a weakening of the traditional foundations of Christian Democrat policy. Catholic associations are looking more and more out of place as the Church itself favours pluralism. Italy is becoming a nation of Catholics in name only, who seldom or never go to Church. Anti-communist idealism has dimmed and is fast disappearing. In its place there remains a no more than historically motivated and, at least to all appearances, no longer justified suspicion of the Communist Party, which has in the meantime reorganized its own structures and revised its attitudes.

Despite all this the DC, shorn of its clerical implications, which today would in any case be an embarrassment to its political position rather than an effective support, remains an influential party, and *the* dominant political party; it continues to run Italian society, albeit in collaboration with non-Catholic non-Communists in the centre and on the left.

Nevertheless, it must be said that a potentially Christian Democrat portion of the electorate was considerably alienated by the 1968–72 shake-up within the party, which was largely the work of Catholics eager for political and cultural progress and renewal. Round about the same time a number of Catholic organizations reached a position to assert at least a relative independence of the DC, the most notable of these being the ACLI and the Catholic trade union.

In this way the DC lost some of its hold, but on the other hand it was able to broaden its appeal so that the party became a more up-to-date one with fewer religious overtones. The change took place in a number of stages. At first the Catholic party did not seem a party for the masses, but was controlled by a small élite. The reorganization of the party in the 1950s and the economic development of the 1960s made the DC much more up-to-date, especially in the North, and it was organized on a more popular basis. Because of the dualism within Italian society and social and economic imbalances this modernization process has never been really completed in the South. There are up-to-date developments there, of course, but there also survive out-of-date organizational structures and ways of running affairs that reflect the family-client tradition, even if its character is more bureaucratic and less personal than in the past.[32]

The change-over was completed in the early 1970s when, as we have seen, the DC became more moderate and lost some of its hold, especially over other organizations and in particular over those which had supported it because of their common links with the Catholic Church.

The Italian Communist Party

30   When the war was over and Fascism fell from power the Marxist sub-culture found its political expression in two parties: the well-established Italian Socialist Party (PSI), and the Italian Communist Party (PCI).

As a political force with a Marxist inspiration the whole Socialist camp has not enlarged its membership very much in the post-war period, but it has held its own. In 1919, 32.2 per cent of the votes cast went to the Socialists; in 1946 the two left-wing parties secured 39.7 per cent of the votes; in 1963 they obtained 39.2 per cent and in 1973 36.8 per cent.

Within the Socialist camp the Communist presence has steadily increased, and it is now the main strength of the opposition parties. At one time it aspired towards a radical transformation of the whole system. In resistance days it was well armed and pursued its objectives in secret, but as time has gone by this aspect of Communism has faded out. The party structure was based at first on an incredible number of cells, but with the passage of time these have lost much of their impact and appeal, and the PCI has adopted a structure more and more like that of the other parties. It is highly centralized and penetrates very effectively into the many different strata of Italian society.

The last time the PCI seemed at all revolutionary was in 1948 when an attempt was made on the leader's life. The party took over several parts of the country by armed force, and caused the government considerable embarrassment.

Since that time the party has been organized quite legally,[33] and the electoral support won by the PCI has increased in this constitutional context. In 1946 the Communists took 18.9 per cent of the votes. In 1948 the Communists and united Socialists (National Democratic Front) obtained between them 31 per cent of the votes. In 1953 the Communists themselves won 22.6 per cent of the votes, in 1958 22.7 per cent, in 1963 25.3 per cent, in 1968 26.9 per cent, in 1972 27.2 per cent.[34] Thus, since 1946 (if we omit 1948 concerning which we have no exact figure for the Communist vote as such) the party has constantly increased its proportion of the votes actually cast in the election.

Those who vote Communist are, however, concentrated in particular areas, and it is in the Centre and towards the North that they are best established and have made most progress (Emilia–Romagna, Tuscany, Umbria and the Marches). In the North itself since 1953 (for this would not be true of 1946) the Communist vote has always amounted to rather less than their average for the country as a whole. Nevertheless, it has increased. In the South and on the islands in 1946 the average number of votes cast for the Communists was well below their national average. Since 1953 the strength of the party has grown considerably in these areas, though its voting successes are still slightly below the national average.[35]

The increase in the party's electoral support has tended to spread this out more evenly through the various social strata. One analysis of political trends in Italy shows that,

> *thanks to a political tradition in its favour and its own large-scale, well-organized efforts the Communist Party is increasing its strength at the elections, both among those groups where it has generally obtained most support in the past, and among others.*[36]

Indeed, for any further expansion to occur in the party's electoral support, it would have to capture the votes of some who have not previously voted for the left at all. Since the early 1960s the PCI seems to admit that it must try to win some support from the centre or the right, but such a strategy conflicts with the traditional image of the party as tied to the Soviet Union, and meets the prejudice of anti-communism which lingers on in the Catholic sub-culture. However, the greatest obstacle to the party's success is the conviction of those who vote for moderation and favour the central parties that the Communist Party must still be regarded as belonging to the extreme left.[37]

As to membership, in 1946 the PCI was already a party for the masses with 1,676,013 members, and its ranks continued to swell – 1,748,722 in 1948; 2,145,317 in 1953, when it reached its peak. The more recent figures have been lower – 1,826,098 in 1958; 1,615,112 in 1963; 1,502,862 in 1967; then up again to 1,700,000 in 1972. This large membership is drawn from different social categories, though mainly from the lower *ceti*. Factory workers accounted for 41.7 per cent in 1951 and 40.2 per cent in 1967; share-croppers, colonists and direct growers for 12.4 per cent in 1967; pensioners for 13.8 per cent the same year.[38]

Until the late 1960s the industrial working-class membership enabled the party to keep its proletarian image. It also had a large following among agricultural workers, though this has rather fallen off. In other social categories the variations in the figures are slight. The three main points to note are that:

(1) Total working-class membership has dropped from about 60 per cent in 1950 to about 40 per cent in the mid-sixties, and continues to go down.

(2) Membership among factory workers is on the decrease, as was admitted in the 1965 Conference on Factory Organizations. If we take actual numbers instead of percentages, the working-class support for the party had dropped from 900,000 to 600,000 members by 1963,[39] at the very time of the exodus from agriculture to industry which increased the number of industrial workers tremendously.

(3) Since 1967 the party is increasingly becoming a party of old men, 24.4 per cent being aged 31–40, 25.2 per cent 41–50 and 30.9 per cent over 50 years old.

Next we can consider the members' geographical distribution. It seems clear from the figures[40] that the majority of Southern peasants are less politically aware than the industrial workers in the North, so that the party can gain little ground among them. Its position in the South is relatively stable because of the cultural difficulties to be overcome, and also, in all probability, because of the large-scale emigration of manual workers towards the North and into Europe. The party stronghold continues to be the three regions at the junction of Northern and Central Italy, and here it has plenty of support, a large membership, and a well-developed organization backed up by ample funds, social approval and a supporting culture. In the

North where the whole structure of society is changing all the time, the party's position remains equally fluid; it has not always won over the new immigrant workers and often loses ground among the well-established sector of the working-class who tend to prefer Socialism.[41]

> *The Communist Party is strongest, not where there are most workers or the most widespread poverty, but where the population is traditionally inclined to socialism, and where, in its handling of local affairs, the party has fitted into the socialist way of life.[42]*

During the 1960s the party made increasing attempts to win over the support of further social groups. Looking back, however, it seems to have had little success with the urban middle *ceti*. Where the industrial society is expanding the party makes little headway 'both because of the competition from the DC and of widespread public opinion in favour of moderate socialist policies'.[43] There has been a slight increase in the percentage of the party-membership belonging to these *ceti*, but it still does not rise above 8–10 per cent. Among the lower strata of the middle *ceti*, such as craftsmen, skilled tradesmen and small contractors, it would seem that the party has made some headway. (The party has never managed to set up an organization specifically for businessmen, but has one for craftsmen.) Furthermore, taking the overall picture into account, the party is losing support in country areas.

Its successes in the elections and its large membership assure the party of being consistently strongly represented in parliament. In 1972 the PCI had 175 deputies and 82 senators to represent it in parliament, making it the second largest Italian political power.

Its supporting organizations are well developed. At grass-roots level there is the Italian General Confederation of Labour (CGIL) and the Cooperative League. The Communist Party directly controls the working-class life of the movement through CGIL; this unfortunately weakens the position of the trade unions and lessens their chances of defending the workers' interests effectively. In 1947 the PCI obtained 52 per cent of the votes at the first CGIL Congress, the Socialist Party coming second with 30 per cent, the Christian group capturing 12 per cent, and the other parties obtaining only negligible support.[44] In the same year the Communist Party took 58 per cent of the votes in the Cooperative League.[45] Having supported the party for a long time, the League eventually declined in importance, with membership dropping between 1952 and 1966 from about 3 to about 2 million, according to available estimates.[46] It seems likely that the movement away from the country of much of the population has further weakened this organization. There are various other pro-Communist organizations, but their membership is not very large.[47] In some areas there are no Communist organizations at all.

What is particularly noteworthy is that the party has never succeeded in creating anything akin to Catholic Action, and is consequently in no position to influence the Italian population during childhood and adolescence. Nevertheless, in those places where it is in power, it tries to be represented in the schools and social services, and also promotes a certain number of reforms, some of which have recently been extremely progressive.

It is time to examine the party machine. The cells have been mentioned already. Historically these were designed 'to bring together those who were already members of the PCI and those sympathetic to its policies'. Today, however, the cell system has been largely abandoned, and sections have been established instead. The change in name acknowledges the relative stability of the present membership level.[48]

In the mid-sixties about 10 per cent, or 160,000 members, were active militants.[49] Today the militants number about 80,000.[50] It is their task to guide and mobilize public opinion, especially around election time. Their efficiency, like that of the party itself, is backed up by professional expertise – often that of people employed in local government, especially in Emilia-Romagna, Tuscany and Umbria.[51] At the present time there are 10,580 sections, and 800 party officials are paid salaries equivalent to those nationally agreed for metal engineers. The party leaders are a select group of about 400 – members of parliament, high officials in the party organization, mayors, provincial officials, trade-union leaders, people at the head of cooperative societies or other pro-communist organizations.[52]

The PCI has its own daily paper, *l'Unità*, an ideological weekly, *Rinascita*, a bi-monthly theoretical journal, *Critica marxista*, and two publishing houses which have been very successful in recent years.[53] Directly or indirectly it also controls some other leading national publishing houses.

The basis for its influence and power is, therefore, quite complex, but the value-system underpinning it has been modified as time has obliged the party to change its ground somewhat. As G. Galli has rightly observed, recent economic developments have meant that the PCI, which used to be strong in parliament because it was strong throughout the country, is now strong throughout the country chiefly because it is strong in parliament, in other words, because it represents a *political* reality in opposition to the DC in the context of an Italian society that has experienced profound social and economic transformations.

The party structure is still highly centralized, and still tries to control the way in which the masses are organized. Certainly until the 1960s the masses, especially in the trade unions, were closely controlled by the party by means of puppet leaders and party officials. More recently the organization has become more flexible and the party thinking less monolithically ideological and politically less doctrinaire. A moderate pluralism is manifesting itself within the party ranks, although not such as to challenge its basic unity.[54] Dialogue between Communists and Catholics has also got under way,[55] and is the outcome of a long, slow evolution.

The social stratification within the party has certainly changed. It is less proletarian; the educational background of the average member is better, and he tends to earn more than before. Of course, the whole electorate has changed, too, mainly because the whole of Italian society is in course of transformation. As a political force the Italian Communist Party is no longer a potentially revolutionary one, but has become a constitutional opposition party, which some authorities claim to be a party committed to 'reform'.

The other political parties

31 Initially the two dominant parties made use of democratic parliamentary institutions for their own ends. The Christian Democrat Party owed much of its success to the support of the highly centralized yet vastly extended organization of the Catholic Church. The Communist Party used the electoral system of a democratic multi-party system intending to dismantle it if ever it won an absolute majority. Thus, the democratic system was important as a working tool. Both major parties, the one in office and that in opposition, were for historical reasons opposed to a bourgeois, free-thinking society, and used the political and juridical institutions it provided in the service of other ideals. This situation has no clear parallel anywhere else in Europe.

Because the two major parties see representative democracy in this way, some observers consider the Italian political system as not really constituting a bi-party system, because although these two parties could theoretically alternate either in office or in opposition, in practice such alternation must be ruled out, because if the PCI ever did secure office it would not just run the present structures in its own way, but would change the entire system of government. We don't need to decide whether such an eventuality is at all likely – perhaps it is not, because of the changes that have now taken place in the thinking, the social composition, the organization and the overall structure of the Italian Communist Party. For the present, at any rate, not yet enough Italians wish to put the theory to the test of experience, and so the Communists are left in opposition.

The political set-up is, then, rather rigid. There are three historical reasons for this: the presence of the Catholic Church which stands behind the DC; the historical development of Socialism in a provincial and Catholic cultural setting – which is why there is a strong Communist party (there are other reasons) instead of a Social Democrat one as in other countries; the free-thinking tradition that brought about the national unification and is the historical reason for the survival of a number of small parties.

For twenty-five years and more there has been no great change in the political situation. While the other industrial nations have opted for a system of two or three parties, Italy has seven or nine, with the same one always in power, principally because it has seemed unlikely that the other major party, the PCI, could accept democratic opposition if it was in office.

As mentioned previously the two major parties are the basis of the entire Italian political system. However, as we have pointed out, there are other parties, and their organization and degree of political support varies over quite a wide range: the Italian Socialist party (PSI),[56] the Italian Social Movement (MSI),[57] the Italian Democratic Socialist Party (PSDI),[58] the Italian Liberal Party (PLI),[59] and the Italian Republican Party (PRI).[60] We need not consider them in detail in the context of this study. We should, however, at least mention in passing that while the Christian Democrats have weakened their position, there has been a certain counterbalancing reinforcement of that of the Socialists in the centre of the Italian political scene.

The situation is one of political stalemate, and the system that operates in other European countries, whereby shifts in the positions in parliament of the major parties ensure economic progress and some measure of improvement in the social services, simply does not work in Italy.

This situation is aggravated by the fact that power within each party tends to be situated at the top instead of originating at grass-roots level. The DC organization once relied heavily on the ideas of the local sections, although it always had a centralized structure, but it has now become 'a party of parliamentarians with people in Rome giving the lead to the various currents'.[61] The PCI has not escaped similar changes, has lost its popular inspiration, and has become in the main a conglomeration of small groups outside parliament with plenty of impractical ideas. Nevertheless, these two parties remain the main actors on the Italian political stage.

C. The trade unions

32   In Italy there are two trade-union organizations, one of them Catholic in origin, the other of Marxist inspiration. The historical reasons for this situation relate to the rise of Socialism in Italy towards the end of the nineteenth century, to the emergence of a new Catholic political élite who were less prejudiced against democratic government, and also to changes in the Church's own opposition to it.

The Catholic trade unions began as associations or societies of workers. Their main aim was mutual assistance, and for some time they were linked together in the *Opera dei Congressi*. In the main these were groups of craftsmen and peasants, and their numbers did not include many factory workers. The development of the unions was, in any case, obstructed by government edicts against them and by repressive laws which between 1864 and 1889 forbade the setting up of trade unions and only allowed strike action to be taken for a 'just cause'.

The first Socialist-inspired *Camere del lavoro* (working-men's chambers) were set up in Italy round about 1890 in the Northern industrial zones, in Milan, Turin and Pavia, mainly to find suitable jobs for their members. Very soon after their foundation they made it their main task to represent the workers' interests and conduct campaigns on their behalf, so that they closely resembled the modern trade unions.[62] As they became more organized a series of strikes were held, and these made the workers aware of the power at their command.[63]

Under Fascism a new trade union was set up with a membership of over 8 million workers. The Fascists linked this with a union of employers and another for artists and professional people in a single national association, the National Corporations Council. The Central Corporate Committee was in a position to run the whole social, economic, political and trade-union life of the country. The Council and Committee were, together with the Fascist Party itself, so many lines of communication between the masses, the two houses of parliament, the government and the Crown. The Fascist phase passed and left few traces behind. After the war the Italian General Confederation of Labour (CGIL) was re-established and catered for all organized groups of workers.

The existence within Italy and, therefore, within the trade-union movement of two sources of inspiration, one Catholic and the other Marxist, soon brought about a split. The result was four trade unions, which we can list in order of their numerical strength: the Communist and Socialist trade union, or CGIL, the Catholic trade union (CISL), the trade union for the Social Democrats and for the politically non-committed – the Italian Union of Labour (UIL), and the Fascist union, the Italian Confederation of National Workers' Trade Unions (CISNAL).[64] The lion's share fell to CGIL and CISL which during the last twenty years have in practice run the political life of the Italian workers, sometimes as rivals, sometimes in collaboration, and sometimes as enemies.

The link between CGIL and the Communist Party was the mainspring of Italian trade-union life in the 1950s. Thus, CGIL's dependence on the party is not just a historical curiosity but a keystone of political praxis. CGIL is the party's main link with its electoral supporters on the shop-floor. Galli believes that in 1966 it could muster more than a million workers, while the party had only 600,000 working-class members. CISL is not in this situation; its membership of 300,000 is much the same as the DC's working-class membership.[65]

CGIL's dependence on the party leads it to adopt defensive positions, partly on political grounds.[66] For quite some time CGIL seldom took any action at factory level, and it was not until 1959 that the possibility of such action was mooted. As late as 1961–3 claims for increased pay were still being expressed in traditional terms as requests for a rise. CGIL has done very little to try and bring about any change in the balance of industrial power, any improvement in working conditions, any modernization of its own organization or of its ideas about its position and responsibility within society.[67] It is still on the defensive.

Yet there was some change in union policies during the 1960s. By spelling out in detail a worker's contractual obligations the union was able to defend his rights more effectively within the more closely supervised setting of an up-to-date and highly technical production line.[68] Thus, it intervened directly in labour problems and questions of organization. In the last few years the trade union is at long last broadening its view of life, becoming relatively independent of the political interests with which it is associated, and is working alongside other unions rather more than before.

The social stratification and political leanings of CGIL have not changed much over the years. In 1966, 43 per cent of the members were industrial workers, 31 per cent agricultural workers, 15 per cent workers in the tertiary sector (including office workers in the public sector: 9 per cent), and 11 per cent pensioners. 'Comparing it with CISL, CGIL is much stronger in industry, considerably stronger in agriculture, clearly weaker in the tertiary sector, but well represented among office workers in public employment.'[69]

The officials in the central organization of the union are 51 per cent communists and 40 per cent socialists from the PSI, the others coming from smaller parties. At local level 75 per cent of trade-union officials in the CGIL are communists, and the others are socialists of one kind or another.[70]

The Catholic union, CISL, despite its initial identity as part of the Marxist-inspired CGIL, quickly discarded the Marxist ideal of the trade-union organization as being directly linked to a political party. Throughout the 1950s the CISL modelled itself on the United States' conception of a trade union as a free association. It also derives from the United States its emphasis on collective bargaining, and the view that it must safeguard the workers' interests and not think of them as being mainly guaranteed by social legislation.[71]

During the 1960s CISL could certainly no longer be regarded as an organization that simply supported the DC, even though it preserved its links with the party's left wing. A sample survey in 1968 indicated that 25 per cent of DC members also belonged to CISL.[72] Many Catholic workers are now more attracted to CISL than before because it has become more independent of the Catholic hierarchy and of the DC. This makes the union less class-conscious and more ready for action.[73] Since the early 1960s the Metal Engineers' Federation has been the most dynamic sector of CISL.

For a long time there has been a certain ambivalence about this trade union. It has links with the Catholic party, but feels the need to remain independent of it. In politics it is rather conservative,[74] and yet it is clearly moving towards progressive positions.[75]

Its first attempts to win over the mass of the workers failed, especially in the industrial sector. Between 1950 and 1961 their membership figures dropped from 40 per cent to 26 per cent of the CISL total.[76]

Since 1968 the union has tended to insist quite clearly on its own independence, despite a certain amount of opposition. 'The traditional link with what is commonly called the Catholic party is entering on a critical period in the thinking of many workers and of many CISL militants, who are now taking up positions extraneous to any party line or, indeed, to any sort of reliance on the party system.' Nevertheless, there are still links between CISL and the left wing of the Catholic party.

> *Obviously the abandoning of previously existing connections has not meant an out-and-out separation, since in 1967 of the four-fifths of CISL leaders who were enrolled members of some political party, 80 per cent belonged to the DC; a similar figure was obtained for the Metal Engineers' Federation in 1971, though in this case only a quarter of the union leaders were members of any particular party.*[77]

The CISL trade-union leader has tended to be very often the outstanding Catholic within his particular local parish. The national leadership of CISL is more conservative because of its close association with bureaucrats and politicians.[78] Conservative elements are also strongly represented in many branches of CISL in the South, partly because of close links there with the DC, and partly because of the economic situation there having until very recently been so different from that in the North.[79]

CISL, therefore, includes both a zone of immobility and a number of dynamic forces. It refuses to adopt a sectarian viewpoint, and as time has gone by has become increasingly reluctant to obey the directives of the ecclesiastical hierarchy.[80] Nevertheless, particularly in certain instances, it is abundantly clear that its predominantly Catholic membership does have a strong effect on the nature of its policies. Moreover, a fair proportion of higher union officials are members of parliament or have other close connections with the ruling Christian Democrat Party.

Despite certain tensions and difficulties within its ranks, however, CISL is increasingly proving itself a union capable of some very hard bargaining indeed. It has its own place within the factory, intervenes in the affairs of individual firms, and has shown itself much more flexible than CGIL, which throughout the 1950s tended to avoid any such direct local intervention because of its class-ideology and its close links with the Communist Party.

Hence, the Catholic-inspired but independent and progressive CISL is sometimes tougher than the Marxist union in its fights for the workers, and its numbers have grown, while its organization has been considerably strengthened. At present its numerical strength seems to have stabilized, as we mentioned previously.

The history of the trade-union movement in Italy reflects the overall developments of society as a whole. Thus, within a dualistic society resting on two distinct value-systems the trade unions could not present a united front, but split into rival bodies that reflected something of the conflict present in the rest of the society, serving to some extent as a political sounding-board.

As the economy improved and society became pluralistic, the situation was sufficiently different for the trade unions to feel free to work together once more. Their integration has never been suggested, and this new attitude symbolizes the changes within the social structure and the modifications of basic values that we have already noted.

Horizons broadened in the early 1960s, when the main unions adopted a common policy in the interests of the working-classes. Ten years of development have paved the way for agreement on a joint programme to bring the unions together, so that workers with different ideologies and of various political persuasions can live and work together, cease to set themselves economic targets that would prevent their fellow citizens from being equally well treated, and strive instead for structural reforms in the interests of overall and evenly distributed economic growth. This is the philosophy that inspires the movement to bring all the unions together, which dates from about 1971.[81]

The Metal Engineers' Federation (FIM) is perhaps the most left-wing union of all, and in it integration is largely an established fact. The Federation is urging CIGL and CISL to accept its lead.[82] On the other hand, integration is opposed by the agricultural day-labourers in CISL, by some unions in UIL, and by some other groups. The political parties are the main obstacles to be overcome; they are afraid that integration would deprive them of their influence within the unions, and of much of their popular support.

The process towards the integration of the Italian trade unions is now well under way, but new problems are already looming on the horizon. The trade-union system is becoming an integral part of the machinery that runs the whole of Italian society. Its efficient and progressive structures and aims increase its capacity to participate in the exercise of social power, even though it may often remain critical of the very nature of power itself. Left-wing trade unions are, therefore, making it their task to criticize, often violently, the present social system – something that was often regarded as the function of all the unions.[83] Integration means different things to union leaders and to those outside parliament and on the shop-floor.[84] There is, in other words, a dualism within the unions themselves. Hence, the increasing number of strikes, and the workers' growing insistence on their own rights.[85]

The way in which the unions operate and their overall significance in society has changed in the course of time, and they are becoming part of its administrative structure instead of merely the defenders of the rights of some particular sectors. Furthermore, the nature of the labour force and of the general make-up of the social pyramid is also evolving. On the basis of available figures it is to be expected that by 1980 workers will number about six and a half million, while there will be about five million university students, students attending polytechnics, graduates and teachers. This suggests some change in the life of the unions.

Italian society has lived through a gestation period of almost a hundred years. It emerges with a life dominated by three forces:

parliament and the government, the political parties and the trade unions. Sometimes these different forces work together, occasionally they are almost indistinguishable, at other times they are in bitter conflict – yet basically they constitute a fairly homogeneous power structure. Within the context of this structure the Christian Democrats, the Communists and the two main trade unions run the country.

At every level there is change – changes in the class-system, the power-system, the horizontal and vertical structures, so we cannot feel at all certain that any of these systems is destined to survive for very long. Nothing, however, can alter the fact that here and now it is the system that underlies Italian society.

D. Power-sharing among the élite

33   Having said a little about the DC, the PCI and the trade unions, which together form the central triangle of political power, and having considered their organization, their parliamentary position, and the nature of their support, we can form some sort of general picture of the Italian political system.

In Italy real political power is confined to a restricted élite. Both the Catholic and the Socialist political organizations are highly centralized, and in both of them there is a certain polarization of influences. A diagram may help to clarify the situation:

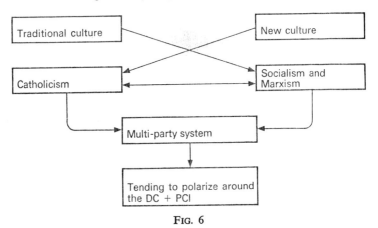

FIG. 6

We have already seen why the cultures and sub-cultures cross-fertilize each other, sometimes to mutual advantage and at others with rather monstrous results, and how the innumerable lines of communication within this whole complex organism operate in a way that makes the social life of the nation enigmatic and Janus-faced – a bipolar society we call Italy.

However, the bipolarity can also be seen as the expression of some rather severe limitations in the cultural élite's creative imagination of alternatives, and of a corresponding weakness among Italian politicians, who are not really as strong a group as one might at first suppose. This point may become clearer if we begin with a general point about the shortage of Italian intellectuals. Obviously they represent a potential source of political leaders, and appear to be distributed as shown in table 6.1.[86] In fact, of course, only a small proportion of elementary or secondary school teachers can be regarded as intellectuals, so that we are really concerned with a number of somewhere between one and two hundred thousand persons.

Table 6.1   Composition of the Intelligentsia, 1969–70 (thousands)

1. *Professional politicians*	
(a) elected to or working in central or local government	30 or 40
(b) party officials	50 or 100
2. *Intellectuals* (properly so called)	
(a) Writers, journalists, and staff of publishing houses together with those organizing cultural groups	10
(b) Elementary school teachers	253.8
Secondary school teachers	302.5
University professors	3.6
Others on university staff	13.1

The majority of those exercising political power are drawn from this group of intellectuals and professional politicians. Those who do come from a different social background are nearly all middle stratum. The middle strata account for about 50 per cent of the membership of the two houses of the Italian Parliament, the Chamber of Deputies and the Senate. Even the Italian Communist Party has a firm base among the less affluent bourgeoisie and among the middle *ceti* in general. About 50 per cent of its members of Parliament are usually of middle-stratum origin, while only about 25 per cent have working-class backgrounds, and this number is going down. Parliament, then, represents the intermediate layers of

Italian society, and the policies it pursues are much as one might expect from representatives of the 'people' with this particular social background.

Parliament aside, there are only about 2000 professional politicians spending their time 'forming the policies of the nation', i.e. exercising any influence of national significance.[87] These professional politicians are never specialists in that field of the nation's life which they are from time to time asked to be responsible for. They are too busy playing politics and fighting for their own survival to have adequate time available to study the problems facing them, and their contacts with the people they allegedly represent become increasingly rare. They keep political power jealously within their own small group and exclude technically qualified people or high-level intellectuals from political life, often because the latter are unwilling to opt for a political ideal as rigid as that represented by either of the two main parties (which partly derive this rigidity from the sub-cultures they represent). The people at large are also, of course, excluded from any say in the formation of policy.

The statistics we have available show that these two thousand policy-makers have acquired an incredibly large number of jobs for themselves and for their collaborators – some of them carry responsibility, others have no work attached to them, some are big, others small; there are positions of great prestige, those with economic influence, and some that serve only to win votes in an election. All these jobs make it difficult for them to do the single worthwhile thing, i.e. form a unified programme for the country's development and implement it swiftly and effectively. They haven't even time just to think about it, and do nothing that really expresses the needs and interests of the general run of the Italian population. Out of these two thousand, an even more restricted group, say fifty or a hundred, take turns in occupying all the key positions in the country, and for at least twenty or thirty years their identities have not changed, apart from a few retirements in old age.

Politicians, then, are a highly stable, restricted, mainly middle *ceto*, the same *ceto* that runs the civil service and the rest of the government machine. As a class they rather tend to set up a power-system or to keep going the one there is, but avoid changing it gradually or making any attempt to transform society; they will introduce a few marginal reforms, usually in a way that means they cannot succeed, as we have already explained.

Nevertheless, some sort of change is taking place. Catholicism and Marxism themselves are, of course, world-wide organizations and ways of life with their own supporting philosophies and value-systems, but in Italy the Catholic and Marxist sub-cultures are much more provincial-minded and narrow on account of their connections with local paganism on the one hand and nineteenth-century popular Marxism on the other. This makes them very poor channels through which to work for social change. Nevertheless, it is the amalgam of conservatism and rebellion in these two sub-cultures that, coupled with the economic miracle, has transformed Italian society and presented us with a whole range of new problems.

The expansion of the mass media and the growth of the consumer society have eroded the foundations of the traditional way of life. People may not deny the old values, but they now know how to find their way round them. The belief-system and the institutional structures of Catholicism are no longer taken for granted, so that Christian Democrat attitudes lack a common focus. The Communist Party, too, has lost its one-time stable ideological basis, and Marxists no longer accept a rigidly conservative culture as the norm.

Thus, in Italy culture and value-systems are in the melting-pot. That is why both Catholic and Marxist organizations and social structures are coming apart at the seams. Catholicism and Marxism were the last surviving mass organizations, and their diminishing influence is a sign that large-scale movements have had their day.

Today, in Italy as elsewhere, the coming of the consumer society has meant the atomization of man, who disassociates himself from all organized allegiances, and becomes a loner in the midst of a crowd, a social atom. Surveys show that when Italians do join associations they prefer a passive role, and that associations are in any case much more loosely structured than in the past, and place fewer demands on their members. In political terms or in terms of the overall running of society they are an irrelevance. At one time most associations aimed mainly at obtaining some sort of political influence or sought to modify people's line of thinking. Today they are more interested in helping the members fill in their free time, keep abreast of cultural developments, enjoy life and improve their economic position. They are still voluntary associations, but their aims are basically quite different.

The whole machinery of Italian democratic life used to be a complex and stable network supported by two sub-cultures. These upheld the values and the claims to social legitimacy of a whole series of organizations, so that all of these were thrown into a crisis by the crisis within the two sub-cultures themselves. Although the voting figures did not show this at once, this was also a crisis for the two main political parties. It may also have been a crisis for democracy itself; it certainly meant the collapse of one form of parliamentary democracy. Thirty years of democracy were not much time to prepare for a crisis of these dimensions. Italian society had hardly had time to adjust to the post-war parliamentary democracy based on universal suffrage, when economic developments obliged the country to seek an alternative.

The rise of technology has accelerated the whole process, and many social structures have quickly lost their apparent stability. The parties and other political organizations have lost the very foundations of their claims to represent things of value and no longer have much real hold on the electorate. For very many years the strength of Catholicism lay with the peasants, and they, as a class, are tending to disappear. The working-classes, too, have changed their nature, and this necessarily makes an immense difference to the whole Socialist movement.

For twenty years now Italian society has been in process of evolution. It has clung to a certain number of principles and has kept some stable institutions but the whole context that gives them meaning has been changing all the time. The different social strata and centres of power have risen and fallen in both importance and size as incomes have fluctuated, technology has advanced by leaps and bounds, and the technostructure has been more finely articulated. Gradually it became impossible to close one's eyes to the fact that this industrial revolution was breaking up the old class structures, ideologies, behaviour patterns and moral codes. Nothing old was sacred, and the new image was veiled and enigmatic.

The same enigma surrounded the changed face of politics, though it more directly expresses the changes that have taken place, responds to them more quickly, and even, to some degree, influences them, directs them, speeds up or obstructs their advance. The general picture is one in which certain elements are unchanged while other features vary more or less rapidly. What is happening within the power structure can be summed up as follows:

(1)   The power structure itself and its relationships with the public administration and with bodies subject to state influence of control remain stable;

(2)   The cultural and popular foundations of this structure, which were laid down at an earlier stage of social evolution, are being increasingly eroded;

(3)   Values are changing, Italians are losing interest in the political machine, scepticism is widespread, authority is viewed with suspicion – a suspicion that was always there but which increases as the current value-systems decline in influence;

(4)   What is technically sound and works in practice now tends to be preferred to all ideological considerations;

(5)   The family-client relationship is thriving, and this social parasitism is in its present form the continuation and the direct heir of a long-standing Southern tradition.

E. A general model of the power-system

34   The final model to conclude our survey of the Italian power-system shows it in a situation of structural crisis. There is no simple way of explaining this crisis solely in terms of the party-political system, nor of the five points we have just mentioned.

To appreciate the significance of the theoretical model we now propose for consideration, the reader must keep in mind all the main features of our whole analysis of Italian society, its structures, its economic reality, its culture, the pressures the client-system places upon it, and all its other elements with their various nuances and limitations. The scheme expresses in visual terms what we have said in the course of the preceding pages, and modifies it to the extent that it is necessarily something of a simplification. The categories we used in the verbal exposition were the equivalents within the power-system of our classification of the horizontal structure which was, it will be remembered, based on various relationships with the means of production, as well as on other factors which we mentioned at the time.

The scheme shows the real centres of power that exert their influence in independence on both the horizontal and vertical structures, so that the evolution of these latter carries with it, as we have seen, a rise or fall in the influence of the various centres of power, whose dynamism both reflects and conditions that of the entire system.

A word or two about how the diagram itself is to be read. There is a symbol at the top of each box, which are numbered from 1 to 15. If

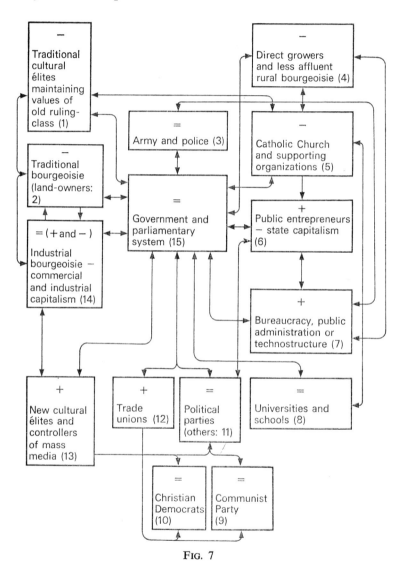

FIG. 7

the importance of a specific sector is stationary we have indicated this with the symbol ' = ', using ' + ' to indicate some growth in importance and ' − ' to indicate a lessening of a given sector's importance. Thus, regarding the Catholic Church, the symbol ' − ' refers to the crisis within it, as the social and economic position of the traditional and especially the rural bourgeoisie is also shown to be diminishing, and is again marked ' − '. On the other hand, if the industrial bourgeoisie is losing ground in the private sector in heavy industry, it is gaining importance in light industry and in medium-sized firms. Hence, we have marked the box ' = (+ and −)'. The importance of the political parties, the army and police is shown to be stationary, ' = ', etc. Other groups are growing in importance, because of the rise of the consumer society, changes in the value-system, modifications in the horizontal and vertical structures, etc. These include the trade unions, the new cultural élites, the bureaucracy and the public administration.

In the new structures of power the forces that are emerging to replace or complement the old are, basically, the trade unions, the administrative organizations and public entrepreneurs. This was only to be expected considering the pragmatic and efficiency-conscious spirit of our times, the secularization of values, and the immediate interests of the middle strata, the non-active members of the population and the tertiary sector of the economy, whose needs the system is, broadly speaking, primarily designed to serve.

For this and other reasons already mentioned, the people who count today are not the great ones of yesterday. Today it is more important to perform a function than to stand by a principle. Technology and science carry more weight than politics. The engineer is more highly regarded than the priest, the manager or the surgeon more highly than the party secretary; the minister responsible for the development programme counts for more than the Prime Minister (*presidente del consiglio*).

Turning from individuals to groups, those sectors that perform a specific function are growing in importance, while others are on the decline, and in every department of society, as within the political parties themselves, functional leadership based on knowledge and skill is coming to be preferred to any amount of personal charisma associated with values.

The power-system is changing, and the model we have provided shows the sort of changes that are taking place.

Notes to chapter 6

1. Friedmann, 1953, p. 225.
2. Moss and Capannari, 1959.
3. Salvatore Giuliano was the last bandit in the nineteenth-century tradition, with his own organized gang living as outlaws in the wilds. He was killed in rather mysterious circumstances in 1952.
4. Camera dei Deputati, 1973, Introduction p. xliii.
5. For these reasons, and also in view of its international obligations, the Church is involved in various sectors, but mainly in: various sorts of money-lending and other financial activities; industry and commerce; buildings and building-sites. The Vatican has the only large-scale network of banks in the private sector, which comprises, as well as the group of Catholic banks in Veneto (perhaps wrongly regarded as a sort of Italian Vendée), such powerful national banks as the Banco Ambrosiano, the Banca di S. Paolo in Brescia, etc. The Vatican has a large interest in certain financial organizations. There are other sectors of banking in which the management tend by tradition to be militant Catholics. This is true of the Banco di Roma and the Banco di Santo Spirito. In the economy itself the Vatican's main interest has for a long time been in the building sector. It used to, but no longer controls one of the largest building firms, the Società Generale Immobiliare Roma. See Ragozzino, 1969.
6. I am grateful for this information to Professor Italo Sandre, who is publishing a study of the problem. There are no published official figures, and these figures are not, therefore, official.
7. The Church's influence in Italy is quite different from elsewhere, and this, coupled with the country's cultural provincialism, has given rise to some peculiar features of Italian society, e.g., the long-standing organization of working-men's societies along the lines of Joseph Mazzini and Joseph Garibaldi. These were outstanding left-wing figures in the campaign to unite Italy, by recourse to arms whenever necessary, and they set up the so-called Brotherhoods of workers. In practice, their members were followers of these colourful leaders, but the societies later developed into something like trade unions. The influence of Socialists such as the rather utopian Proudhon and Louis Blanc, represented in Italy by intellectuals like Carlo Pisacane, was slight, and they won little popular support. Anarchism and Marxist-Socialism came later, and it was not until 1870 that they began to gain ground over the Mazzinian movements. Catholic working-class movements and Catholic political theory along democratic lines did not really get off the ground until after 1890.
8. The biggest revolts were the Socialist rising in Sicily towards the close of the century and the Anarchist one in Lunigiana in Tuscany in 1894. Both were put down by force. There were also a number of large strikes towards the end of the nineteenth century.
9. The DC was founded in the summer of 1942 by Alcide De Gasperi and is heir to the tradition of the pre-Fascist Popular Party and of other Catholic groups. The manifesto of Milan of 25 July 1943 promulgated the Party's existence as a public fact and asked Catholics to support its policies and programme.
10. After the 1949 Congress of Venice it became a characteristic of Christian Democrat policy to accept quite readily the directives of the Church, and to make its attitudes its own. Under the leadership of Pope Pius

XII, the Catholic Church at that time adopted a rigid policy regarding Marxism. De Gasperi's pre-eminence in Catholic party circles during these years also expressed the need to maintain a severely anti-communist attitude. The organizational links between the Catholic party and the Church are quite obvious, if we remember that for many years the parish was the grass-roots basis of the party's activities.

11. When the Christian Democrats were already in power they tried to acquire the political supremacy once and for all on the Italian political stage by the so-called Majority Law of 1953 which provided that any party obtaining 50.01 per cent of the votes cast in a general election should be entitled to a particularly high percentage of seats in Parliament.

12. It was mainly in the late 1950s that the Catholic party was brought up to date, with considerable reorganization at local level in order to become more representative of society as a whole.

13. As a preface to our discussion of the social structure of the Christian Democrats and of the Communist Party we must draw the reader's attention to the fact that our information is approximate rather than exact. Apart from the usual general reviews of electoral, administrative and political affairs we have taken our data from party publications or from figures released on the occasion of the congresses and national conventions. Obviously, they may be distorted in some ways, and numbers may easily be exaggerated. Both parties' estimates of the social stratification of voters can at best be no more than reliable approximations. Similar qualifications apply to the trade union figures.

14. The notion that the DC represents the interests of Catholics as a whole and is the only alternative to Communism has, in our opinion, frequently brought it many extra votes at the elections, when it has been supported by many with quite moderate political views.

15. These figures refer to elections of members of the Chamber of Deputies. Source: ISTAT *Compendio statistico*, 1946, 1962, 1972.

16. For an analysis of these figures see Brunetta, 1972, p. 301. See also, as regards the 1972 figures, Spreafico, 1972, p. 541.

17. See Galletti, 1973.

18. The situation in post-war Italy is quite different from in pre-Fascist days. Instead of the moderate Catholic voters being some of those who gave their support to a liberal bourgeois group, a liberal electorate with moderate opinions now supports a Catholic leadership. See Galli, 1966, p. 111.

19. See *La DC dopo il primo ventennio*, p. 178.

20. See the research referred to by Sani, 1973, pp. 561ff.

21. See Galletti, 1973, p. 28.

22. See *L'organizzazione partitica del PCI e della DC*, pp. 390ff.

23. *Ibid.*, pp. 390–91.

24. 'When agricultural workers transfer to industry without leaving the district it may be presumed that this leads to no large-scale dropping-off in their support of either the Christian Democrat or the Communist party.' *Ibid.*, p. 430.

25. Galli, 1966, p. 75.

26. Fabiani, 1974, p. 24.

27. Cazzola claims that 'voting preferences are influenced more by the level of economic development and the sort of political organization it brings with it than by the presence of a Catholic or Socialist sub-culture.' Cazzola, 1972, p. 583.

28. *Ibid.*, p. 587.

29.　A certain political stagnation within the Christian Democrat Party results from the influence upon it of various of its self-governing supporting organizations.

30.　Galli, 1966, p. 191.

31.　'In 1949 the Christian Democrats were able to mobilize considerable support in country districts because most direct growers belonged to one of their peasant organizations. Thanks to such supporting groups the Catholic party has not only succeeded in controlling certain features of the country's economic development but has also won over a certain proportion of the lower middle-classes, including some craftsmen and merchants.' *Ibid.*, p. 191.

32.　See Spreafico, 1972, p. 550.

33.　The Communist Party participated in every post-war government from 1944 to 1947, and contributed to the work of the Constituent Assembly. This was a temporary alliance with the bourgeoisie in the interests of more rapid economic reconstruction. In other words, the party subordinated the working-classes' revolutionary aspirations to the need for increased productivity.

34.　ISTAT data – See *Compendio statistico*, 1946, 1962, 1972.

35.　See Brunetta, 1972, p. 304.

36.　Sani, 1973, p. 566.

37.　A sample survey in 1968 and 1972 found the following percentages of persons interviewed saying they would never vote for these political parties:

	PCI	PSU	DC	MSI
1968	54.7	3.8	9.8	31.7
1972	41.9	5.1	9.2	43.8

Those opposed to the Christian Democrats were probably anti-clericals. The results on the whole confirm the moderate views of the Italian electorate and their preference for central political positions. See Sani, 1973, pp. 568ff.

38.　See *L'organizzazione partitica del PCI e della DC*, p. 328; Magri and Maone, 1969, pp. 28–40, especially pp. 28 and 30; *L'Unità*, 1 October 1972.

39.　The Communist Party's membership among factory workers halved between 1946 and 1963. See Galli, 1966, pp. 158–9.

40.　See Magri and Maone, 1969, p. 30.

41.　A comparison of the number of voters in the different parts of the country with the percentage of the Communist party membership resident in the area can be used to assess in which zones the Communists are making most progress. In the mid-sixties they were certainly doing much better in the Centre of Italy than anywhere else. See *L'organizzazione partitica del PCI e della DC*, pp. 328–9.

42.　Galli, 1966, p. 157.

43.　*Ibid.*, p. 160.

44.　*Ibid.*, p. 224.

45.　*Ibid.*, p. 224.

46.　We shall see that this is also true of the CGIL.

47.　It cannot be denied that the cultural organizations of the PCI, like the party itself, have had an important role in making the masses aware of various social, political and cultural issues.

48.　See Galli, 1966, pp. 164–5.

49.　*Ibid.*, p. 165.

50.　See Galli, 1971, p. 26.

51.　The Communist Party, as we have seen, runs most things in these areas. In the early 1950s it was also able to exert some power in local administration and in trade-union and associated organizations throughout the country generally, gradually extending its influence.

52. Only the Communist Party publishes its accounts. In 1973 it spent all its income, which amounted to 9380 million lire, coming mainly from the subscriptions of party-members and of those representing it in parliament. A certain proportion of party funds also come as a result of its part in promoting trade with the Eastern bloc.

53. Editori Riuniti is the most important of these.

54. The group most sympathetic to the student protest movement, *Il Manifesto*, broke away from the party in 1969, but failed to gain any parliamentary representation in the 1972 elections. Thus, the PCI still has almost a monopoly of left-wing opposition.

55. It was during the party's XI Congress held in Rome in 1966 that the notion of dialogue and collaboration with Catholics crystallized and was first made public.

56. In discussing the PCI we have said quite a lot about the Italian Socialist Party (PSI), which together with the PSDI represents moderate left-wing opinion in Italy. Recent estimates place its membership at some 560,000 (see Fabiani, 1974, p. 24). It has its own daily paper, *L'Avanti*, and a monthly ideological journal, *Mondo Operaio*. It has 61 deputies and 36 senators in parliament, making it the third force in Italian politics. During the 1950s it was quite well supported in elections, and in the early 1960s still commanded about 12–14 per cent of the votes, though this seems to have dropped now to about 9.6 per cent. See ISTAT, *Compendio statistico*, 1972. The local sections of the PSI are quite active, and the party has about 300 permanent officials. It is mainly in the North that it is influential and has its main possibilities of expansion.

57. The MSI was founded mainly by ex-Fascists, and serves as a focus for right-wing forces. Recent estimates place the membership at 420,000. It is the fourth party in the country with 56 deputies and 26 senators. It has a daily paper, *Il Secolo d'Italia*, and directly or indirectly controls at least two publishing houses and a few weekly magazines. It had some success with other right-wing forces in the 1972 elections and took 8.7 per cent of the votes. (ISTAT, *Compendio statistico*, 1972.) Most of its support is drawn from the less affluent middle strata and from the lumpenproletariat. In particular it has the sympathy of 'office-workers unsure of their jobs, self-styled contractors, small shop-keepers and land-owners, all of whom have been hit by an economic crisis in their particular field'. (Spreafico 1972, p. 548.) The party's Southern lumpenproletarian supporters are those who have been suddenly thrust haphazard into a new urban environment, and live in social chaos on the margins of the real life of the town. Apart from a limited amount of traditional right-wing support, the MSI obtains most of its votes from people suffering from economic difficulties or undergoing some other social hardship. (*Ibid.*, p. 549.) We have no detailed information about the party's organization. Its budget amounts to 5 billion lire a year (Fabiani, 1974, p. 24). It meets its expenses by the sale of the party newspaper, helped out by contributions from industrialists and farmers and from Fascist countries abroad.

58. The PSDI has 200,000 members, and a weekly journal, *Umanità*. It hoped to recommence publication of its former daily paper, *Giustizia*, before the end of 1974. It has 29 deputies and 12 senators, but not much local activity. Its annual expenditure of 1200 million lire is partly met by donations from North-American trade unions. See Fabiani, 1974, p. 24.

59. The PLI has 130,000 members, one weekly, *La Tribuna*, 20 deputies and 10 senators. Local sections are very few. It spends about one billion lire each year, which it obtains mainly from Fiat and the Confindustria. See Fabiani, 1974, p. 24.

60. The PRI has 100,000 members, one daily, *La voce repubblicana*, 15 deputies and 5 senators. Its annual budget fluctuates between seven and eight hundred million lire. It relies for financial support on large industrial concerns, and especially on Fiat. See Fabiani, 1974, p. 24.

61. Ardigò, 1973a, pp. 321–32, especially p. 321.

62. The first congresses of the *Camere del lavoro* were held between 1893 and 1901. In 1901 the chambers were organized on a national scale. Professional associations and associations for specific categories of workers developed alongside them, for instance for typographers, for railwaymen, for builders, for those employed in the chemical industries. The Italian Federation of Metal Workers was also formed in 1911.

63. The number of strikes increased as follows – in 1895, 126 with 19,307 workers taking part; in 1901, 1042 with 196,540 on strike; in 1907, 1891 with 321,499 involved in industrial action. There were also a few general strikes – the first in 1904, the second in 1911 to protest against the colonizing of Libya (clearly a politically motivated one); both failed. It is noteworthy that the railwaymen refused to take part in the second general strike. There was a third general strike in 1914, immediately before the country became a nation at war.

64. Trade-union sources and some non-official figures suggest that CGIL had 5 million members in the 1950s, and 3½ million in the mid-sixties. Galli also favours these figures (1966, p. 225). The present membership is about 3,700,000, while CISL has 2,410,000, which roughly corresponds to Galli's figure for the mid-sixties (1966, p. 192). At present UIL has 1,100,000 members, either Socialists, Social Democrats, or Republicans. During 1971 the Social Democrats and Republicans together had a slight majority in the union's leadership – 39 out of 75. UIL is not well represented in the factories, where its efforts are concentrated in the larger concerns. CISNAL now has about 200,000 members with very few in the factories, hardly any at all in the North. Its stronghold is the sector of public-service office workers, especially in Rome and Naples.

65. Galli, 1966, p. 236.

66. Like the unsuccessful struggle for control in Fiat factories in 1955. During the next seven years there were no more strikes in this firm.

67. While CGIL draws its rather elderly and conservative higher-ranking, though not top-ranking, officials from the political parties, CISL has full-time union workers who press for change and are quite independent of party responsibilities. See *La DC dopo il primo ventennio*, p. 116.

68. See Baglioni, 1966, for a fuller discussion of this point.

69. Galli, 1966, p. 225.

70. *Ibid.*, p. 226.

71. See *La DC dopo il primo ventennio*, pp. 109ff.

72. Merkl, 1971, p. 331.

73. See Turone, 1973, p. 339.

74. Local groups of strongly anti-communist members, especially in traditionally strong Catholic areas, still play an important part in the internal functioning of CISL. See *La DC dopo il primo ventennio*, p. 115.

75. CISL lost no time in organizing itself on a thoroughly professional basis, stressed the need for awareness of the union's place in the member's

life, emphasized the value of sound technical, economic and social under-standing of one's overall situation, and mobilized a large number of professional union activists. Another thing in its favour is its readiness to benefit from recent research, especially in the economic and legal fields. Its most progressive members come from federations of workers in food-production, textiles and engineering. We should also mention some im-portant unions that support it in Milan, Brescia and Ravenna. *Ibid.*, p. 110.

76. Accornero, 1973, p. 23. In the mid-sixties 23 per cent of CISL members came from agriculture, 26 per cent from industry, 51 per cent from the tertiary sector, of whom 27.2 per cent were office workers in government service. (Galli, 1966, p. 192.) This trend is still in evidence, and the CISL remains stronger in the tertiary sector than in the industrial field. Most new members are office workers in government service (+276 per cent between 1950 and 1968 in contrast with +38 per cent for industrial workers). In places that are less industrialized CISL is well represented in the towns, only moderately well represented in agricultural centres, and not at all well represented in provincial capitals or large industrial centres. (Accornero, 1973, p. 23.)

77. *Ibid.*, pp. 23–24.

78. See *La DC dopo il primo ventennio*, p. 115.

79. *Ibid.*, p. 115.

80. The Catholic Association of Italian Workers, which until recently maintained close links with the Church's hierarchy and has a rather religious orientation for a workers' association, not long ago tried to push the Catholic trade unions towards the left. Since 1968 it has tended to withdraw from the influence of the hierarchy, and to develop its own attack on capitalism, inspired largely by the student protest campaign. This has triggered off some violent reactions in Catholic circles.

81. This proposal became quite precise at Florence in November 1971 on the occasion of the joint meeting of the General Councils of CGIL, CISL and UIL. Some further progress has been made. See Turone, 1973, p. 510, where there is a leisurely discussion of the various moves towards an integration of all the unions.

82. Within CISL, FIM had in 1966 about 160,000 members, a three-fold increase of the 1959 figure while within CGIL it had about 320,000 members. (*La DC dopo il primo ventennio*, p. 117.) The Metal Engineers moved very close to organic union in 1972 with the setting up of the Metal Engineers' Working-Men's Federation (FLM). (Turone, 1973, p. 517.)

83. The workers' campaigns and the union conflicts of 1969 have led to the setting up of new structures to represent the workers within the factories so that they can participate more fully in what is going on. These are the factory councils with delegates representing the workers. See Albanese, Liuzzi and Perella, 1973, for a full treatment.

84. Today there seem to be two ways of integrating the unions. The more radical approach is to transform their whole organization so that it includes the factory councils and the new area structures within it, and allows the general membership a large say in policy decisions. A less ambitious project is merely the integration of the present union structures, with some degree of devolution of power from the top towards the base.

85. Since 1967 the number of labour disputes in Italy has increased steadily – 2658 in 1967; 3377 in 1968; 3788 in 1969; 4162 in 1970; and 5598 in 1971. The severity of the conflict has also intensified. In 1967 the number of workers involved in strikes or other disputes was only 2,243,000. This

doubled to 4,862,000 in 1968, and reached its peak in the Autumn Heat of 1969 when 7,507,000 workers were involved. The main focus of conflict was the factory situation. See ISTAT, *Compendio statistico*, 1972.

86.   Sylos Labini, 1973, p. 101.
87.   Galli, 1966, p. 321.

CONCLUSIONS

Out of Underdevelopment into Crisis

35   To describe the main features of Italian society is, at least to some extent, to describe the crisis at present afflicting it, and to relate that crisis to its origins. This crisis, as we have seen, impinges not only on social structure and the power-system, but also confronts the criteria of legitimacy and the value-system generally with a new challenge. The picture takes in both economic growth and in some areas a lack of efficiency. Italian society was split in two from the outset, and has never managed to free itself from this dualism. The very rapidity of its development has made its administrative structures inadequate and unable to cope with the new problems of economic life in a fresh situation.

Against this background of a crisis in values and a scarcely-functioning social organization, we have witnessed the increasing tendency towards political and social disinvolvement, the modern counterpart of the people's long-standing hostility to authority and the heir to the structures imposed upon Italian society in the last century when the country was 'united' without being consulted or considered.

Today, at all events, the more Italian society comes to resemble a technostructure for administration and production coupled with a subsidiary servostructure, the more the citizens are uninvolved and keep their distance. Sometimes they have no choice, sometimes they have; individuals, *ceti*, classes and groups re-enact in a modern idiom the roles assigned to them by what remains from the culture of underdeveloped Italy. Moreover, the new values are themselves in crisis even before society has had time to assimilate them, and the traditional hostility to community life, to authority and to organization augments the conflicts between rival groups, and against them all.

This society no longer seems to show any interest in its own future. There is no concern for values, work or social life; no opposition to the parasitic and private abuse of the government machinery or of the bureaucratic system generally; no reliable plans for development, change and renewal over the long term. If any plans do exist they are either impossible to realize or people are just unable to carry them out. Society shrugs off the collapse of its moral code and the erosion of the value-system that was its essential foundation and the basis of its legitimacy. Both religion and respect for the institution of the family have been jettisoned without tears, and no plausible alternative set of values has been proposed, let alone accepted. Thus, it is with considerable apprehension that we look towards the future in a society that, despite all these short-comings, continues to evolve and expand and even blossom in a climate of reasonable tolerance and something approaching democracy.

The social structure is, if we examine it in detail, certainly inefficient, counterproductive, unbalanced, split right down the middle, devoid of long-term plans, etc. Nevertheless, it somehow manages to work, and in a mere twenty or thirty years an underdeveloped society has become developed; a semi-agricultural country has become an advanced industrial nation; the hegemony of an élite has become some sort of popular democracy.

There is a sort of logic behind the development of Italian society, its crisis and the general disenchantment, and it is possible to spell out the situation in some detail. In the course of this study we have described its various features, and here we can recall the main ones very briefly:

(a) Development is taking place in an unbalanced economic system, which means that the development itself is uneven.
(b) Confronted with such a situation of uneven development the value-system of underdevelopment fails to transform itself consistently or to present a united front throughout the country. Instead, alongside a radically different social and economic system, we find at least two value-systems in positions that are

here more and there less entrenched – the underdeveloped system and the modern one. Hence, there are no longer any unambiguous or clear-cut criteria of legitimacy on the basis of which the social and institutional systems can be accepted or rejected, but different groups, indeed different individuals, behave in the light of mutually contradictory moral and social criteria. As a result, credibility is a commodity in increasingly short supply.

(c) All these economic and social factors combine into widespread attitudes of lethargy, hostility, non-involvement, and so constitute a substantial threat to the whole system.

(d) Nothing now remains strong enough to withstand the pressures of the parasitic *ceti* in various sectors who are thriving on the collapse of the old class-system. Nobody can stem the advancing tide of bureaucratic expansion, officials who consume much and produce nothing, except perhaps for a very high price – their numbers are in many sectors three times those found in other equally industrialized countries.

The parasites' attack is mainly launched from the less developed zones of the country, but relies for its expansion on the funds readily made available by the industrialized parts of Italy. In countries that have been completely industrialized there is not the same urge to swell the ranks of such parasitic *ceti*, since they can no longer mask their activities as 'public service'. On the other hand, underdeveloped nations cannot afford them. It is only when a country is unevenly developed that we can find both the means (supplied by the developed areas) and the motivation (life in an underdeveloped area) for their existence. The consequences of this fact for Italy we have already seen in some detail.

(e) Another result is the serious inefficiency of such basic sectors as social welfare, hospitals, and education. An advanced society must have schools to produce the labour force it needs, but they, like hospitals and institutions for social welfare, can very easily be inefficient themselves and produce all too little.

(f) All this means that the servostructure is in most respects inefficient, and that there is even less efficiency to be found in the bureaucratic system on which, of course, any industrial society must rely.

(g) The apathy and disenchantment increasingly shown towards the power-structure and the servostructure as a whole are also infecting the body of society. There is a lack of interest in the material means of production; scientific and technical progress lessens the need for manual work and brings with it a shift towards the tertiary and non-active sectors of the economy, but what we are now witnessing is simply a lack of interest in work as such.

Since Italy became a single nation this is the greatest crisis she has yet had to face.

More generally, in following the development of Italy, we have seen the upheavals that transformed it economically, culturally, socially and politically, so that the whole power-system was changed. The structure before our eyes today is very different from that with which united Italy began, and we trust the reader now has a clear picture of its main contours, its highlights and the shadows hanging over it.

There has been a price to pay as well as benefits to be reaped in this process of transformation which has changed an underdeveloped society into the seventh or eighth power in the industrial world. Can any realistic balance-sheet be drawn up?

In a single century, disenchantment with a system of values that, in some respects, had shown itself able to give a meaning to its own existence and to that of those who based their lives on its acceptance has stripped Italy of her defence mechanisms and of her sense of her own identity, which previously enabled her to live a meaningful life despite her insecurity, her anxieties and the many threats to her survival. For the Italy of former days was poor, violent, unjust.

In the new order of things freedom has been enlarged, the value of the individual person is acknowledged and each can give life his own meaning. Power is no longer brutally tyrannical, but is shared by many. Social controls are less rigid, and increased educational provision together with a more even distribution of consumer goods have dissolved many grounds for social conflict. Life is easier both materially and morally, despite the inefficiency and the dishonesty of the administration. Yet in this society life has become colourless and monotonous, and no one seems able to give it any real meaning. Loneliness and insecurity are widespread, and often reach dramatic proportions.

Can anyone weigh such things in the balance? Can anyone say whether the gains compensate adequately for all that has been lost?

Anybody who passed his childhood in the immediately post-war years can recall the poverty and injustice of those days, the daily battle against violence, oppression and systematic banditry. Today society has advanced, and we have the welfare state, so that such situations no longer exist. Meanwhile, the Italian himself has also changed, very deeply.

Some say, perhaps rightly, that the coming of the welfare state has robbed the Italians of their happiness. It may be that new injustices have replaced the old ones – injustices that are less obvious, more subtle, but that in their own way still do violence to the individual personality.

Thus, in the Italian case, too, we have to ask whether it was a good thing to pay such a high price for such slight advantages as development has brought in the shape of higher standards of living. Would it not be possible to fashion a different sort of society, with a different structure and different values, one that is still different from all that has gone before, but that leaves room for happiness, for humanity, or, if we don't want to use big words, one that leaves people free to live in peace?

Is this not, after all, independently of all considerations of ideology and structure, the essential aim of every society and of every man setting out on that journey into history that is at once both a personal and a social adventure?

Bibliography

Unattributed articles and reports

'Alcuni dati sulla consistenza del movimento contadino italiano', *Critica marxista*, 1970, 1–2, pp. 436–41.
Analisi metodologica delle statistiche economiche in Italia, 1972, Milano, Comunità.
La DC dopo il primo ventennio, 1968, Padova, Marsilio.
L'organizzazione partitica del PCI e della DC, 1968, Bologna, Il Mulino.
'Partecipazione degli italiani adulti alla vita religiosa', *Bollettino Doxa*, 1973, 17–18, pp. 248–9, 258–9.
Il potere militare in Italia, 1971, Bari, Laterza.
Scuola e mercato del lavoro, 1973, Bologna, Il Mulino.
'La selezione nella scuola dell'obbligo', *Inchiesta*, 1973, III, 10, pp. 70–3.

Acerbo, G. (1961) 'L'agricoltura' in *L'economia italiana dal 1861 al 1961*, Milano, Guiffré.
Accornero, A. (1973) 'La questione democristiana. Le contraddizioni di fronte al processo di unità sindacale', *Rinascita*, XXX, 21.
Acquaviva, S. S. (1962) 'Democrazia politica e società industriale', *Terzo Programma*, 4, pp. 57–99.
— (1969) *Automazione e nuova classe*, Bologna, Il Mulino, 3rd edn.
— (1971a) *L'eclissi del sacro nella società industriale*, Milano, Comunità.
— (1971b) *Una scommessa sul futuro*, Milano, ISEDI.
— (1972), 'Italy' in H. Mol, *Western Religion. A Country-Sociological Inquiry*, The Hague, Mouton, pp. 305–24.
— (1976) *The Eclipse of the Holy in Industrial Society*, Oxford, Blackwell.
Acquaviva, S. S. and Eisermann, G. (1971) *La Montagna del sole. Il Gargano: rottura dell'isolamento e influenza dei mezzi di informazione di massa in una società in transizione*, Milano, Comunità.
— (1974) *Der Einfluss der Fernsehen in der Gesellschaft von Heute und Morgen*, Stuttgart, Enke Verlag.
Acquaviva, S. S. and Guizzardi, G. (1971) *Religione e irreligione nell'età postindustriale*, Roma, Ave.
— (1973a) 'Essays on a model aimed at an empirical verification of new religious attitudes', *The Contemporary Metamorphosis of Religion*, Lilla, CIRS, pp. 485–99.
— (1973b) (eds.) *La secolarizzazione*, Bologna, Il Mulino.

Bibliography 221

Albanese, L., Liuzzi, F. and Perella, A. (1973) *I consigli di fabbrica*, Roma, Editori Riuniti.
Alberoni, F. (1970) *Classi e generazioni*, Bologna, Il Mulino.
— (1972) 'La nuova classe imprenditoriale pubblica', *Sociologia*, VI, 3, pp. 7–31.
— (1973) 'Società nazionale e imprese multinazionali: Sistema concettuale per alcune ipotesi previsionali', *Tempi moderni*, XV, 13, pp. 5–11.
Alberoni, F. and Bonin, L. (1971) 'L'Italia dopo il '68: la ricostruzione dei ceti', *Tempi moderni*, XIII, 8, pp. 114–17.
Amendola, G. (1968) *La classe operaia italiana*, Roma, Editori Riuniti.
— (1973) 'La classe operaia nel decennio 1961–71', *Critica marxista*, XI, 6, pp. 3–20.
Anderson, G. (1957) 'Il comparaggio, the Italian Godparenthood Complex', *Southwestern Journal of Anthropology*, XIII, 2.
Anselmi, S., Di Toro, C. and Montuori, F. (1967) 'Sviluppo edilizio, rendita fondiaria e urbanistica', *Problemi del socialismo*, 1, pp. 340–53.
Ardigò, A. (1973a) 'Stratificazione sociale e potere politico in Italia', *Aggiornamenti sociali*, 4, pp. 321–32.
— (1973b) 'Le classi sociali in Italia: per una proposta del movimento operaio. Intervento di verifica critica', *Quaderni di azione sociale*, 8, pp. 545–55.
— (1974) 'Evoluzione, crisi e prospettive della presenza politico-sociale dei cattolici in Italia', *Aggiornamenti sociali*, 6, pp. 29–64.
— (1975a) 'La famiglia tra classe e ceto', *Il punto*, III, 3, pp. 20–26.
— (1975b) *La stratificazione sociale*, 2nd edn, Bologna, Patron.
Avveduto, S. (1968) *La società scientifica*, Milano, Etas Kompass.
Aymone, T. (1973) *Scuola dell'obbligo e città operaia*, Bari, Laterza.

Baglioni, G. (1966) *Il conflitto industriale e l'azione del sindacato*, Bologna, Il Mulino.
— (1972) 'Una borghesia in formazione; gli imprenditori italiani nell' inchiesta industriale del 1870–1874', *Studi di sociologia*, 2, pp. 185–218.
Balbo, L. (1973) 'Le condizioni della vita familiare', *Inchiesta*, III, 1, pp. 10–26.
Balbo, L. and Chiaretti, G. (1972) 'Le classi subordinate nella scuola di massa', *Inchiesta*, II, 6, pp. 23–38.
Banca d'Italia (1973) *Assemblea generale dei partecipanti*, Roma, Centro stampa Banca d'Italia.
Banfield, E. (1958) *The Moral Basis of a Backward Society*, Glencoe, The Free Press.
Barbagallo, C. (1929) *Le origini della grande industria contemporanea*, Firenze, La Nuova Italia.
Barbagli, M. (1973) 'Scuola e mercato del lavoro', pp. 11–32 in *Scuola e mercato del lavoro*.
Barzini, L. (1966) *Gli italiani*, Milano, Mondadori.
Bendix, R. and Lipset, S. M. (1953) *Class, Status and Power*, Glencoe, The Free Press.
Benvenuti, F. (1962) 'La riorganizzazione del pubblico impiego in Italia', *Il Politico*, 27, pp. 342–57.
Bergonzini, L. (1973) 'Casalinghe o lavoranti a domicilio?', *Inchiesta*, III, 10, pp. 50–4.
Berlinguer, G. and Terranova, F. (1972) *La strage degli innocenti*, Firenze, La Nuova Italia.

Bini, G. (1971) 'Falsa coscienza e problemi reali della crisi della scuola', *Critica marxista*, X, 5–6, pp. 193–222.

Birnbaum, N. (1969) *The Crisis of the Industrial Society*, London, Oxford Univ. Press.

— (1971) *La crisi della società industriale*, Padova, Marsilio.

Bocca, G. (1969) *Storia d'Italia nella guerra fascista*, Bari, Laterza.

Bolacchi, G. (1963) *Teoria della classi sociali*, Roma, Edizioni Ricerche.

Bonanni, M. (1971) 'Scienza, industria e organizzazione in Italia', *Tempi moderni*, XIII, 8, pp. 33–6.

Bova, S. and Rochart, G. (1971) 'Le forze armate in Italia', *Inchiesta*, I, 2, pp. 3–27.

Braghin, L. (1973) *Le diseguaglianze sociali*, Milano, Sapere.

Brunetta, G. (1972) 'Le elezioni politiche dal 1946 al 1968 – Retrospettiva Statistica', *Aggiornamenti sociali*, XXIII, 4, pp. 295–308.

Brusco, S. (1973) 'Prime note per uno studio del lavoro a domicilio in Italia', *Inchiesta*, III, 10, pp. 33–49.

Bulferetti, L. and Costantini, C. (1966) *Industria e commercio in Liguria nella età del Risorgimento (1700–1861)*, Milano, Banca Commerciale Italiana.

Burgalassi, S. (1967) *Italiani in chiesa*, Brescia, Morcelliana.

— (1968) *Il comportamento religioso degli italiani*, Firenze, Vallecchi.

Cafagna, A. (1962) *Il nord nella storia d'Italia*, Bari, Laterza.

Cafiero, S. and De Rita, G. (1962) *Trasformazioni sociali e culturali in Italia e loro riflessi sulla scuola*, Milano, Guiffré.

Cafiero, S. and Marciani, G. E. (1968) 'Le zone povere nella politica di sviluppo' in Svimez (1968) *Il Mezzogiorno nelle ricerche della Svimez, 1947–67*, Milano, Guiffré, pp. 643–67.

Caizzi, B. (1965) *Storia dell'industria italiana dal secolo XVIII ai giorni nostri*, Torino, UTET.

Caizzi, R. (1968) *Industria, commercio e banca in Lombardia nel XVIII secolo*, Milano, Banca Commerciale Italiana.

Camera dei Deputati (1953) *Atti della commissione parlamentare di inchiesta sulla disoccupazione in Italia*, Roma.

— (1953) *Atti della commissione parlamentare di inchiesta sulla miseria in Italia, e suoi mezzi per combatterla*, Roma.

— (1955) *Documenti della commissione parlamentare di inchiesta sulle condizioni dei lavoratori in Italia*, Roma.

— (1961) *Documento della commissione parlamentare di inchiesta sulle condizioni dei lavoratori in Italia*, Roma.

— (1973) *Testo integrale della relazione della commissione parlamentare di inchiesta sul fenomeno della Mafia*, Roma, Cooperativa scrittori.

Cancian, E. (1961) 'The Southern Italian Peasant: World View and Political Behavior', *Anthropological Quarterly*, XXXIV, 1.

Capecelatro, E. C. A. (1972) *Contro la 'questione meridionale'. Studio sulle origini dello sviluppo capitalistico in Italia*, Roma, Samonà Savelli.

Car Boara, L. (1964) *Pluripartitismo e struttura democratica dello stato partitocratico*, Bologna, Forni.

Catelli, G. P. (1973) *Scuola, ambiente, lavoro*, Bologna, Consorzio Provinciale per L'Istruzione Tecnica.

Cazzola, F. (1972) 'Partiti, correnti e voto di preferenza', *Rivista Italiana di Scienza Politica*, II, 3, pp. 569–88.

Censis (1973) *VII Relazione generale sulla situazione economica del paese, 1972*, Roma, Poligrafico dello stato.

Centro Karl Marx (1969) *Sviluppo capitalistico e forza lavoro intellettuale*, Milano, Jaca Book.

Cervellino, E. (1962) *Lucania tradizionale*, Cava de' Tirreni, Di Mauro.

Clough, S. B. and De Rosa, L. (1964) *The Economic History of Modern Italy*, New York and London, Columbia Univ. Press.

— (1971) *Storia economica dell'Italia moderna*, Bologna, Cappelli.

Clough, S. B. and Livi, C. (1956) 'Economic Growth in Italy: An Analysis of the Uneven Growth of North and South', *Journal of Economic History*, 16, pp. 334–49.

Compagna Francesco (1967) *La politica delle città*, Bari, Laterza.

Consiglio Nazionale dell'economia e del lavoro (1969) *VI Rapporto sulla situazione economica del paese*, Milano, Angeli.

— (1973) *VII Rapporto sulla situazione sociale del paese*, Roma, Censis.

Consiglio Superiore dell'economia e del lavoro (1973) *VII Rapporto sulla situazione economica del paese*, Roma, Censis.

Corbetta, P. G. and Riccardi, F. (1972) 'Analisi di alcuni aspetti del processo di secolarizzazione in un quartiere urbano', *Studi di sociologia*, 1, pp. 29–79.

Corrain, C. (1962) 'Ricerche etnografiche sul Gargano', *Rivista di etnografia*, XVI, pp. 1–15.

Crespi, P. (1966) *Una società fra costume e storia*, Milano, Guiffré.

Croce, B. (1928) *Storia d'Italia dal 1870 al 1915*, Bari, Laterza.

Dal Pane, L. (1958) *Storia del lavoro in Italia dagli inizi del secolo XVIII al 1815*, Milano, Guiffré.

Daneo, C. (1967) 'Struttura e ideologia del ceto medio', *Problemi del socialismo*, 2, pp. 1216–43.

— (1972) *Agricoltura e sviluppo capitalistico in Italia*, Torino, Einaudi.

D'Anna, V. (1971) 'Gli operai contadini e la proletarizzazione', *Inchiesta*, I, 3, pp. 19–27.

D'Antonio, M. (1973) *Sviluppo e crisi del capitalismo italiano 1951–72*, Bari, De Donato.

D'Ascenzi, G. (1973) *Coltivatori e religione*, Bologna, Edagricole.

De Claricini, S. (1964) 'Chi dirige e chi legge la stampa quotidiana in Italia', *Rassegna di sociologia*, V, 2, pp. 251–73.

Del Carria, R. (1970) *Proletari senza rivoluzione. Storia delle classi subalterne italiane dal 1860 al 1950*, Milano, Oriente.

De Marchi, F. (1965) *La burocrazia centrale in Italia*, Milano, Guiffré.

— (1966) 'Organizzazione e burocrazia', *Questioni di sociologia*, Brescia, II, pp. 361–419.

De Meo, G. (1970) *Evoluzione e prospettive delle forze di lavoro in Italia*, Milano, ISTAT.

— (1973) 'Evoluzione e prospettive delle forze lavoro in Italia' in Leon and Marocchi (eds).

De Rosa, G. (1966) *Il Partito popolare italiano*, Bari, Laterza.

De Rosa, L. (1973) *La rivoluzione industriale in Italia e il Mezzogiorno*, Bari, Laterza.

De Simone, C. (1970) 'Sulla funzione burocratico-poliziesca dell'istituto prefettizio', *Critica marxista*, 3, pp. 168–77.

Dickinson, R. (1955) *The Population Problem of Southern Italy*, Syracuse, Syracuse Univ. Press.

Dina, A. (1967) 'I tecnici nella società contemporanea', *Problemi del socialismo*, 2, pp. 1406–16.

— (1969) 'Condizione del tecnico e condizione operaia nella fabbrica: dall'oggettività alla scelta politica', *Classe*, June, pp. 88–134.

— (1970) 'La delega di potere agli specialisti e il rifiuto della funzione', *Classe*, November, pp. 73–93.

Donolo, C. (1972) 'Sviluppo ineguale e disgregazione sociale. Note per un'analisi delle classi nel Meridione', *Quaderni Piacentini*, 47, pp. 101–128.

Dorso, Guido (1950) *La Rivoluzione meridionale*, Torino, Einaudi.

Dragò, N. (1973) *La scienza come profitto*, Bari, De Donato.

Eckhaus, R. S. (1961) 'The North-South Differential in Italian Economic Development', *Journal of Economic History*, September.

Eisermann, G. (1964) 'Die Bedeutung des Fremden für die Entwicklungsländer', *Schmöller Jahrbuch für Gesetzgebung Verwaltung und Volkswirtschaft*, LXXXIV, 3, pp. 301–22.

— (1964) 'Die Rolle des Unternehmers in den Entwicklungsländern, *Wirtschaft Gesellschaft*, 1, pp. 23–57.

— (1964) *Wirtschaft und Gesellschaft*, Stuttgart, Enke Verlag.

— (1968) *Soziologie der Entwicklungsländer*, Stuttgart, Kohchanner.

Ellis, R. S., Lane, W. C. and Olsen, W. (1963) 'Inter-Community Measure of Social Stratification', *American Sociological Review*, 4, pp. 272–79.

Emma, R. and Rostan, M. (1971) *Scuola e mercato del lavoro*, Bari, De Donato.

Esposto, A. (1970) 'Il ruolo politico delle classi dominanti agrarie', *Critica marxista*, VIII, 1–2, pp. 237–62.

Fabiani, R. (1974) 'La tasche bucate', *Panorama*, XII, 409, pp. 22–8.

Farneti, Paolo (1970) *Imprenditore e società*, Torino, Edizione l'Impresa.

Ferrabino, A. (1934) *L'Italia Romana*, Milano, Mondadori.

Ferrari Bravo, L. and Serafini, A. (1972) *Stato e sottosviluppo, il caso del Mezzogiorno italiano*, Milano, Feltrinelli.

Ferrarotti, F. (1970) *Roma da Capitale a periferia*, Bari, Laterza.

— (1972) *Per una sociologia alternativa*, Bari, De Donato.

Friedmann, F. G. (1953) 'The world of la miseria', *Partisan Review*, XX.

Fuà, G. (ed) (1969) *Lo sviluppo economico in Italia*, vol. 3, Milano, Angeli.

— (1973) *Lo sviluppo economico in Italia*, vol. 1, Milano, Angeli.

Galletti, V. (1973) 'La questione democristiana. Le basi sociali e i collegamenti di massa', *Rinascita*, XXX, 21, pp. 28–9.

Galli, G. (1966) *Il bipartitismo imperfetto*, Bologna, Il Mulino.

— (1971) 'Il PCI rivisitato', *Il Mulino*, XX, 213, pp. 25–52.

— (1972) 'Il governo invisibile e l'Italia', *Tempi moderni*, XIV, 11, pp. 3–10.

Gallino, L. (1970) 'L'evoluzione della struttura di classe in Italia', *Quaderni di sociologia*, XIX, 2, pp. 115–54.

Gannagé, E. (1962) *Économie du développement*, Paris, Presses universitaires de France.

Garavini, S. (1970) 'Le nuove strutture democratiche in fabbrica e la politica rivendicativa', *Problemi del socialismo*, XII, 44, pp. 36–52.

— (1973) 'Sono un milione gli sfruttati del "lavoro nero" ', *Rinascita*, XXX, 18, pp. 6–7.

Garin, E. (1963) *La cultura italiana tra '800 e '900*, Bari, Laterza.

Gattullo, M. (1971) 'Riforme scolastiche e scuola di massa', *Inchiesta*, I, 4, pp. 3–25.

Geertz, C. (1963) *Concerning the Role of Education in Development. Old Societies and New States*, (III), Glencoe, The Free Press.

Germani, G. (1963) *Clase Social Subjectiva e Indicadores Objetivos de Estratificacion*, Buenos Aires, Collection Datos, Instituto de Sociologia.

Gerschenkron, A. (1955) 'Notes on the rate of industrial growth in Italy, 1881–1913', *Journal of Economic History*, XV, 4, pp. 360–75.

— (1962) *Economic Backwardness in Historical Perspective*, Cambridge, Mass., Belknap-Harvard.

Golzio, S. (1942) *L'industria dei metalli in Italia*, Torino, Einaudi.

— (1951) *Sulla misura delle variazioni del reddito nazionale italiano*, Torino, Einaudi.

Gorrieri, E. (1973) *La giungla retributiva*, Bologna, Il Mulino.

Gramsci, A. (1955) *L'ordine nuovo, 1919–20*, Torino.

Graziani, A. (1962) 'Dualismo e sottosviluppo nell'economia italiana', (rec.) *Nord e Sud*, 2, pp. 24–32.

Grifone, P. (1971) *Il capitale finanziario in Italia*, Torino, Einaudi.

Guerra, G. (1967) 'Il capitalismo nelle campagne', *Problemi del socialismo*, 2, pp. 1362–1478.

Hartwell, M. (1971) *The Industrial Revolution and Economic Growth*, London, Methuen.

Illuminati, A. (1967) *Sociologia e classi sociali*, Torino, Einaudi.

ISTAT (Instituto centrale di statistica):
Annuario di statistiche demografiche, various years, Roma.
Annuario di statistiche industriali, 1972, vol. XVI, Roma.
1° censimento generale dell'agricoltura: 15.4.1961, 1962, Roma.
2° censimento generale dell'agricoltura: 25.10.1970, 1971, Roma.
IX censimento generale della popolazione: 4.9.1951, vol. 5, 1957, Roma.
X censimento generale della popolazione: 15.10.1961, vol 7, 1968, Roma.
XI censimento generale della popolazione: 24.10.1971, 1973, Roma.
Compendio statistico italiano, various years, Roma.
Indagine speciale sulle abitazioni al luglio 1969, 1970, Roma.
Sommario di statistiche storiche italiane 1861–1965, 1966, Roma, Poligrafico dello stato.
'Sviluppo della popolazione italiana dal 1861 al 1961', *Annali di statistica*, 1965, series VIII, vol. 17, Roma.

Jorgenson, D. W. (1961) 'The Development of a Dual Economy', *The Economic Journal*, 6.

Jovine, D. B. (1958) *La scuola italiana dal 1870 ai nostri giorni*, Roma, Editori Riuniti.

Kuznets, S. (1971) *Economic Growth of Nations. Total Output and Production Structure*, Cambridge, Mass., Belknap-Harvard.

La Palombara, J. (1964) *Interest Groups in Italian Politics*, Princeton, Princeton Univ. Press.

Leon, P. and Marocchi, M. (eds) (1973) *Sviluppo economico italiano e forza lavoro*, Padova, Marsilio.

Lettieri, A. (1967a) 'Sviluppo economico, progresso tecnico e occupazione (1960–66)', *Problemi del socialismo*, 1, pp. 436–54.

— (1967b) 'Caratteristiche e prospettive dello sviluppo industriale', *Problemi del socialismo*, 2, pp. 1317–33.

Libertini, L. (1968) *Integrazione capitalistica e sottosviluppo. I nuovi termini della questione meridionale*, Bari, Laterza,

Lloyd, P. C. (1971) *Classes, Crises and Groups. Themes in the Sociology of Developing Countries*, London, MacGibbon & Kee.

Lopreato, J. and Lococo, D. (1959) 'Stefaconi, un villaggio agricolo meridionale in relazione al suo mondo', *Quaderni di sociologia*, 34, pp. 239–60.

Lopreato, J. (1961) 'Social Stratification and Mobility in a South Italian Town', *American Sociological Review*, XXVI, 4.

— (1965) 'Social Mobility in Italy', *American Journal of Sociology*, LXXI, 3, pp. 311–14.

— (1967) *Peasants no More: Social Class and Social Change in an Underdeveloped Society*, New York, Chandler.

Lutz, V. (1962) *Italy. A Study in Economic Development*, London, Oxford Univ. Press.

Luzzatto, G. (1932, 1960) *Storia economica dell'età moderna e contemporanea*, Padova, Cedam.

— (1949) *Storia economica d'Italia*, Roma, Leonardo.

Luzzatto, Fegiz P. (1967) *Il volto sconosciuto dell'Italia*, Milano, Guiffré.

Lydall, H. (1968) *The Structure of Earnings*, Oxford, Clarendon Press.

Magri, L. and Maone, F. (1969) 'L'organizzazione comunista. Strutture e metodi di direzione', *Il Manifesto*, I, 4, pp. 28–40.

Maranini, G. (1967) *Storia del potere in Italia, 1848–1967*, Firenze, Vallecchi.

Marucco, D. and Agosti, A. (1970) 'Il movimento sindacale in Italia. Gli ultimi anni (1945–1969)' in *Fondazione Luigi Einaudi, Annali*, Torino, III, pp. 227–84.

Marzano, F. (1969) *Un'interpretazione del processo di sviluppo economico dualistico in Italia*, Milano, Guiffré.

Meldolesi, L. (1972) *Disoccupazione e esercito industriale di riserva in Italia*, Bari, Laterza.

Merkl, P. H. (1971) 'Partecipazione ai sindacati e ai partiti in Germania Occidentale e in Italia', *Rivista Italiana di Scienza Politica*, I, 2, pp. 325–66.

Merli, S. (1969) 'La grande fabbrica in Italia e la formazione del proletariato industriale di massa', *Classe*, June, pp. 1–87.

— (1973) *La formazione del proletariato industriale*, Firenze, La Nuova Italia.

Ministero degli Affari Esteri (1967) *Problemi del lavoro italiano all'estero*, Roma.

Ministero degli interni (no date) *Direzione generale dell'Amministrazione civile*.

Ministero del Bilancio e della Programmazione economica (1969) *Progretto 80*, Milano, Feltrinelli.

Monticelli, L. G. (1965) *I movimenti migratori italiani*, Roma, Ucci.

Morandi, C. (1965) *I partiti politici nella storia d'Italia*, Firenze, Le Monniere.

Morandi, R. (1959) *Storia della grande industria in Italia*, Torino, Einaudi.

Mori, G. (1967) 'L'industria toscana fra gli inizi del secolo e la guerra di Libia', in *Studi di Storia dell'industria*, Roma, Editori Riuniti.

Morosini, G. (1970) 'Ideologia practica della tecnocrazia pubblica', *Classe*, November, pp. 41–71.

Moss, L. W. and Capannari, S. C. (1959) 'A Sociological and Anthropological Investigation of an Italian Rural Community', *IV World Congress of Sociology*, Milano, Isa.

Mottura, G. and Pugliese, E. (1971) 'Agricoltura capitalistica e funzione dell'inchiesta', *Inchiesta*, I, 3, pp. 3–18.

— (1973) 'Mercato del lavoro e caratteristiche dell'emigrazione italiana nell'ultimo quindicennio' in Leon and Marocchi (eds).

Neufeld, M. (1961) *Italy: School for Awakening Countries*, Ithaca, Cornell Univ. Press.

Organisation mondiale de la santé (1967) *Annuaire de Statistique*.

Oriani, A. (1929) *Lotta politica in Italia*, Bologna, Cappelli.

Ossowski, S. (1963) *Class Structure in the Social Consciousness*, London, Routledge, English translation from Polish.

Paci, M. (1972) 'Le contraddizioni del mercato del lavoro', *Inchiesta*, II, 6, pp. 3–19.

Pagani, A. (1960) *Classi e dinamica sociale*, Centro di ricerche economiche e sociali, Istituto di Statistica Università di Pavia.

— (1970) 'L'immagine della struttura di classe nella popolazione italiana', *Quaderni di sociologia*, XIX, 2, pp. 155–81.

Pareto, V. (1951) *I sistemi socialisti*, Torino, Utet.

Parillo, F. (1970) *Lo sviluppo economico italiano*, Milano, Guiffré.

Parsons, T. (1951) *The Social System*, Glencoe, The Free Press.

— (1953) 'A Revised Analytical Approach to Social Stratification' in Bendix and Lipset.

Pasolini, P. P. (1974) 'Gli italiani non sono più quelli', *Corriere della Sera*, June 10, p. 1.

Pelliciari, G. (ed) (1970) *L'immigrazione nel triangolo industriale*, Milano, Angeli.

Pesenti, A. (1969) 'Impresa pubblica e sviluppo', *Critica marxista*, 1, pp. 72–90.

Petralla, R. (1967) 'Mezzogiorno e migrazioni interne', *Problemi del socialismo*, 2, pp. 1400–5.

Piancastelli, Corrando (1971) *Rapporto dal Mezzogiorno*, Ravenna, Longo.

Pizzorno, A. (1959) 'Le classe sociali' in A. Pagani (ed) *Antologia di scienze sociali*, vol. 1, Bologna, Il Mulino.

— (1966) 'Familismo amorale e marginalità storica, ovvero perché non c'è niente da fare a Montegrano', *Community Development*, 15, pp. 55–66.

— (1971) 'I sindacati nel sistema politico italiano: aspetti storici', *Rivista trimestrale di Diritto Pubblico*, XXI, 4, pp. 1510–59.

Prandstraller, G. P. (1967) *Gli avvocati italiani, inchiesta sociologica*, Milano, Comunità.

Principe, Q. (1959) 'Diocesi di Padova, pratica religiosa (1744–53)', *Sociologia religiosa*, III, 3, pp. 151–66.

Principe, Q. and Acquaviva, S. S. (1956) 'Un primo contributo alla sociologia storico-religiosa del padovano', *Studia Patavina*, 1, pp. 140–53.

Ragazzi, G. (1969) 'La dinamica dei salari nell'industria manifatturiera italiana 1953–65', in F. Forte, *Saggi di Economia*, Milano, Einaudi.

Ragozzino, G. (1967) 'La riorganizzazione del capitale finanziario', *Problemi del socialismo*, IX, 24–25, pp. 1334–61.
— (1969) 'Le finanze del Vaticano', *Problemi del socialismo*, XI, 40, pp. 434–46.
Ricci, A. and Salierno, G. (1971) *Il carcere in Italia. Inchiesta sui carcerati, i carcerieri e l'ideologia carceraria*, Torino, Einaudi.
Romano, S. F. (1965) *Le Classi sociali in Italia*, Torino, Einaudi.
Romeo, R. (1961) *Breve storia della grande industria in Italia*, Rocca S. Casciano, Cappelli.
— (1973) *Mezzogiorno e Sicilia nel Risorgimento*, Napoli, Edizione Scientifiche Italiane.
Roscani, B. (1969) 'La rendita edilizia in Italia', *Critica marxista*, 6, pp. 27–45.
Russi, A. (1971) 'I censimenti in agricoltura', *Inchiesta*, I, 3, pp. 23–27.

Salierno, G. (1973) *Il sottoproletariato in Italia*, Roma, Samonà e Savelli.
Salvemini, G. (1955) 'La piccola borghesia intellettuale nel Mezzogiorno d'Italia (1911)', in *Scritti sulla questione meridionale*, Torino, Einaudi, pp. 412–26.
Sani, G. (1973) 'La strategia del PCI e l'elettorato italiano', *Rivista Italiana di Scienza Politica*, III, 3, pp. 551–80.
Saraceno, P. (1968a) 'La mancata unificazione economica italiana a cento anni dall'unificazione politica' in Svimez, *Il Mezzogiorno nelle ricerche della Svimez, 1947–1967*, Milano, Guiffré, pp. 437–73.
— (1968b) 'La politica di sviluppo in un'area sottosviluppata nell'esperienza italiana' in Svimez, *Il Mezzogiorno nelle ricerche della Svimez, 1947–1967*, Milano, Guiffré, pp. 709–55.
Schramm, W. (1964) *Mass Media and National Development*, Stanford, Stanford Univ. Press.
Scoppola, P. (1971) *La Chiesa e il fascismo*, Bari, Documento e interpretazioni.
Scortegagna, R. (1972) 'Tradizione e cambiamento nel Veneto cattolico', *Rocca*, 19, pp. 29–31.
Sereni, E. (1947) *Il capitalismo nelle campagne*, Torino, Einaudi.
— (1966) *Capitalismo e mercato nazionale in Italia*, Roma, Riuniti.
Serpieri, A. (1947) *La struttura sociale dell'agricoltura italiana*, Roma, INEA.
Seton-Watson, C. (1967) *Italy from Liberalism to Fascism: 1870–1925*. London, Methuen.
Sindaco di Roma (1971) *Situazione delle locazioni in Italia*, Roma, Camera dei Deputati, Servizio Commissioni Parlamentari.
Spadolini, G. (1967) *Il Tevere più largo*, Napoli, Morano.
Spinetti, G. S. (1964) *Parlamentarismo e burocrazia*, Bologna, Zanichelli.
Spreafico, S. (1972) 'Le elezioni politiche italiane del 7 maggio 1972', *Rivista Italiana di Scienza Politica*, II, 3, pp. 525–68.
Stefanelli, R. (1970) 'La classe operaia italiana negli anni '70', *Classe*, February, pp. 3–35.
Svimez (1960) *Aspetti sociali e cultura dello sviluppo economico della Sardegna*, Milano, Guiffré.
— (1963) *Le migrazioni interne del Mezzogiorno. Rapporto Generale sulla ricerche*, Roma, Ed. Svimez.
Sweezy, P. M. (1962) *Il presente come storia*, Torino, Einaudi.
Sylos Labini, P. (1972) *Sindacati, inflazione, produttività*, Bari, Laterza.
— (1973) 'Sviluppo economico e classi sociali in Italia' in P. Farneti, *Il sistema politico italiano*, Bologna, Il Mulino.

Tarle, E. V. (1950) *La vita economica dell'Italia nell'età napoleonica*, Torino, Einaudi.

Tarrow, G. S. (1967) *Peasant Communism in Southern Italy*, New Haven and London, Yale Univ. Press.

Tawney, R. H. (1962) *Equality*, London, Allen and Unwin.

Tocci, C. (1971) *Terra e riforme nel Mezzogiorno moderno*, Bologna, R. Patron.

Toniolo, G. (1969) 'Patterns of Industrial Growth and Italy's Industrialisation from 1894 to 1913', in G. Franco (ed), *Rendiconto del comitato per il potenziamento in Venezia degli studi economici*, Padova, Cedam, vol. 1, pp. 265–7.

— (1973) (ed) *Lo sviluppo economico italiano 1861–1940*, Bari, Laterza.

Tremelloni, R. (1947) *Storia dell'industria italiana contemporanea. Dalla fine del settecento all'unità italiana*, Torino, Einaudi.

Trivulzio, A. and Buffardi, A. (1967) 'Pianificazione scolastica e riforma', *Problemi del socialismo*, IX, 17, pp. 455–68.

Turone, S. (1973) *Storia del sindacato in Italia 1943–1969*, Bari, Laterza.

Università di Padova (1966) *Reports of Sociology Department.*

Villari, P. (1962) *Mezzogiorno fra riforme e rivoluzione*, Bari, Laterza.

Villari, R. (1961) *Mezzogiorno e Contadini nell'età moderna*, Bari, Laterza.

Vöchting, F. (1951) *Die Italienische Südfrage*, Berlin, Drucker & Humbolt.

Warner, A. *et al.* (1949) *Social Classes in the United States*, Chicago, Chicago Univ. Press,

Wenner, G. (1953) *L'industria tessile salernitana dal 1824 al 1918*, Salerno, Salernitane.

Zamagni, V. (1973) 'Istruzione e sviluppo economico in Italia 1861–1913' in Toniolo (ed).

Index

ability, and income, 61; *see also* education

agriculture, and capitalism, 123, 124; decline of, 23, 24, 28, 29–30, 34–5, 120, 123, 124; economic imbalance, 26; functions within, 165–6; and industry, 68, 69; intensive production methods, 166; and land ownership, 121–2

Albania, 15

Alberoni, F., on economic position, 131; on scientific research, 161

anarchism, 208

Ardigò, A., on *ceti*, 59

army, and bureaucracy, 146–7; expenditure, 167, 168; and Fascism, 167; structure of, 167; in value system, 147

Austria, scientific research in, 161

authority, hostility to, 4, 5, 172, 215; *see also* government, politics, power

automation, and boom in tertiary sector, 36; and highly skilled worker, 71; and industrial bureaucracy, 61; and specialization, 73; *see also* industrialization

Bari, 27

behaviour, patterns of, recent changes in, 82–5, 110; and religion, 104

Belgium, and Italian bureaucratic structure, 139; scientific research in, 161

Biological Research, Centre for, 161

Birnbaum, N., on cultural traditions, 93

birth control, 110

Blanc, Louis, 208

building trade, labour force in, 68–9, 88

bureaucratic structure, centralization of, 140, 158; and child-care, 148; debts, 144, 145; expansion of, 50, 60, 137–9, 165; exploitation of, 57–9; history of, 139–40; in industry, 61; and loss of productivity, 143–4, 165; parasitic nature of, 142–4, 146, 157, 159, 164, 217; and power, 136ff; and private sector, 163; Southern element in, 2, 140–1; and technology, 159, 160

Burgalassi, S., on religion, 103

Canada, scientific research in, 161

Capannari, S. C., on hostility to government, 172

capital investment, income from, 41–2, 43

capitalism, international, 131; private, 131, 134; progress of, 5, 10; state, 131, 134

Catholic Action groups, and Christian Democrat party, 175, 176; drop in membership, 176–7

Catholic Association of Italian Workers (ACLI), 175, 184, 213

Catholic sub-culture, conservative elements in, 185–6; dominance of, 112; and Fascism, 179; and politics, 175–7, 179; provincial minded, 203; in retreat, 115; and traditional value system, 114; *see*

231